Patterns of REVISION

Inviting 6th GRADERS into Conversations That Elevate Writing

Travis Leech and Jeff Anderson

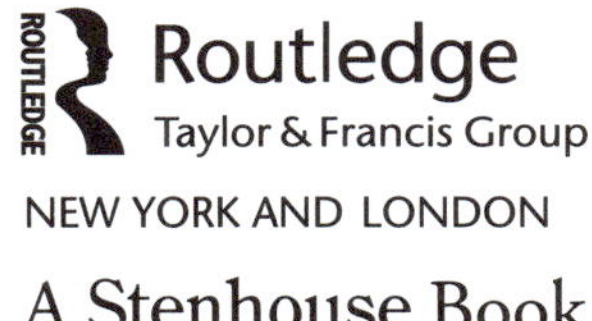

NEW YORK AND LONDON

A Stenhouse Book

Designed cover image: Page2, LLC, Morristown, NJ

First published 2025
by Routledge
605 Third Avenue, New York, NY 10158

and by Routledge
4 Park Square, Milton Park, Abingdon, Oxon, OX14 4RN

Routledge is an imprint of the Taylor & Francis Group, an informa business

ISBN: 9781625316370 (pbk)
ISBN: 9781032682013 (ebk)

DOI: 10.4324/9781032682013

Typeset in ITC Berkeley Oldstyle, ITC Franklin Gothic Std, Wendy LP Std
by Page2, LLC, Morristown, NJ

Access the Support Material: www.routledge.com/9781625316370

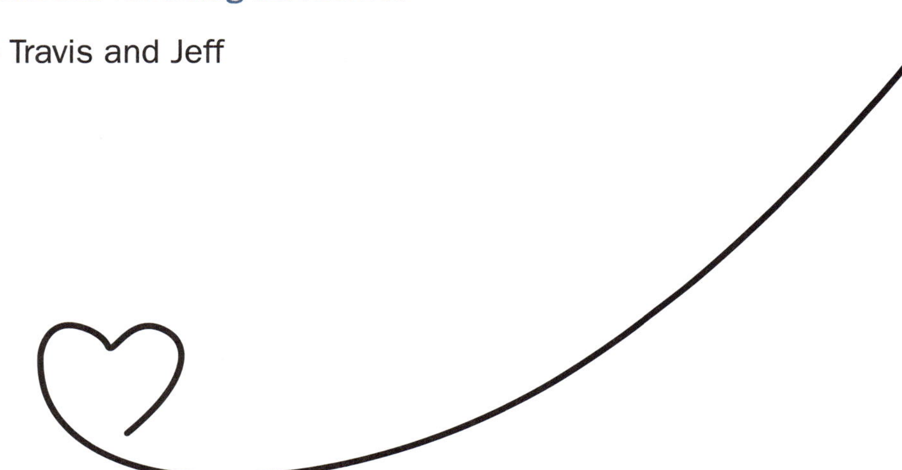

To Whitney LaRocca for being awesome!

– Travis and Jeff

Contents

Acknowledgments

Patterns of Revision would not have been possible without everyone who helped us make it a reality. Teachers whose willingness to try some of our ideas and have open dialogue about it was essential to creating truly practical lessons. The feedback we received led us to revise, revise, and revise some more. This book is a direct result of the magic of revision.

We want to give a HUGE shout out to the teachers and staff who graciously opened their classroom doors for us or tried out lessons and shared honest feedback with us, including Heather Trible, Melissa Contreras, Kristina James in Northside Independent School District, Katie White and her middle school crew in Blue Springs School District, and Nicola Hart, Celeste Parker, Jennifer Shroeder, and Elizabeth Hamrick in Frisco Independent School District. We appreciated the opportunity for collaboration and honest feedback from both you and your students. You really helped shape the flow and level of complexity of these lessons for middle schoolers.

We are grateful to Stenhouse for your support throughout this process. Thank you so much to Emily Hawkins, Shannon St. Peter, and Lynne Costa for the love and care you have given to our *Patterns* family. Thanks to Lauren Davis, Samantha Meagher, Melanie Moy, and the incredible production team for taking up the mantle of support as we moved this book toward the finish line.

Whitney La Rocca, our trailblazer, we owe you a debt of gratitude for getting into the weeds early with the elementary version of this resource. Your brilliant mind, unwavering effort, and constant positivity set the tone for this collaborative work.

To Mark Overmeyer, who provided thoughtful feedback and remained by our side through the marathon of writing and revising this resource. We are so excited to have you on board!

To Malene Golding for her skillful eye in helping us tighten up our message and ensure consistency throughout each lesson within this book.

To the expert mind of Terry Thompson who has remained close by and a phone call or text away throughout this project. We thank you, Terry, for your continued patience and support! We love you.

To our families, thank you for putting up with us, especially when we had deadlines hanging over our heads! We are so fortunate to have you in our lives, and we are thankful to have you as our biggest cheerleaders. Love you so much!

– Travis and Jeff

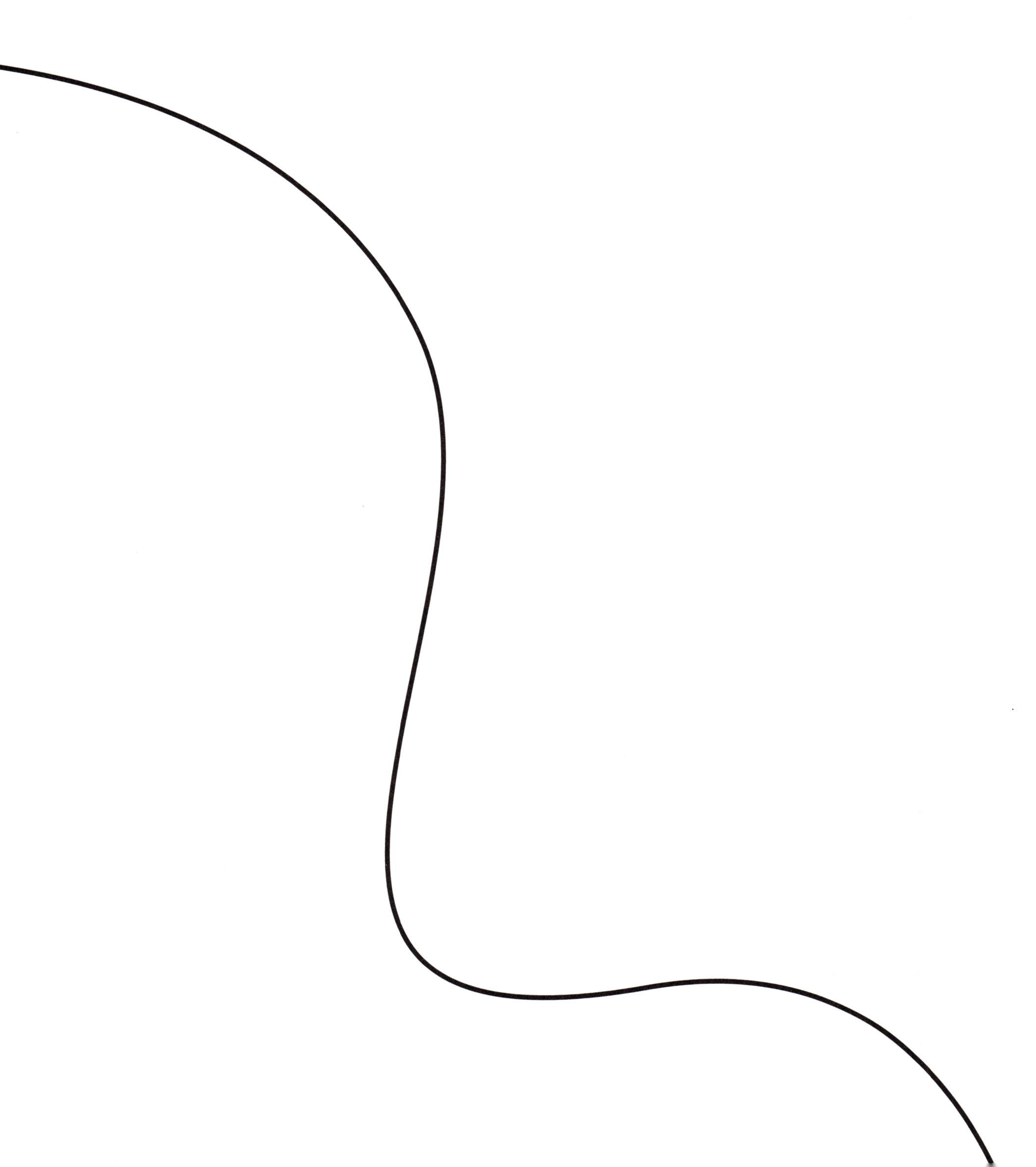

Introduction

OWNING the *Patterns of Revision*

Remember one thing: That you should not leave this Earth until you have made it a little more beautiful, a little lovelier, a little more loving.

– Osho

"Revise?" Jacob's nose scrunches, as if revising smells rank.

To be fair, most middle-school students don't clamor to revise. In fact, they downright resist it.

"What do you mean?" Jacob snaps. "I just wrote it!"

"Revising can make our writing better," Travis offers.

"*Better?*" Jacob is not buying it. "But it's already done. You didn't even *read* it yet."

"Yes, but I will," Travis says. "Writing is not a one-and-done thing. Revision is when and where writers figure out how to improve."

"You're trying to sound all nice, sir, but you're blowing it, you're saying it's wrong before you even read it."

"I see you, Jacob," Travis empathizes. "I appreciate what you accomplished here—you have written the first draft. But when I read my writing a few times before I share it with anyone, I can usually find ways to make it stronger."

"Mine is strong enough," Jacob pushes his quickwrite toward Travis.

No doubt you've had similar, almost heated conversations with your writers, struggling to keep your revision hopes from dying on the vine when it all just seems so abstract. These types of interactions in middle school classrooms seem more like an argument than a discussion. We don't have to win this fight, but we can make revision make sense to students. We can make revision accessible. We can give them concrete ways to revise, moving from abstract to practical actions. Indeed, that is our aim for *Patterns of Revision*.

"*How* do you revise?" students plead.

We know how you feel. We've been in similar situations, struggling to land on the right words to "get" kids to actually revise, not merely pretend to do so. Therefore, in this *Patterns of Revision* resource, we want to offer helpful, concrete, doable solutions—something more than abstract generalizations, something more than advice lobbed at middle school writers like wadded-up balls of paper:

- Revise for clarity
- Develop this (part, sentence) more
- Organize your writing
- Structure is key
- You're all over the place (Focus!)

Revision Truths

Longer is not always better.

Although it's true revision can make a text longer (adding detail or clarity), sometimes things need to be deleted (cutting extraneous details to make writing focused to communicate an intended message).

In *Patterns of Revision*, our goal is to show you how to help your middle-grade writers access these revision strategies with the tools that already exist in your classroom:

- Using model texts
- Engaging in open-ended discussions
- Reading aloud their own words
- Discovering through inquiry
- Learning through exploration
- Playing and experimenting

Getting middle school kids' hands and minds engaged in the act of revising is the central aim of every component of the *Patterns of Revision* process. In each lesson, we demonstrate what writers can actually *do* to revise—repeatable, practical, applicable choices, explored and named, and used and evaluated. Students can apply these strategies in their writing regardless of genre or the assignment in front of them. They also don't need a draft to be complete to begin incorporating them. Revising is ongoing.

So where do we start?

It's important for students to know that we don't revise to achieve perfection. Revision isn't really about correction; it's about making sense and so much more:

- Deleting unneeded words or parts
- Rearranging sentences and paragraphs
- Adding connector words and punctuation to make relationships between and among words and ideas
- Using the power of verbs and verb forms to tighten or enhance a message
- Talking through changes and permutations to hear how they sound and better evaluate their effectiveness

Revision Truths

Shorter isn't always better either.

Writers aim to be as brief as possible, so that our message is heard. Even though brevity is often better, sometimes shorter is sparse, unclear, undeveloped, or incomprehensible.

We opened this introduction with an epigraph that highlights the idea of doing "a little more." That's the way we think about revision—a process writers use to make their writing "a little more beautiful" or "a little lovelier." (We know. That's not very concrete yet—but hang on.) Our goal is to show middle graders how to make their writing a little more effective and, with each experiential lesson, build a repertoire of options or choices (author's purpose and craft), that they can own, and that will help them most clearly convey their meaning to their readers—or even answer multiple-choice revision test questions. The *Patterns of Revision* process—Deleting, Rearranging, Adding connectors, Forming new verbs, and Talking it out— will ensure they can not only revise, but have a process they can use comfortably and skillfully on revision multiple-choice test items.

We also strive to ensure the entire learning experience around revision is "a little more loving." To that point, we're hyper aware of how revision is often talked about—and it's usually anything but loving. Do we lament or lift it? Do we malign or praise its gifts? Do we present revision as an absolute right-or-wrong proposition, or do we celebrate it as a set of powerful options that we can use as writers to effectively share our voices and communicate our passions? Because when the words fall just right, revision can inspire us with a little more awareness of options we can bring to future pieces. This is what we want our middle graders to feel.

Experiences like these fortify their confidence and help them further identify as writers.

Talk It Out: The Power of Conversation to Move Writers Forward

Revision Truths

Revision isn't corrective.

While revision makes writing better (most of the time), it isn't about fixing writing as much as it is about playing with the order, effectiveness, and clarity of words, phrases, and paragraphs. Writers revise to make sure what they write is what they mean. As always, it's about meaning and effect— not right or wrong.

We believe in the power of talk, which is why conversation is the foundation of everything in this resource—the lessons, the strategies, the philosophy. Conversation is rehearsal. And since talk plays such a critical role in every lesson, you'll notice speech bubbles placed as a constant reminder of the importance of talk to the *Patterns of Revision* process.

Inquiry, discovery, and interaction naturally blossom out of student talk. Talking revisions out is freeing. We are far more likely to start, stop, restart, play, and recast when we are talking instead of writing. Talk feels more temporary. When we make time for the joyous generation of ideas that come as a result of talking, we build writers' revision repertoires. These conversations writers have become an internal part of their independent thinking process (Vygotsky 1978).

"But what if my kids don't talk?" you might wonder.

Middle graders will talk, but they may need your help directing that talk in a productive way. Model how to talk out revision. Give them various opportunities to join in discussions with you and each other across multiple revision lessons. Processing time is important for engagement and retention. Give middle grade writers space and grace for their conversations to unfold. Practice extending your wait time to give them a minute to start talking; resist the ever-present urge to jump in too soon or too often to rush things along. It's better that only a little bit of natural conversation bubbles up than for us to control it. It's their rehearsal; it's about starts and stops. Thinking can take silence, but it also needs to be unbound to allow ideas to bump against each other and take form. When we read our writing aloud or talk it out, we test our message for clarity and effectiveness. If you jump into their conversations too quickly to prompt, then students won't experience the productive struggle necessary to learn how to revise. Instead, they'll just wait for you to tell them what to revise.

Since talk is so central to the *Patterns of Revision* process, and is critical in each lesson, we incorporate moments for talk across every chapter. That's because, in reality, the whole book's foundation is talk. To support this, we also include a full-page printable that can be used for display or for pasting in your students' notebooks (see **Talk chart**, page 14).

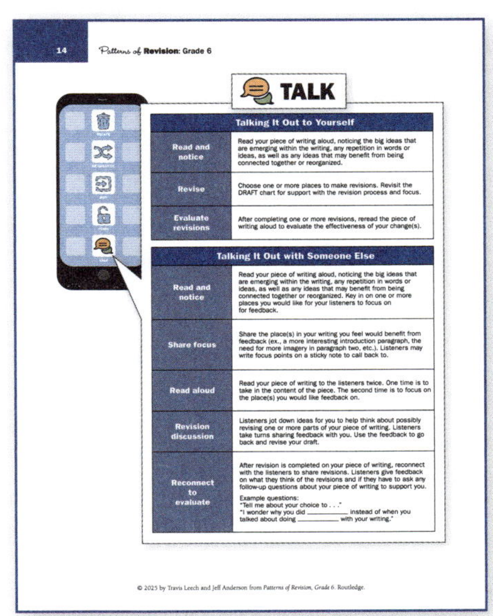

We break the DRAFT mnemonic into individual parts of the process—delete, rearrange, add connectors, and form new verbs, but it all begins and ends with talk.

Teaching the *Patterns of Revision*

The good news is that we can revise in innumerable ways: this is the beauty and freedom of revision. On the other hand, these infinite choices can also be revision's curse. Endless options can render revision overwhelming and thorny to teach—or *do*. We, our children, or any writer who considers the sheer amount of revision possibilities can easily become paralyzed, frozen by trying to do it "right."

How do we help middle-grade writers decide what to do?

We expose them to options—a high-impact, specific set of revision patterns that are based upon meaning-driven decisions and the desired effect we wish to have upon our readers. We read aloud; we model. We invite students deeper into this work. They experiment and play. They share and compare. They *do*. In *Patterns of Revision*, we intend to set writers and teachers up for success. We start with literature that demonstrates what revision can do for writing. Then we invite writers to try out the *Patterns of Revision* strategy with us, with other writers, and then on their own—all while having critical discussions about the effects of our revisions.

Another way we avoid the analysis paralysis that comes with so many choices is to narrow the focus for deep study. To that end, the lessons that follow zero in on specific doable actions, helping students realize, from the inside out, how words and the order or groupings we put them in change meaning and effect. As the lessons progress, these actions build on one another, cumulatively, to fill revisers' repertoires with options: we invite them to constantly stretch beyond what they can do now, so they can easily reach the next place.

Initially, we embolden writers to take risks and play with writing a bit at a time, with specific lessons to build their stores of options and prepare them for the cumulative work of revision. The secret of these bite-sized chunks of revision instruction is that they unlock fear by narrowing things a bit, so revision doesn't feel insurmountable or incomprehensible. Eventually, students try two, three, or four revision strategies, each grounded in a foundation

Tip

Talk it out! An oral test drive of our writings illuminates clumsy parts, wonderful parts, and confusing parts. Revision is talking through your writing, either internally or externally. Repeated opportunities to see the simple act of talk in play across multiple writing experiences help students develop habits for these external conversations about meaning and effect, and these habits eventually become internal.

Revision Truths

Revision patterns do exist, and they leave writers clues for what is possible.

There are plenty of effective revision patterns writers can consider, and you can showcase them through the mnemonic DRAFT (Delete, Rearrange, Add connectors, Form new verbs, and Talk it out) which Jeff included in his books *10 Things Every Writer Needs to Know* (2011) and *Revision Decisions* (2014) with Debbie Dean.

Tip

Remember, the fifth strategy of "talking it out" permeates everything we do in the *Patterns of Revision* process. Talk helps adolescent writers generate ideas and reason. Because it is integrated across the entire DRAFT mnemonic, we do not include a separate set of lessons for the **T** (talk it out.)

of talk and integrated into the mnemonic, DRAFT, illustrated below. We call this the **Reviser's DRAFTboard**.

- **D**elete unnecessary information
- **R**earrange
- **A**dd connectors
- **F**orm new verbs
- **T**alk it out

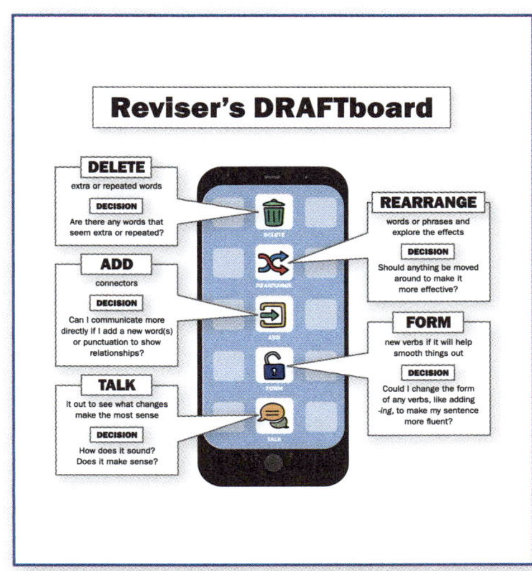

The lessons that follow are built across this mnemonic. As you work through them with your writers, remember that the lines between these options are fuzzy and naturally bleed over from one action to another. For instance, to combine sentences, or to put ideas together, an important, research-based vehicle for revision application (Graham and Perin 2007), writers often delete unneeded or repeated words as they rearrange sentences and ideas. Each action may, in turn, cause a cascade of new actions:

- inserting new connector punctuation such as a comma or colon,
- incorporating new connector words such as conjunctions like *but, and, or, when, while, until,*
- forming new verbs to compensate for deleted information or words (you need to trust us for now),
- rearranging the words or ideas to make sense.

Changes force us to try exciting new possibilities, especially when we treat revision as a generative exercise of choices as we evaluate what works best at the micro- and macro-level. In this book, we introduce each revision strategy individually for deep study. But in reality, they work synergistically across the entire revision process. To that end, the last set of lessons in Part 2 extend those individual strategy lessons, looking at them collectively in what we call combination lessons. Sentence combining uses all of our revision strategies (DRAFT) and provides meaningful practice that writers will transfer to their own work—if we are intentional.

> **66** Throughout each lesson, from start to finish and every step along the way, talking it out will play the most vital instructional role. **99**

And finally, as you get started, remember this revision work is wrapped up in the power of conversations. Throughout each lesson, from start to finish and every step along the way, talking it out will play the most vital instructional role.

With all this in mind, let's explore the *Patterns of Revision* lesson structure a bit further.

Tip

Best Practice *as* Test Practice: As teachers, we crave engaging and engrossing revision strategies that follow best language arts practices such as conversation that raises awareness of choices and effects in mentor texts. Best practices also highlight the value of focus and clarity and most importantly tap into students' existing language pool to accelerate revision access and application. Hands-on sentence text manipulation and opportunities to talk about, apply, and discover new understandings about revision in larger applications thread through all twenty lessons included in this book. And all these conversations around effective options provide writers with the strategies they'll need on any multiple-choice or open-ended test question you put in front of them.

Patterns of Revision Lesson Overview

When looking for powerful mentor text in literature, oftentimes Newbery medal winners are a rich place to find powerful examples of effective writing. We imagine Newbery-winning author Tae Keller wrote more than one draft of *When You Trap a Tiger* (2020). Students need to be shown options or possibilities of what revising can do. In the example that follows, we highlight a few of Keller's sentences to give you a helicopter view of the ultimate structure of the lessons contained in this resource. After a quick instructional overview, each lesson proceeds across seven components, each building on the next to encourage collective community experiences and conversations around a particular revision strategy (see Figure I.1):

- Setting Context
- Naming the Revision Strategy
- Modeling the Strategy
- Collaborating Through Conversation
- Quickwrite Opportunity
- Applying Revision
- Sharing Results

Figure I.1

Each lesson in this book follows the same format.

How Do We Engage Writers in Revision?		
Lesson Process	**Why?**	**How?**
Setting Context	When students engage with a model text, they are more likely to consider the effectiveness of the author's choices.	• Provide some background about the model text, including a part of it read aloud. • Create a need for the revision strategy.
Naming the Revision Strategy	When looking at student writing, it can be easy to get bogged down in fixing this, that, and everything else. Narrowing the focus to a small, manageable number of revision strategies helps writers access bite-sized chunks.	• Brush up on revision standards and decide what is appropriate for students. • Name and highlight the strategy that will be modeled in the particular lesson.
Modeling	Students need to see the target to hit it. Modeling writing behaviors demonstrates strategies and gives students clarity as they move toward application.	• Model the revision strategy. • Talk out possible decisions writers could make and how they generate them. • Reveal concrete ways to improve writing and solve writing problems.
Collaborating Through Conversation	Since everyone works on the same sentence(s), this collaboration gives more opportunities for shared discussion and demonstrates the many possible outcomes of revision. Creating writing together and comparing and contrasting a variety of writing moves broadens student perspectives. Post-collaboration reflection cements and clarifies concepts.	• Provide a structured opportunity for writers to get their feet wet, playing and experimenting with revision work. • Provide opportunity for writers to share their work with each other to uncover numerous revision solutions. • Facilitate post-revision reflection to tie the work to a revision concept.
Quickwrite Opportunity (Optional)	Writers need writing to work with in order to apply their current understanding of the revision strategy highlighted in the lesson. If students don't have easy access to a writing piece, using these writing prompts that are thematically-connected to the lesson's text will help students generate just-in-time writing to use for Applying.	• Provide lesson entry point options for writers. • Give writers clarity around where to draft their writing. • Provide time for writing, and if possible model drafting writing yourself.
Applying Revision	Revision becomes an integrated part of students' writing process when they are nudged to apply the strategies to their own compositions. Successful revision application also builds writers' confidence in their ability to craft quality writing.	• Provide concrete ways to nudge writers into using the modeled and practiced skill to solve their own writing problems. • Offer time and space for writers to apply their learning to their writing.
Sharing Results	Sharing and celebrating the revisions students make in their own writing makes students feel valued, and they will want to continue to revise other pieces in the future.	• Provide time for students to share their revisions with each other. • Celebrate their work with clapping, music, and/or displays.

Setting the Context with Read-Aloud

In each lesson, we kick things off by setting the context. Travis might say something like, "This book is about what happens when your story-telling Grandma gets sick and has to move in with your family." Then, to further set the context, he reads aloud another section of Tae's book:

I can turn invisible.

It's a superpower, or at least a secret power. But it's not like in the movies, and I'm not a superhero, so don't start thinking that. Heroes are the stars that save the day. I just disappear.

See, I didn't know, at first, that I had this magic. I just knew that teachers forgot my name, and kids didn't ask me to play, and one time at the end of fourth grade, a boy in my class frowned at me and said, *Where did you come from? I don't think I've ever seen you before.*

Throughout the past few weeks, Travis has taken students through revision at the paragraph level—Deleting, Rearranging, Adding whole sentences, and Forming new verbs—and now feels that his students are ready for the ultimate revision strategy: combining sentences, which takes all of the recent lessons and invites middle graders to do this same work at the sentence level while thinking how ideas might be combined. He focuses on the next sentence from the read-aloud. Here is the sentence as it appears in Keller's *When You Trap a Tiger* (2020):

> I wrap myself in invisibility and rest my forehead against the back-seat window, watching raindrops slide down the side of our old station wagon.

Travis lifts this sentence and briefly makes it less effective, deconstructing it for the purpose of teaching how combining can make a piece less repetitive and more concise. To that end, he untangles all of Keller's great text. (Forgive us, Tae. Don't worry, we'll eventually share your awesome sentence, but not just yet.)

> ***Original:*** I wrap myself in invisibility and rest my forehead against the back-seat window, watching raindrops slide down the side of our old station wagon.
>
> ***Unrevised:*** I wrap myself in invisibility.
> I rest my forehead.
> I rest it against the window.
> The window is in the back-seat.
> I watch raindrops slide down the side of our station wagon.
> The station wagon is old.

Naming the Revision Strategy

Travis chooses this time after setting the context to share a specific revision strategy.

"Sometimes writing has too many words."

"Amen!" Justice says.

"When revising." Travis smiles. "One thing we can always do is use DRAFT strategies to help us." Travis shares the **Reviser's DRAFTboard** with his students. This **DRAFT chart** is a sneak peek of the dashboard that defines the same DRAFT mnemonic that your students will eventually use after they've been introduced to the strategies individually in Part 1. "So far, we've learned how to delete, rearrange, add, and form new verbs when we revise. Now we can do that same thing, but we'll look closer at which words are repeated that we can delete and how we might rearrange what we have left. Let's look back at Tae Keller's writing. In her next sentence, Keller wants to make her reader feel more about the nature of observing and staring. Let's look over her ideas and see how we might use DRAFT to revise some parts that may not work so well."

Modeling the Strategy

Travis displays the "unrevised" version of Keller's sentence:

> I wrap myself in invisibility.
>
> I rest my forehead.
>
> I rest it against the window.
>
> The window is in the backseat.
>
> I watch raindrops slide down the side of our station wagon window.
>
> The station wagon is old.

He asks questions like, "What do you notice about these six sentences? Are there any words that aren't needed or necessary for the author to get their point across? Could we take out, or delete, any words?"

As students share out their responses to his prompt, Travis models deleting. "You've noticed that there are a few words repeated. Repetition isn't always a problem, but here I wonder if we could take out some of the repeated words."

"I see the word *I* four times," Xavier says.

"True," Travis says. "Maybe we could take a few of them out."

"There are two *thes*," Marshawn announces.

"Let's see what happens if we delete a few of these *Is* and *thes*," Travis shares his thoughts aloud: *I wrap myself in invisibility.* I'm going to leave this first pronoun *I* and get rid of the others. If I look at the following second and third sentences, I can get rid of both an *I* and a *rest* by combining these sentences.

I wrap myself in invisibility.

I rest my forehead.

~~I rest it~~ against the window.

I wrap myself in invisibility.

I rest my forehead against the window.

"Another thing we can do to compress writing or delete some words is to form a new verb, changing *rest* to *resting*. If we change *rest* to *resting*, it gives the reader the feeling of blankly staring forward. One thing a participle, *–ing* verb, does is show an ongoing nature. *Rest* to *resting*. This also allows me to connect the first two sentences by changing the period after the first sentence to a comma and forming the new verb (*rest* to *resting*) after the comma.

I wrap myself in invisibility.

I *rest* my forehead against the window.

I wrap myself in invisibility, *resting* my forehead against the window.

"What are some ways we could rearrange or revise this?" Travis scans the students' faces. "Talk with your elbow partners and talk it out together." After a few minutes, Travis invites groups to share.

With Travis's guidance, the class of writers collaborate to consider what's left of the unrevised version of the model:

I wrap myself in invisibility, resting my forehead against the window.

The window is in the backseat.

I watch raindrops slide down the side of our station wagon.

The station wagon is old.

"Take the challenge: Combine all four sentences remaining and make them all into one sentence."

The class works together to continue revising, while Travis moves around the room and talks with various groups of students. After noticing most students have completed revising, he gathers the class back together, and they work together to draft a single whole class version.

"Good work. Do you want to see Tae Keller's final version?" Travis asks. They are, in fact, dying to see it. Travis invites the group to compare their revision with Keller's:

> ***Class Version:*** I wrap myself in invisibility, resting my forehead against the backseat window, watching raindrops slide down the side of our old station wagon."
>
> ***Original Version:*** I wrap myself in invisibility and rest my forehead against the backseat window, watching raindrops slide down the side of our old station wagon.

As students compare and contrast their sentences with Keller's original, the group naturally starts to learn about options and choices we can make as writers. For example, sometimes when we delete, the revision needs the help of a connector sentence, word, or phrase, or maybe we can delete repeated words by forming new verbs.

Note, the goal here isn't matching, changing, or challenging Keller's original; instead, we're studying it so we can think through revision possibilities and options, so we can learn from her brilliant process.

Collaborating Through Conversation

Next, Travis invites the students to dive in and use conversation as a way to think about combining sentences using DRAFT in another excerpt from the same text. In groups, they work from another unrevised selection he's deconstructed from Keller's book. (You can find all needed lesson printables and displays at the end of each lesson.)

> She's sitting in the passenger seat.
>
> Her feet are slammed against the glove compartment.
>
> Her knees are smashed into her chest.
>
> Her whole body is curled around her glowing screen.

Travis begins, "Take a minute to carefully read the four sentences a couple of times with your group. Read it to yourselves and read it aloud. What do you notice?"

Students talk through the sentences and start crossing through anything that seems unneeded, such as repeated words like *her* and *are*. "Work together to think through how you might reflect all of this information in one clear sentence. Could we cut words? Bring in some connector punctuation or words?" Once students have read through the sentences and started cutting and combining, they decide what to write down as a new version.

Student groups share their revisions with others in the class, comparing and contrasting different options and effects. Finally, after students share, Travis invites them to look over Tae Keller's original model sentence, continuing to explore how varying versions can accomplish more or less impactful levels of meaning.

> She's sitting in the passenger seat with her feet slammed against the glove compartment, knees smashed into her chest. Her whole body is curled around her glowing screen.

> **❝** This exploration is very important: when we study an author's original sentence, it is not because it is the right answer but because it is an answer. This is how we learn powerful language patterns: by listening to and reading other writers' work. There is no right or wrong answer; there are only options. **❞**

This exploration is very important: when we study an author's original sentence, it is not because it is the right answer but because it is an answer. This is how we learn powerful language patterns: by listening to and reading other writers' work. There is no right or wrong answer; there are only options.

Quickwrite Opportunity

We find that applying new revision strategies to something in a writer's notebook or file of works, digital or otherwise, is essential. If your students aren't currently working on a piece of writing, we provide a brief, optional writing opportunity at this point in each lesson to help students generate some authentic drafts to revise. Our quickwrites (Reif 2018) are thematically or topically related. Please don't force this option if you have writing to work with. When it comes to quickwrites, Linda Reif says it best:

Quickwrites offer an easy and manageable writing experience that helps both students and teachers find their voices and develop their confidence, as they discover they have important things to say. This quick exercise pulls words out of the writer's mind. I am always surprised at the precision of language, level of depth and detail, and clarity of focus I hear when a student reads a three-minute quickwrite out loud.

If you decide to use the quickwrite prompts to get students writing, where you offer this quickwrite opportunity has flexibility within the provided lesson structure. While we believe moving from writing directly into applying our understanding of a revision strategy is highly effective, there are also other places where quickwrites work just as effectively to connect students to this process:

- Inviting students to complete a quickwrite before introducing the text and read-aloud for the lesson can prime the pump for the class to think about the content being covered in the lesson.
- Inviting students to complete a quickwrite directly after the read-aloud can strengthen engagement for students as the class moves into working with the revision strategy.

These are just two possible entry points into using the quickwrites. What's most important is that students have writing to work with as they move into applying revision.

Applying Revision

Later, students will return to their own writing and look for a place where they can combine sentences or ideas. But before that, Travis chooses to model making revisions to his own writing. The next day, Travis opens the class by reviewing what they've discovered so far and displays some sentences in his writer's notebook.

> Adults spend tons of time worrying kids aren't happy. They don't think they're happy enough.
> When you do have some fun, it's always at the wrong time.

"I love to write," Travis says. "But when I do write, if I go back and look at it later, I can usually find some ways to make it more effective. One way I can do this is to remove unnecessary ideas and sentences. First, I always look for repeated words that could be deleted. Do you see some here?"

Jamaica says, "Well, it's not really repeated, but *they* and *adults* are the same thing."

"Brilliant!" He circles *adults* and *they*. "So . . . if we took out one of these words . . . someone talk out some ways we could make this into one sentence."

Students talk it out and Travis writes down some options. Then, together, the class chooses which version is the clearest and best. Travis concludes the discussion by inviting students to go into their notebooks or any piece of writing, old or new, and look for places in their writing where they might revise some sentences: combine them using DRAFT.

Sharing Results

After they've had some time to apply the revision strategy of combining in a few of their pieces, students share and celebrate their own revisions, the *befores* and *afters*, comparing and contrasting effects and celebrating the hard work of their revisions. The goal in this stage is twofold. Sharing builds students' confidence as writers through positive interactions with classmates. Sharing also demystifies revision from something difficult or stress-inducing to something that is low-stakes and helpful. These repeated celebrations convince writers: "This is something I can do."

Now that we've explored its lesson structure, let's take a look at how to use this book and what's to come.

Revising at the Sentence, Paragraph, and Whole-Text Level

Every revision strategy presented in *Patterns of Revision* can be applied at the word, phrase, sentence, paragraph, or whole text levels. For example, the lessons in Chapter 3 highlight adding in new information to help the text progress from idea to idea. We present this concept by adding new sentences at the paragraph level, but revising by adding could happen just as surely at the sentence level, with students adding specific words to help clarify meaning. Sometimes, writers even notice that entire pieces will need an additional paragraph to support their main point more clearly. The teaching in *Patterns of Revision* provides the opportunity for teachers to be flexible and responsive to students' needs. If you feel your writers are ready to explore adding clarifying words at the sentence level, follow that instinct. You can easily spin out from the lessons presented here to zoom in and out on these various levels of revision with your writers (see the *Patterns of Revision* Quick List of Lesson Components, page 16).

How to Use the *Patterns of Revision Resource*

Revision Truths

Revision requires time and thought.

One quick change isn't really revising and stretching. Revision is about making writing better, but this requires deep thought, conversation, and reflection as writers read aloud, talk things out, and explore different choices along with their effects to make sure they're saying exactly what they want their readers to understand. In short, revision is a generative activity.

This is one of those books where you *must* read the introduction. We made it short, but it's packed with information that will help you find success with *Patterns of Revision* in your classroom. Although each lesson follows the same format (see page 15), this book is written in an order of progression, moving from deleting, rearranging, and adding entire sentences, phrases, or words at the paragraph level to combining ideas at the sentence level.

> **Part 1** lessons follow the DRAFT mnemonic revision strategies of Deleting, Rearranging, Adding, and Forming new verbs introducing one at a time in concrete and manageable bite-sized chunks.
>
> **Part 2** builds from these to include sentence-combining lessons, which apply DRAFT in a more blended way, calling upon the revision strategies students explored in Part 1 but bringing them together in larger contexts.

Now it's time to dive into the lessons in Chapters 1–5. Remember, they are built on talk and generation of possibilities. Make your classroom a safe place to experiment in the free flow of ideas. The lessons will help your middle-grade writers reflect on purpose and effect, enhancing their abilities to revise in any setting. When choosing lessons that will best meet the needs of your students, here is a list of things to consider:

1. Read the lesson overview for each chapter. This will explain how the set of lessons differs from the others.
2. Explore the ***Patterns of Revision*** **Quick List of Lesson Components chart** located in Figure I.2 on page 16. This will help you zoom in on the individual lesson components while giving you an overview of how the lessons in each chapter are alike and different, as you teach the *Patterns of Revision*.
3. Each lesson will range from a minimum of forty-five minutes to an hour. Lessons could easily spill into the next day or be planned across several days. Use your discretion to adjust their pacing based on the needs of your middle graders and the flexibility of your schedule.
4. Display pages and printables are included right in the lesson for which they're needed, so you can easily locate them for display or pasting into student notebooks.

5. Since the processes in this book center on talk, make sure you allow plenty of wait time after you ask questions, and provide plenty of silence after their answers to see if the students will add more. You can always sum everything up at the end.

6. You will likely find teaching the DRAFT revision strategies more manageable if you progress through the lessons in order. However, as always, we encourage you to chart a course that makes the most sense based on the needs of the student writers you work with every day.

7. As you work through the twenty lessons included in Part 1 and Part 2, recognize that they are just a starting point. They aren't intended to be comprehensive. As you develop your instructional muscles for the steps in each lesson, you'll be ready to stretch beyond them, using the structures we introduce here to plan your own *Patterns of Revision* lessons—driven by your students' ongoing needs and grounded in mentor texts your writers enjoy, celebrate, and love.

Finally, remember during the entire revision process to have fun with your students. Play. Experiment. Talk it out. Try new ways of writing. Allow this process to grow your writing community and elevate the ways you and your students think about the power of revision.

In silence there is eloquence.
Stop weaving and see how the pattern improves.

– Rumi

# TALK

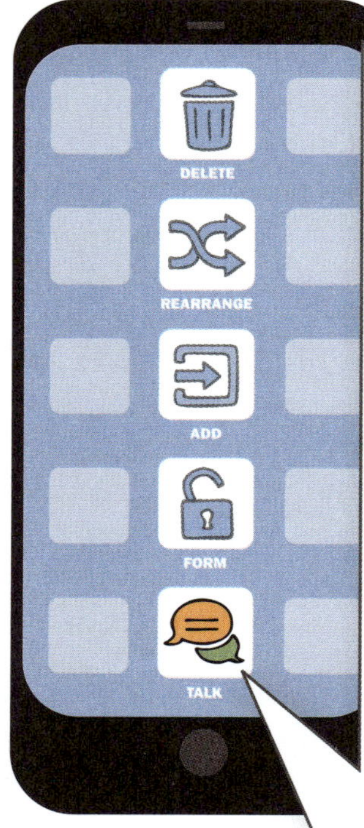

Talking It Out to Yourself

Read and notice	Read your piece of writing aloud, noticing the big ideas that are emerging within the writing, any repetition in words or ideas, as well as any ideas that may benefit from being connected together or reorganized.
Revise	Choose one or more places to make revisions. Revisit the DRAFT chart for support with the revision process and focus.
Evaluate revisions	After completing one or more revisions, reread the piece of writing aloud to evaluate the effectiveness of your change(s).

Talking It Out with Someone Else

Read and notice	Read your piece of writing aloud, noticing the big ideas that are emerging within the writing, any repetition in words or ideas, as well as any ideas that may benefit from being connected together or reorganized. Key in on one or more places you would like for your listeners to focus on for feedback.
Share focus	Share the place(s) in your writing you feel would benefit from feedback (ex., a more interesting introduction paragraph, the need for more imagery in paragraph two, etc.). Listeners may write focus points on a sticky note to call back to.
Read aloud	Read your piece of writing to the listeners twice. One time is to take in the content of the piece. The second time is to focus on the place(s) you would like feedback on.
Revision discussion	Listeners jot down ideas for you to help think about possibly revising one or more parts of your piece of writing. Listeners take turns sharing feedback with you. Use the feedback to go back and revise your draft.
Reconnect to evaluate	After revision is completed on your piece of writing, reconnect with the listeners to share revisions. Listeners give feedback on what they think of the revisions and if they have to ask any follow-up questions about your piece of writing to support you. Example questions: "Tell me about your choice to . . ." "I wonder why you did _____________ instead of when you talked about doing _____________ with your writing."

Figure I.1

Each lesson in this book follows the same format.

How Do We Engage Writers in Revision?		
Lesson Process	**Why?**	**How?**
Setting Context	When students engage with a model text, they are more likely to consider the effectiveness of the author's choices.	• Provide some background about the model text, including a part of it read aloud. • Create a need for the revision strategy.
Naming the Revision Strategy	When looking at student writing, it can be easy to get bogged down in fixing this, that, and everything else. Narrowing the focus to a small, manageable number of revision strategies helps writers access bite-sized chunks.	• Brush up on revision standards and decide what is appropriate for students. • Name and highlight the strategy that will be modeled in the particular lesson.
Modeling	Students need to see the target to hit it. Modeling writing behaviors demonstrates strategies and gives students clarity as they move toward application.	• Model the revision strategy. • Talk out possible decisions writers could make and how they generate them. • Reveal concrete ways to improve writing and solve writing problems.
Collaborating Through Conversation	Since everyone works on the same sentence(s), this collaboration gives more opportunities for shared discussion and demonstrates the many possible outcomes of revision. Creating writing together and comparing and contrasting a variety of writing moves broadens student perspectives. Post-collaboration reflection cements and clarifies concepts.	• Provide a structured opportunity for writers to get their feet wet, playing and experimenting with revision work. • Provide opportunity for writers to share their work with each other to uncover numerous revision solutions. • Facilitate post-revision reflection to tie the work to a revision concept.
Quickwrite Opportunity (Optional)	Writers need writing to work with in order to apply their current understanding of the revision strategy highlighted in the lesson. If students don't have easy access to a writing piece, using these writing prompts that are thematically-connected to the lesson's text will help students generate just-in-time writing to use for Applying.	• Provide lesson entry point options for writers. • Give writers clarity around where to draft their writing. • Provide time for writing, and if possible model drafting writing yourself.
Applying Revision	Revision becomes an integrated part of students' writing process when they are nudged to apply the strategies to their own compositions. Successful revision application also builds writers' confidence in their ability to craft quality writing.	• Provide concrete ways to nudge writers into using the modeled and practiced skill to solve their own writing problems. • Offer time and space for writers to apply their learning to their writing.
Sharing Results	Sharing and celebrating the revisions students make in their own writing makes students feel valued, and they will want to continue to revise other pieces in the future.	• Provide time for students to share their revisions with each other. • Celebrate their work with clapping, music, and/or displays.

Figure I.2

	Patterns of Revision Quick List of Lesson Components					
Lesson Sets	**Part 1** (Pages 21–156)					**Part 2** (Pages 157–245)
Revision Strategies	**Delete**	**Rearrange**	**Add Connectors**	**Form new verbs**	**Talk**	**Combining**
Setting the Context	Identify and lift an engaging piece of authentic writing to serve as a model. Introduce the model excerpt to writers, giving some background information and building interest.	Identify and lift an engaging piece of authentic writing to serve as a model. Introduce the model excerpt to writers, giving some background information and building interest.	Identify and lift an engaging piece of authentic writing to serve as a model. Introduce the model excerpt to writers, giving some background information and building interest.	Identify and lift an engaging piece of authentic writing to serve as a model. Introduce the model excerpt to writers, giving some background information and building interest.		Part II pulls the thread of **DRAFT** through the rest of the lessons, weaving in strategies from all the lessons and conversations that have come before. As always, the lessons in this set start with lifting and introducing an engaging piece of authentic writing for study and discussion.
Naming the Revision Strategy	Establish and define **deleting** as a powerful revision strategy, naming it as the purpose for the lesson with a continued focus on the model text.	Establish and define **rearranging** as a powerful revision strategy, naming it as the purpose for the lesson with a continued focus on the model text.	Establish and define **adding connectors** as a powerful revision strategy, naming it as the purpose for the lesson with a continued focus on the model text.	Establish and define **forming new verbs or verb endings** as a powerful revision strategy, naming it as the purpose for the lesson with a continued focus on the model text.	Conversation is so key that we introduce "**talking it out**" early in the introduction of *Patterns of Revision* and fold it into every lesson of this book.	Name that revisers ultimately use all the **DRAFT** strategies and note how some decisions prompt additional choices that need to be made. Emphasize this strategy is about finding a combination that works. There is no one right answer.
Modeling the Strategy	Demonstrate the power of **deleting unneeded or repetitive sentences, words, or phrases**, studying the choices the author of the model text made, talking, thinking, creating, and sharing.	Demonstrate the power of **rearranging words and sentences to help make our writing more organized and structured**, studying the choices the author of the model text made, talking, thinking, creating, and sharing.	Demonstrate the power of **adding connector sentences, words, and punctuation to help make writing easy to follow**, studying the choices the author of the model text made, talking, thinking, creating, and sharing.	Demonstrate the power of **forming new verbs or verb endings**, studying the choices the author of the model text made, talking, thinking, creating, and sharing.		Demonstrate **combining multiple strategies** in one revising event—reading through options, referring back to the DRAFT mnemonic, making critical decisions, and talking them out while continually considering meaning and effectiveness.
Collaborating Through Conversation	Working together and using a new text excerpt, writers talk through possibilities for **deleting unnecessary or repetitive, sentences, words, or phrases**.	Working together and using a new text excerpt, writers talk through revision possibilities, **rearranging and moving sentences around and reorganizing them** to see what effect it has on the reader.	Working together and using a new text excerpt, writers talk through possibilities for **adding in new information, sentences, words, or phrases** to connect ideas in a clear way.	Working together and using a new text excerpt, writers talk through revision possibilities, **forming new verbs or verb endings**.		Working together and using a new text excerpt, revisers think through possibilities for **combining multiple sentences into one** while calling back to previously learned revision strategies (DRAFT), trying them out, talking them through, and using all this to Make effective, meaning-centered revision decisions.

Figure I.2 *(continued)*

Patterns of Revision Quick List of Lesson Components						
Lesson Sets	**Part 1** (Pages 21–156)					**Part 2** (Pages 157–245)
Revision Strategies	**Delete**	**Rearrange**	**Add Connectors**	**Form new verbs**	**Talk**	**Combining**
Quickwrite Opportunity (Optional)	If students don't have easy access to a writing piece, the writing prompts found within the lessons in this chapter offer choices for students to generate just-in-time writing they can use to practice **deleting unnecessary or repetitive sentences, words, or phrases**.	If students don't have easy access to a writing piece, the writing prompts found within the lessons in this chapter offer choices for students to generate just-in-time writing they can use to practice **rearranging and moving sentences around and reorganizing**.	If students don't have easy access to a writing piece, the writing prompts found within the lessons in this chapter offer choices for students to generate just-in-time writing they can use to practice **adding in new information, sentences, words, or phrases to connect ideas in a clear way**.	If students don't have easy access to a writing piece, the writing prompts found within the lessons in this chapter offer choices for students to generate just-in-time writing they can use to practice **forming new verbs or verb endings**.		If students don't have easy access to a writing piece, the writing prompts found within the lessons in this chapter offer choices for students to generate just-in-time writing they can use to practice **combining sentences** using their understanding of the revision strategies (DRAFT).
Applying Revision	Writers try out the strategy in their own writing by returning to previous drafts or pieces from their writing notebooks to revise using the power of **deleting** to make their writing effective, talking through options either internally or with peers.	Writers try out the strategy in their own writing by returning to previous drafts or pieces from their writing notebooks to revise using the power of **rearranging** to make their writing effective, talking through options either internally or with peers.	Writers try out the strategy in their own writing by returning to previous drafts or pieces from their writing notebooks to revise using the power of **adding connectors** to make writing easier to follow talking through options either internally or with peers.	Writers try out the strategy in their own writing by returning to previous drafts or pieces from their writing notebooks to revise using the power of **forming new verbs or verb endings** to make their writing effective, talking through options either internally or with peers.	Conversation is so key that we introduce **"talking it out"** early in the introduction of *Patterns of Revision* and fold it into every lesson of this book.	Revisers try out **combining** strategies in their own writing by returning to previous drafts or pieces from their writing notebooks. They revise using a **combination of all or a collection of the DRAFT revision strategies** —deleting, rearranging, adding, forming new verbs, and, of course, talking it out either internally or with peers.
Sharing Results	Writers share and celebrate by reading aloud from their new pieces while revisiting the newly learned revision strategy and talking through how their choices to **delete unnecessary sentences, phrases, or words** affect meaning and make their pieces stronger.	Writers share and celebrate by reading aloud from their new pieces while revisiting the newly learned revision strategy and talking through how their choices to **rearrange sentences, phrases, or words** affect meaning and make their pieces stronger.	Writers share and celebrate by reading aloud from their new pieces while revisiting the newly learned revision strategy and talking through how their choices to **add new details to connect** affect meaning and make their pieces stronger.	Writers share and celebrate by reading aloud from their new pieces while revisiting the newly learned revision strategy and talking through how their choices to **form new verbs or verb endings** effect meaning and make their pieces stronger.		Revisers share and celebrate by reading aloud from their new pieces while talking through the individual **DRAFT revision strategies** they considered and how their ultimate decisions enhance their message and make their piece stronger. As always, steer this conversation toward choice and effect. There isn't one right answer.

Connecting the *Patterns of Revision* to the *Patterns of Power*

If you've come to this book by way of our previous work in the *Patterns of Power* series, this book is not intended as a replacement but rather a supplement to that family of resources. ***Patterns of Power*** focuses on studying authors' use of grammar and mechanics to create meaning and effect. ***Patterns of Revision*** follows a similar structure to *Patterns of Power* in that it asks students to directly apply new concepts in the context of their own writing. *Patterns of Revision* can easily be used in concert with the ongoing work you're doing with grammar instruction—or its lessons can stand on their own. As in *Patterns of Power*, the carefully orchestrated lessons in this book provide all you need, including curated excerpts from authentic literature and culturally nourishing texts (Qarooni 2023) to spark powerful revision conversations along with twenty lesson plans with correlating printables, displays, and step-by-step visual instructions to generate engaging experiences to make revising with depth accessible and memorable to middle schoolers.

Patterns of Revision Lesson	Lesson Type	Goal Focus	Mentor Text Title	Patterns of Power, Grades 6–8 Connection
6.1 Make Like a Toilet and Get the Sentence Out of Here	Delete	Delete unnecessary or repetitive information that obscures meaning	*Poop Happened! A History of the World from the Bottom Up*	
6.2 We've Got an Urge to Purge	Delete	Delete unnecessary or repetitive information that obscures meaning	*Space Case*	
6.3 Tuning Up Our Writing	Delete	Delete unnecessary or repetitive information that obscures meaning	*The Boy Who Harnessed the Wind: Young Readers Edition*	
6.4 Finding the Ripest Order	Rearrange	Rearrange ideas and sentences to ensure a logical progression	*Hello, Universe*	*PoP* Lesson 7.1: If You Continue…The Conditional Mood
6.5 Kicking Around Sentence Order	Rearrange	Rearrange ideas and sentences to ensure a logical progression	*The Big Book of Soccer*	
6.6 Itching to Rearrange	Rearrange	Rearrange ideas and sentences to ensure a logical progression	*Itch! Everything You Didn't Want to Know About What Makes You Scratch*	

(continued)

Patterns of Revision Lesson	Lesson Type	Goal Focus	Mentor Text Title	Patterns of Power, Grades 6–8 Connection
6.7 Connecting Ideas with a Flash of Brilliance	Add	Add information and ideas for coherence and clarity	*The Miscalculations of Lightning Girl*	
6.8 Adding an Extra Dash of Connection	Add	Add information and ideas for coherence and clarity	*The Complete Cookbook for Young Chefs: 100+ Recipes that You'll Love to Cook and Eat*	
6.9 Inventing Connections to Link Sentences	Add	Add information and ideas for coherence and clarity	*Girls Think of Everything: Stories of Ingenious Inventions by Women*	*PoP* Lesson 13.5: Conjunctivitis Connections: Conjunctive Adverbs
6.10 The Remarkable Journey of Forming New Verbs	Form New Verbs	Form new verbs to compress repetition, connect ideas, and improve clarity	*The Remarkable Journey of Coyote Sunrise*	*PoP* Lessons 7.4 or 9.1: Participial Phrases
6.11 Trading Voice	Form New Verbs	Form new verbs to compress repetition, connect ideas, and improve clarity	*The Season of Styx Malone*	*PoP* Lesson 8.1: Subjects Come First: The Active Voice
6.12 We're Popping and Locking with Verbs	Form New Verbs	Form new verbs to compress repetition, connect ideas, and improve clarity	"The Definition of Cool" from *Black Boy Joy*	*PoP* Lesson 10.6: Dashing Through the Sentence: Dash Interruption *PoP* Lessons 6.1 or 6.6: Complex Sentences w/ Dependent Clause Openers
6.13 Saving the Best Content	Combine	Combine ideas to avoid redundancy, add clarity, and improve fluency	"The Save" from *The Hero Next Door*	*PoP* Lesson 6.5: Comma Who, or No Comma Who? A Relative Pronoun Closer
6.14 Combining Isn't as Tough as My Sister	Combine	Combine ideas to avoid redundancy, add clarity, and improve fluency	*Time Villains*	*PoP* Lesson 5.2: The Compound Sentence and And *PoP* Lesson 10.1: This, That, and the Other: Serial Commas *PoP* Lesson 6.1: When Introductory Clauses… Subordinate Opener

(continues)

(continued)

Patterns of Revision Lesson	Lesson Type	Goal Focus	Mentor Text Title	Patterns of Power, Grades 6–8 Connection
6.15 Don't Get Stranded in Revision	Combine	Combine ideas to avoid redundancy, add clarity, and improve fluency	*They Lost Their Heads: What Happened to Washington's Teeth, Einstein's Brain, and Other Famous Body Parts*	*PoP* Lesson 6.1: When Introductory Clauses…Subordinate Opener *PoP* Lesson 10.4 or 10.5: Semicolons
6.16 Adventures in Combining	Combine	Combine ideas to avoid redundancy, add clarity, and improve fluency	*Shipwreck at the Bottom of the World: The Extraordinary True Story of Shackleton and the Endurance*	*PoP* Lesson 10.4 or 10.5: Semicolons *PoP* Lesson 7.5: Creating a Setting (Prepositional Phrases)
6.17 Combining is No Secret: Use DRAFT!	Combine	Combine ideas to avoid redundancy, add clarity, and improve fluency	*Code Breaker, Spy Hunter*	*PoP* Lessons 7.2 or 7.3: Interrupters with Commas *PoP* Lesson 10.6: Dash Interruption
6.18 Don't Let Sentence Combining Plague You	Combine	Combine ideas to avoid redundancy, add clarity, and improve fluency	*Legend*	*PoP* Lesson 13.1: Compound-Complex Sentences *PoP* Lesson 4.5: Don't Allow a Noun with Two Verbs to Startle You
6.19 Getting A Complex Understanding of Revision	Combine	Combine ideas to avoid redundancy, add clarity, and improve fluency	*Thirst*	*PoP* Lesson 6.2 & 6.1: Complex Sentences
6.20 Zooming in on Revision	Combine	Combine ideas to avoid redundancy, add clarity, and improve fluency	*New From Here*	

Part 1

EXPLORING Patterns of REVISION in Bite-Sized CHUNKS

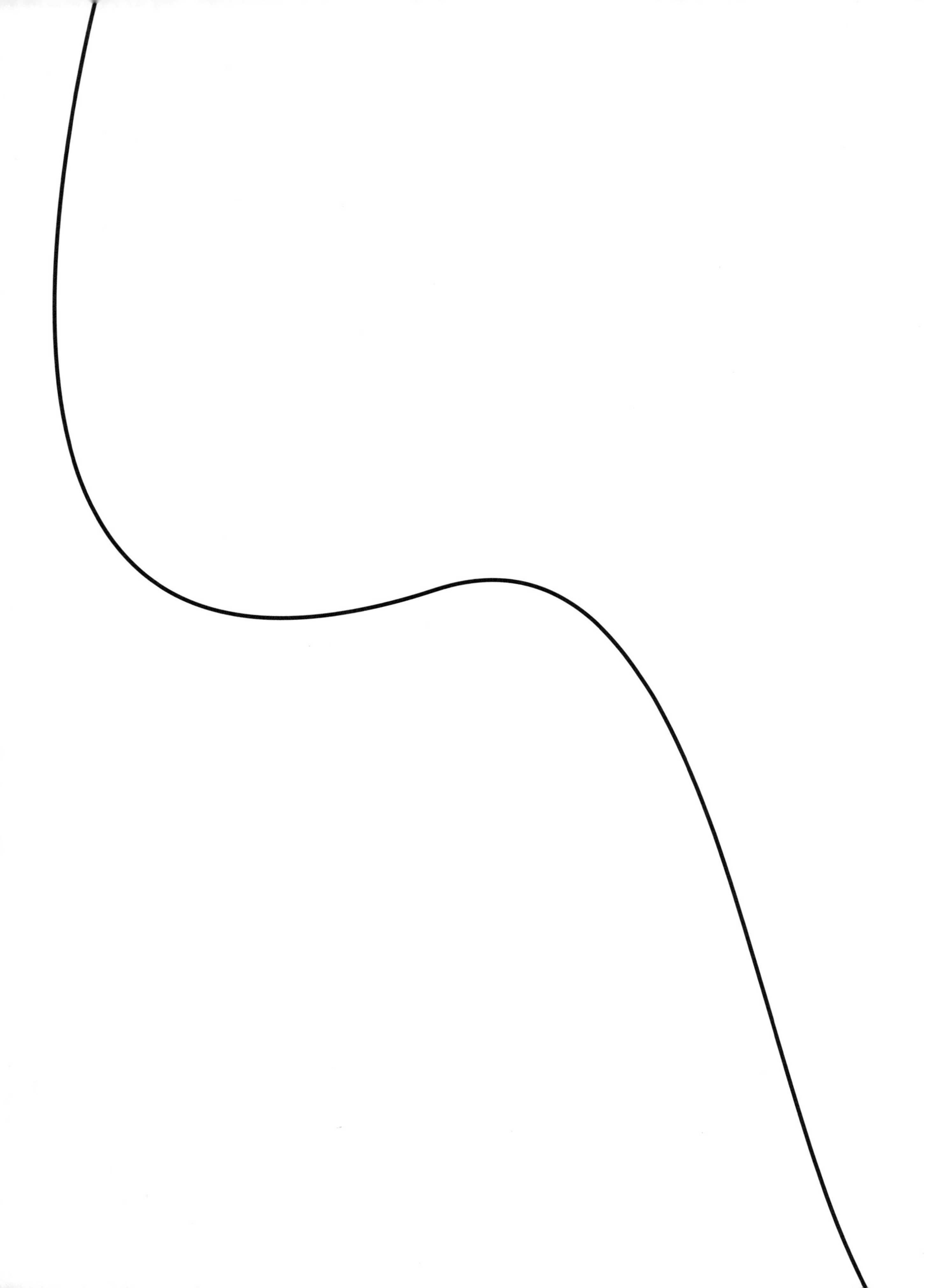

1

Invitation to
DELETE UNNECESSARY INFORMATION

*Getting rid of clutter gives writing its due space: space for thought, space for
readers to soak in what's important, space for what matters most. When we clear out the clutter,
our best thoughts surface and shine.*

– Jeff Anderson, *10 Things Every Writer Needs to Know*

We like to ground the lessons in this chapter with an initial exploration of the word *necessary*. We begin by asking students to share what they think the word *necessary* means. Invariably someone will say something like, "You *have* to do something."

"So, if something is necessary, you *have to* do it. It's important. It's needed. Now think about the prefix *un-*." Students turn to a neighbor and discuss what the prefix *un-* usually does to a word when attached to the beginning of it. The discussion usually produces some responses like "*Un-* almost always means *not*," or "*Un* can mean "*the opposite of.*"

Then, we ask writers to consider how adding *un-* to the beginning of the word *necessary* changes the meaning. We discuss how the opposite of necessary means something you don't need or *have to* do. Now we're cooking with gas.

In this chapter, we include three starter lessons to help students begin to think about parts of their writing that are unnecessary—inclusions they don't need because they're ineffective, repetitive, or things that aren't required in order for their piece to make sense.

As you lead your middle-grade writers through the work of deleting words, phrases, and sentences presented across this chapter, your conversations may naturally evolve to include the idea that revisers can also choose to delete larger chunks of text-like whole paragraphs. For specific guidance in extending discussions with your writers beyond these lessons to the paragraph level, see the **Delete chart** on page 24. Students may keep a copy of this chart in their writing folder, glue a copy into their writing notebook, or access a copy hanging in your classroom.

All the lessons in this chapter follow a similar format. We include a sentence with extra information that *doesn't belong* in the paragraph, and we then invite students to consider which sentence should be deleted and why. First, we try one out together, then writers try a different one in small groups or with partners. To conclude the lesson, students return to their own writing to delete unnecessary details, sentences, or words that get in the way of meaning for readers. We learn by doing, so let's start deleting.

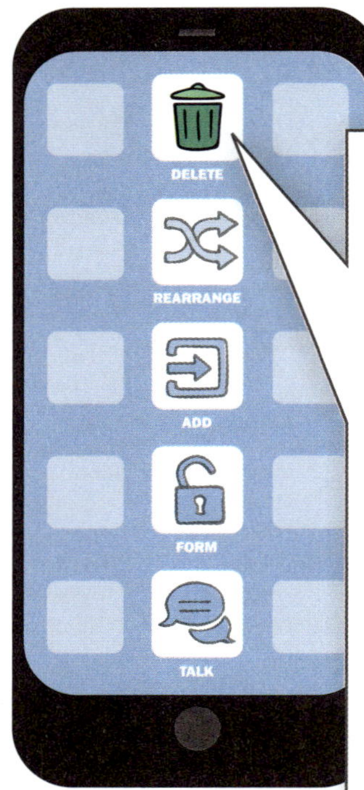

DELETE

Deleting at the **Sentence** Level

Get rid of **WORDY WORDS**
(words that don't say much or are repetitive)

Check your writing for word pairs that actually do the same thing. Delete the extra word.

Examples:

fall down	**BECOMES**	fall
past history	**BECOMES**	past
unexpected surprise	**BECOMES**	surprise
cancel out	**BECOMES**	cancel

Use a single word to say the same thing as the pair or group of words.

Examples:

said loudly	**BECOMES**	yelled
at the present time	**BECOMES**	now

If you are looking to cut words that don't do much work, check your writing for some of the words below. They don't always need to be deleted, but can be easily removed without affecting meaning.

Examples:

absolutely	quite
all	really
completely	sort of
definitely	totally
just	very
kind of	would

Deleting at the **Paragraph** Level

Find your focus
- Read or reread one paragraph you wrote.
- Think about and decide what you think is the main topic or focus of the paragraph.
- Write or say the main focus of the paragraph in one word, phrase, or sentence.

Check your writing for extra ideas not related to your main focus
- After deciding on a main focus, reread your paragraph. Are there any parts of the paragraph that don't match your focus?
- If not, move on to looking at the next paragraph of your composition.
- If so, you have some choices to make:
  – Move these extra ideas somewhere else, either connected to another paragraph or into a new paragraph or another piece of future writing.
  – If these ideas don't fit anywhere, delete them.

6.1 Make Like a Toilet and Get the Sentence Out of Here

Lesson Overview

Revision goal connected to standards:

Develop and strengthen writing by deleting unnecessary or repetitive information that obscures meaning.

Model Text

Poop Happened! A History of the World from the Bottom Up
- Written by Sarah Albee
- Illustrated by Robert Leighton

Teacher Considerations

We often ask writers to identify places in their writing that may seem unclear or ineffective to readers. When we take a closer look, a common reason the piece is unclear or ineffective is because extra information exists within paragraphs that is unrelated to the topic. To help them gain confidence in deleting information that doesn't belong, we invite writers to approach revision with conversations and thinking around meaning and effect, instead of what's right and what's wrong.

We start this set of lessons with the engaging nonfiction text *Poop Happened! A History of the World from the Bottom Up* by Sarah Albee. We find Albee's nonfiction titles fascinate sixth grade students, and they are designed to invite all types of readers into the content.

Since this will likely be the first *Patterns of Revision* lesson you provide for your sixth-grade students in the school year, you may choose to add more guidance during the discussion. If you do, be sure to leave ample time for authentic conversations, keeping this lesson focused on your students' thoughts and discoveries rather than a checklist of tasks.

Setting the Context

To set a context, read aloud the excerpt of Sarah Albee's *Poop Happened! A History of the World from the Bottom Up* in which she chronicles the wonders of the toilet (Shh! We've added a sentence that doesn't belong.):

Take a good look at your toilet. Have you ever really thought about how it works? It may not look like much, but it's an engineering marvel. How did a knight wearing fifty pounds of armor go to the bathroom?

 **Revision Strategy**
Delete repeated or unnecessary information.

Modeling

Display **6.1 Unnecessary Sentence: Part I**, which includes each sentence from the model excerpt (and a sentence unrelated to the topic that needs to be deleted) numbered in order. Ask students, "What is this paragraph mostly about?" or "What is the central idea of this paragraph?" Then share with students that one sentence in this paragraph does not support this big idea. "Something is off in this paragraph. Let's check each sentence, one by one, to see if it ties back to the author's message of this paragraph." Think aloud while you model taking out each one of the sentences to examine its effect on meaning.

Students talk it out for each sentence using the following questions to prompt the conversation:

- How would deleting this sentence affect the meaning? WHY?
- Do we need this sentence? WHY or WHY NOT?

Through discussion, the students determine that sentence #4 doesn't belong because it is not connected to the focus of the first three sentences (a toilet), but instead focusing on the broader topic of a knight trying to use the bathroom. Using the display page, **6.1 Unnecessary Sentence: Part II**, reveal the original excerpt from *Poop Happened!* and compare how the different version affects meaning.

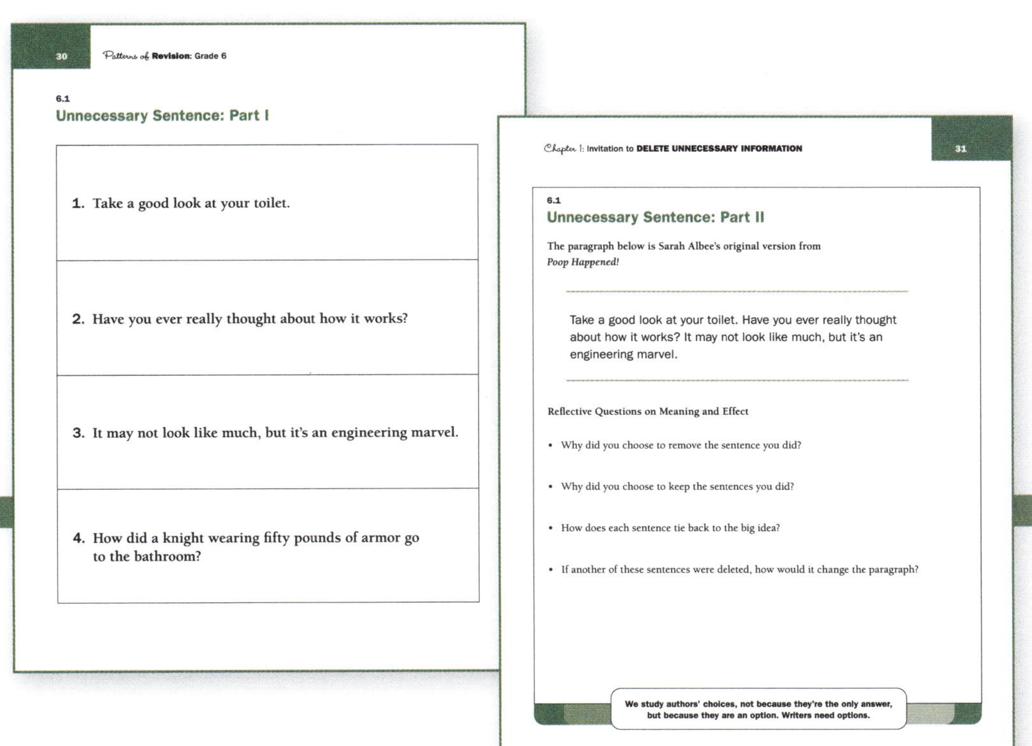

Collaborating Through Conversation

Organize students into pairs or small groups. Display **6.1 Invitation to Delete Unnecessary Information: Part I**. You may choose to prepare the sentences for your students to manipulate on sentence strips, index cards, or electronically. Students collaborate through conversation to delete the unnecessary sentence from another paragraph from *Poop Happened!* To help students talk it out, remind them to explore how each sentence supports or ties into the message of the paragraph and to look for information that may be repeated. By justifying their thinking, students take ownership of their decisions to delete or keep information.

When ready, students compare their deletion choices with others in class, talking through their decisions together. The point here is for them to discuss WHY they made the choice. Display the author's original text using **6.1 Invitation to Delete Unnecessary Information: Part II** for comparative analysis. Refer to the reflective questions to facilitate a conversation about meaning and effect.

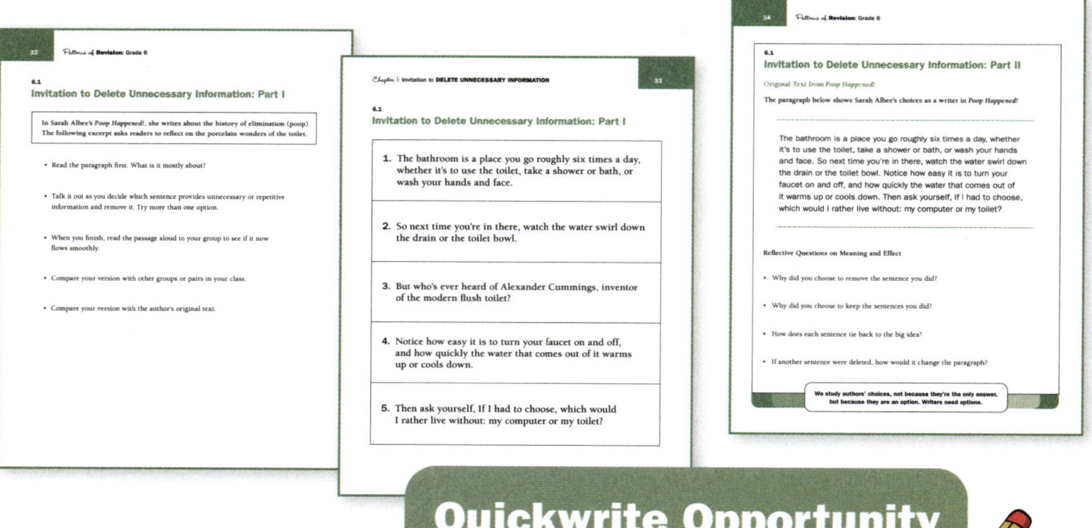

Quickwrite Opportunity (Optional)

1. What is one item that exists in your home that you couldn't live without? Explain what's important about this item and what life would be like if it didn't exist. (Some options to prompt student thinking could include *refrigerator, microwave, computer, TOILET, air conditioning, etc.*)

2. Answer the author's question from the Collaborating Through Conversation work: *If I had to choose, which would I rather live without: my computer or my toilet?* Explain your choice.

Applying Revision

To set your students up for applying this revision strategy in their own writing, return to a piece of writing from your own notebook, a class piece that you've been working on, or use one of the writing prompts above to generate a piece of writing right now. Then, engage your students in a live demonstration highlighting a paragraph of writing, deciding what the paragraph is about, and then checking sentence-by-sentence to make sure you've stayed on topic. Model how to look at one sentence at a time and elicit support from your students as you make decisions about deleting. This modeling with classroom input will reinforce the idea that these revision strategies apply to all writers and can strengthen all writing.

Students return to their own writing or their writer's notebooks and play with deleting unnecessary information and noticing its effect. Invite them to choose one section or paragraph to revise at a time. Some learners may find it helpful to write each sentence on a strip of paper or sticky note so they can physically manipulate their writing, deciding if each sentence connects to the meaning of the piece. It may help students to talk it out with a partner or with themselves as they consider their own central ideas and information that are needed and not needed. Some may decide nothing needs to be deleted. In this case, remind them to move on to other sections of their pieces to do this same work.

Sharing Results

Set your writers up for sharing success by posting discussion starters/stems to use as a starting point for discussion. Students choose a stem, use it as the start of their discussion, and add their own content to finish the stem. Here are some sentence starter/stem options:

- Something I chose to delete in my writing . . .
- I chose to delete ______________ because . . .
- One revision I made is . . .

6.1

Unnecessary Sentence: Part I

1. Take a good look at your toilet.

2. Have you ever really thought about how it works?

3. It may not look like much, but it's an engineering marvel.

4. How did a knight wearing fifty pounds of armor go to the bathroom?

6.1

Unnecessary Sentence: Part II

The paragraph below is Sarah Albee's original version from
Poop Happened!

Take a good look at your toilet. Have you ever really thought about how it works? It may not look like much, but it's an engineering marvel.

Reflective Questions on Meaning and Effect

* Why did you choose to remove the sentence you did?

* Why did you choose to keep the sentences you did?

* How does each sentence tie back to the big idea?

* If another of these sentences were deleted, how would it change the paragraph?

We study authors' choices, not because they're the only answer, but because they are an option. Writers need options.

6.1

Invitation to Delete Unnecessary Information: Part I

In Sarah Albee's *Poop Happened!*, she writes about the history of elimination (poop). The following excerpt asks readers to reflect on the porcelain wonders of the toilet.

- Read the paragraph first. What is it mostly about?

- Talk it out as you decide which sentence provides unnecessary or repetitive information and remove it. Try more than one option.

- When you finish, read the passage aloud to your group to see if it now flows smoothly.

- Compare your version with other groups or pairs in your class.

- Compare your version with the author's original text.

6.1

Invitation to Delete Unnecessary Information: Part I

1. The bathroom is a place you go roughly six times a day, whether it's to use the toilet, take a shower or bath, or wash your hands and face.

2. So next time you're in there, watch the water swirl down the drain or the toilet bowl.

3. But who's ever heard of Alexander Cummings, inventor of the modern flush toilet?

4. Notice how easy it is to turn your faucet on and off, and how quickly the water that comes out of it warms up or cools down.

5. Then ask yourself, If I had to choose, which would I rather live without: my computer or my toilet?

6.1

Invitation to Delete Unnecessary Information: Part II

Original Text from *Poop Happened!*

The paragraph below shows Sarah Albee's choices as a writer in *Poop Happened!*

The bathroom is a place you go roughly six times a day, whether it's to use the toilet, take a shower or bath, or wash your hands and face. So next time you're in there, watch the water swirl down the drain or the toilet bowl. Notice how easy it is to turn your faucet on and off, and how quickly the water that comes out of it warms up or cools down. Then ask yourself, If I had to choose, which would I rather live without: my computer or my toilet?

Reflective Questions on Meaning and Effect

- Why did you choose to remove the sentence you did?

- Why did you choose to keep the sentences you did?

- How does each sentence tie back to the big idea?

- If another sentence were deleted, how would it change the paragraph?

> **We study authors' choices, not because they're the only answer, but because they are an option. Writers need options.**

6.2 We've Got an Urge to Purge

Lesson Overview

Revision goal connected to standards:

Develop and strengthen writing by deleting unnecessary or repetitive information that obscures meaning.

Model Text

Space Case
- Written by Stuart Gibbs

Teacher Considerations

As we continue facilitating discussions with our students around choices writers make, we consider a common reason a piece of writing may be unclear or ineffective: it includes distracting, repetitive information. To help students gain confidence in deleting information that doesn't belong, we invite writers to continue to approach revision with conversations and thinking around meaning and effect, instead of what's right and what's wrong.

We love Stuart Gibbs' book *Space Case* because of the humorous personality Gibbs develops in his narrator, Dashiell (Dash) Gibson. It's an engaging mystery set on the moon that includes equal parts humor and suspense. Sixth graders love not only this book, but they also devour the rest of the series. Also, we promise the rest of the lessons won't be about toilets!

Setting the Context

In the book *Space Case*, author Stuart Gibbs describes Moon Base Alpha, a livable space station that has been built on the moon. We get to hear all about this base from the perspective of the main character, Dashiell (Dash) Gibson, who is particularly eager to share his feelings about the bathrooms. You'll read a little bit about the bathrooms of Moon Base Alpha from the book to your students. We've added a sentence that repeats information and doesn't belong, but don't tell your students. You'll reveal the original version later.

The living quarters are all in one section of the base, but the geniuses who designed MBA put the bathrooms on the opposite side. The "logical" explanation for this was that the bathrooms would be closer to the work and dining areas, where we—in theory—would spend most of our awake time. Unfortunately, this means that when the urge to purge strikes in the middle of the night, you have to get dressed, leave your quarters, cross the base, use the complicated toilet, and then head back again. The whole process of using the toilet takes a lot of time. It can take fifteen minutes—or more if the toilet jams, which happens far more often than anyone predicted. Everyone at MBA loathes the entire process.

Prompt your students with, "Sometimes when we write, we include information that doesn't really belong, or when we try to elaborate or add details, we repeat the same information in a different way. This can be confusing for our readers. Do you feel like there is some information that doesn't belong or says the same thing—like it repeats information?"

Revision Strategy

Delete repeated or unnecessary information.

Modeling

Display **6.2 Unnecessary Sentence: Part I**, which includes each sentence from the model excerpt (and a repetitive sentence that needs to be deleted) numbered in order. For students that could benefit from physically manipulating them, you may choose to display the individual sentences on index cards or sentence strips—or even electronically. To invite the thinking that is involved in deleting unnecessary or repetitive information, share the **Delete chart** found on page 24 with your students. You may choose to have them glue this chart into their notebooks for future reference. Invite your students to pay close attention to the bottom half of the chart: Deleting at the Paragraph Level. Then return to the excerpt from *Space Case* and ask, "What is this paragraph mostly about?" Guide your students through a discussion about choosing which sentence doesn't really belong and why. "Something is off in this paragraph. Let's check each sentence, one by one, to see if each sentence says something different about the toilets at Moon Base Alpha." Think aloud while modeling how to reread, taking out a different sentence each time and talking the change through to examine its effect on meaning. Students will likely notice that some of the information is repeated.

Students talk it out for each sentence using the following questions to prompt the conversation:

- How would deleting this sentence affect the meaning? WHY?
- Do we need this sentence? WHY or WHY NOT?

Through discussion, students may share that sentences 4 and 5 are saying essentially the same thing. Keep in mind that it's not about right or wrong, but rather what is most effective. Continue asking questions using the prompts to help students consider how, although it may make sense in the excerpt, both sentences aren't necessary. Using the display page, **6.2 Unnecessary Sentence: Part II**, reveal the original excerpt from *Space Case* and compare how the different version affects meaning.

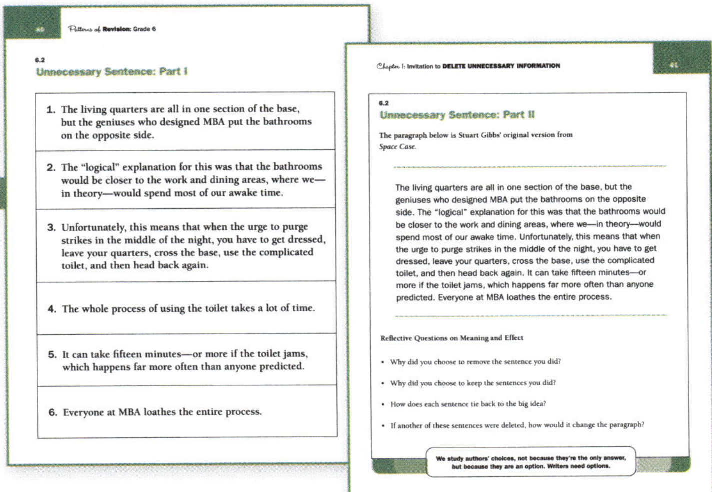

Collaborating Through Conversation

Organize students into pairs or small groups. Display **6.2 Invitation to Delete Unnecessary Information: Part I**. You may choose to prepare the sentences for your students to manipulate on sentence strips, index cards, or electronically. Students collaborate through conversation to delete the unnecessary sentence from another paragraph from *Space Case*. To help students talk it out, remind them to explore how each sentence supports or connects to the message of the paragraph and to look for information that may be repeated. By justifying their thinking, students take ownership of their decisions to delete or keep information.

When ready, students compare their deletion choices with others in class, talking through their decisions together. The point here is for them to discuss WHY they made the choice. Display the author's original text using **6.2 Invitation to Delete Unnecessary Information: Part II** for comparative analysis. Refer to the reflective questions to facilitate a conversation about meaning and effect.

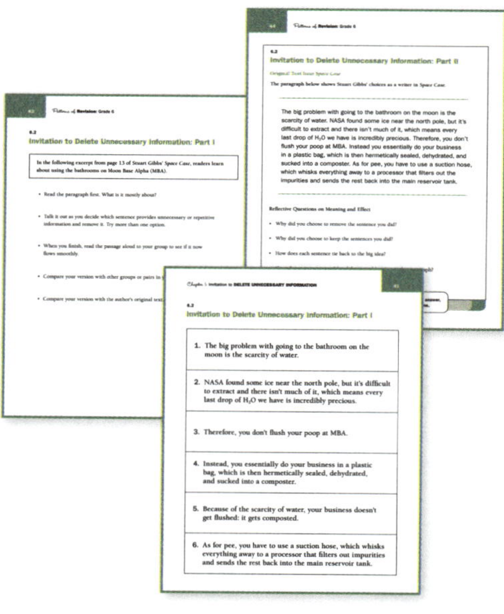

Figure 6.2

Students discuss which information doesn't belong.

Quickwrite Opportunity (Optional)

1. Would you want to live in a space colony on the moon? What might go into someone's decision to live on the moon? What might be some of the pros and cons of living on the moon?
2. Describe what an important place in your life looks like. Then, write about a memory that took place at this important place.

Applying Revision

To set your students up for applying this revision strategy in their own writing, you may choose to return to a piece of writing from your own notebook or a class piece that you've been working on. If necessary, you may want to use one of the prompts above to generate a piece of writing in the moment. Then, engage your students in a demonstration of searching for information that is either repeated or simply does not belong. Model how to look at one sentence at a time and elicit support from them as you make decisions about deleting. This modeling with input from the class will reinforce the idea that these revision strategies apply to all writers and can strengthen all writing.

Students then return to their own writing (either drafts on the computer, or in their writer's notebooks) and play with deleting unnecessary or repetitive information while gauging the effects of such removals. To help them focus, encourage writers to choose one section or paragraph to revise at a time. It may help individuals to talk it out with a partner or in their heads as they consider whether information is needed or not needed. Some students may decide nothing needs to be deleted. In this case, encourage them to move on to other sections of their pieces and continue the process. You can also invite them to consider repetitive words. Invite them to circle words they notice they are using often so they can see the possibilities for deletion. Writers have options.

Sharing Results

Writers share their revisions with others and celebrate their work by naming how their revisions will help their readers understand their writing more clearly. Listeners paraphrase what they heard the speaker say, then affirm if the speaker met their revision goal of helping their reader understand their writing more clearly. Listeners can choose a sentence starter below to begin their feedback, adding their ideas to finish the stem. Here are some sentence starter/stem options:

- What I heard you say was . . .
- What I'm hearing is . . . Is that correct?
- One thing you did to help me better understand your writing is . . .

6.2

Unnecessary Sentence: Part I

1. The living quarters are all in one section of the base, but the geniuses who designed MBA put the bathrooms on the opposite side.

2. The "logical" explanation for this was that the bathrooms would be closer to the work and dining areas, where we—in theory—would spend most of our awake time.

3. Unfortunately, this means that when the urge to purge strikes in the middle of the night, you have to get dressed, leave your quarters, cross the base, use the complicated toilet, and then head back again.

4. The whole process of using the toilet takes a lot of time.

5. It can take fifteen minutes—or more if the toilet jams, which happens far more often than anyone predicted.

6. Everyone at MBA loathes the entire process.

6.2

Unnecessary Sentence: Part II

The paragraph below is Stuart Gibbs' original version from
Space Case.

The living quarters are all in one section of the base, but the geniuses who designed MBA put the bathrooms on the opposite side. The "logical" explanation for this was that the bathrooms would be closer to the work and dining areas, where we—in theory—would spend most of our awake time. Unfortunately, this means that when the urge to purge strikes in the middle of the night, you have to get dressed, leave your quarters, cross the base, use the complicated toilet, and then head back again. It can take fifteen minutes—or more if the toilet jams, which happens far more often than anyone predicted. Everyone at MBA loathes the entire process.

Reflective Questions on Meaning and Effect

- Why did you choose to remove the sentence you did?

- Why did you choose to keep the sentences you did?

- How does each sentence tie back to the big idea?

- If another of these sentences were deleted, how would it change the paragraph?

We study authors' choices, not because they're the only answer, but because they are an option. Writers need options.

6.2

Invitation to Delete Unnecessary Information: Part I

In the following excerpt from page 13 of Stuart Gibbs' *Space Case*, readers learn about using the bathrooms on Moon Base Alpha (MBA).

- Read the paragraph first. What is it mostly about?

- Talk it out as you decide which sentence provides unnecessary or repetitive information and remove it. Try more than one option.

- When you finish, read the passage aloud to your group to see if it now flows smoothly.

- Compare your version with other groups or pairs in your class.

- Compare your version with the author's original text.

6.2

Invitation to Delete Unnecessary Information: Part I

1. The big problem with going to the bathroom on the moon is the scarcity of water.

2. NASA found some ice near the north pole, but it's difficult to extract and there isn't much of it, which means every last drop of H_2O we have is incredibly precious.

3. Therefore, you don't flush your poop at MBA.

4. Instead, you essentially do your business in a plastic bag, which is then hermetically sealed, dehydrated, and sucked into a composter.

5. Because of the scarcity of water, your business doesn't get flushed: it gets composted.

6. As for pee, you have to use a suction hose, which whisks everything away to a processor that filters out impurities and sends the rest back into the main reservoir tank.

6.2

Invitation to Delete Unnecessary Information: Part II

Original Text from *Space Case*

The paragraph below shows Stuart Gibbs' choices as a writer in *Space Case*.

The big problem with going to the bathroom on the moon is the scarcity of water. NASA found some ice near the north pole, but it's difficult to extract and there isn't much of it, which means every last drop of H_2O we have is incredibly precious. Therefore, you don't flush your poop at MBA. Instead you essentially do your business in a plastic bag, which is then hermetically sealed, dehydrated, and sucked into a composter. As for pee, you have to use a suction hose, which whisks everything away to a processor that filters out the impurities and sends the rest back into the main reservoir tank.

Reflective Questions on Meaning and Effect

- Why did you choose to remove the sentence you did?

- Why did you choose to keep the sentences you did?

- How does each sentence tie back to the big idea?

- If another sentence were deleted, how would it change the paragraph?

> **We study authors' choices, not because they're the only answer, but because they are an option. Writers need options.**

6.3 Tuning Up Our Writing

Lesson Overview

Revision goal connected to standards:

Develop and strengthen writing by deleting unnecessary information that obscures meaning.

Model Text

The Boy Who Harnessed the Wind: Young Readers Edition
- Written by William Kamkwamba and Bryan Mealer
- Illustrated by Anna Hymas

Teacher Considerations

In this lesson, as with the previous two lessons, we engage students in conversations about meaning and effect as they think about what information belongs in their writing, and what information could be deleted. Additionally, we use this lesson to show writers that when we delete, it doesn't mean the information is going away forever. It often doesn't belong in that place, but it could go somewhere else. We tell writers to simply cross through unnecessary information in their own pieces, as opposed to fully erasing or deleting it. This way, they can refer back to it later in their writing, or in another piece, to see if there is a better place for it.

Setting the Context

To set the context, read aloud the excerpt of William Kamkwamba and Bryan Mealer's *The Boy Who Harnessed the Wind* in which the narrator, William, describes how he and the members of his community at the time interacted with the radio.

Since we didn't have electricity or television, the radio was our only link to the world outside our village. The same was true in many other parts of Africa. In most places you go, whether it's deep in the forest or in the city, you'll see people listening to small portable radios. At the time, Malawi had two stations called Radio One and Radio Two, both run by the government. In addition to giving us the news and sports, they also played Malawian reggae music and American rhythm and blues, along with Chichewa gospel choirs and Sunday church sermons.

Prompt your students with, "Sometimes when we write, we include information that doesn't really belong in that place. This can be confusing for our readers. Let's take a look and see what information in this paragraph may not belong here, in this place."

 **Revision Strategy**
Delete repeated or unnecessary information.

Modeling

Display **6.3 Unnecessary Sentence: Part I**, which includes each sentence from the mentor excerpt (as well as an unnecessary sentence that needs to be deleted) numbered in order. You may choose to write these sentences on sentence strips, index cards, or digitally for physical manipulation during the lesson.

To spark some thinking around deleting unnecessary information, ask students, "What is this paragraph mostly about?" Then share with your students that one sentence in this paragraph does not support the event described. "Something is off in this paragraph. Let's check each sentence, one by one, to see if it ties back to the event described in this paragraph." Think aloud while modeling how to reread, taking out a different sentence each time and talking the change through to examine its effect on meaning.

Students talk it out for each sentence using the following questions to prompt the conversation:

- How would deleting this sentence affect the meaning? WHY?
- Do we need this one? WHY or WHY NOT?

Through discussion, students determine that sentence #5 doesn't belong because it provided additional information that really isn't necessary to the topic being developed in the paragraph. It could possibly go somewhere else in the book, but not here. Display the original excerpt from *The Boy Who Harnessed the Wind* using **6.3 Unnecessary Sentence: Part II**, and compare how the different version affects meaning.

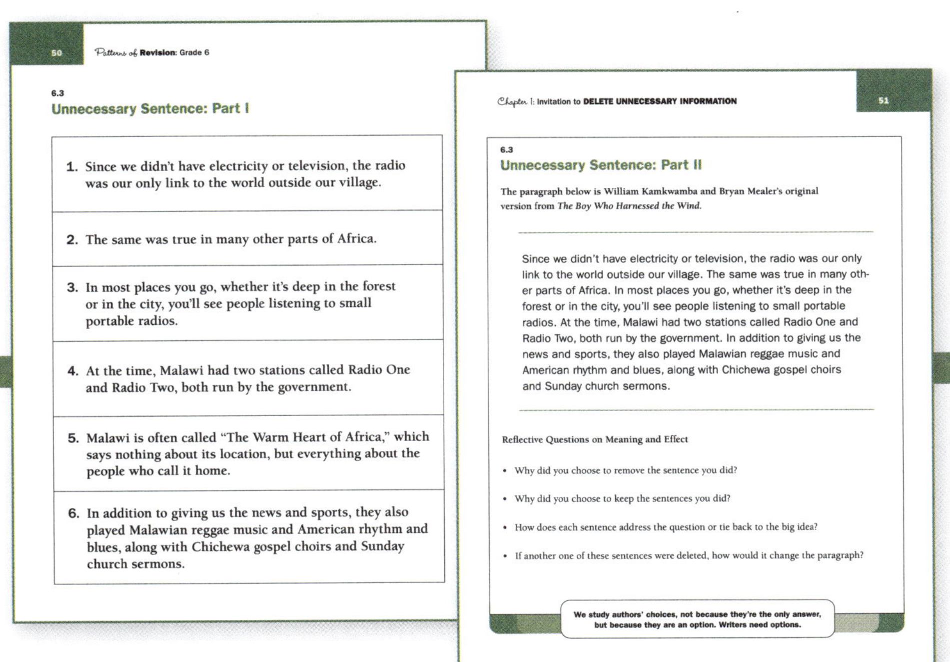

Collaborating Through Conversation

Display **6.3 Invitation to Delete Unnecessary Information: Part I**. In pairs or small groups, students follow the directions provided and collaborate through conversation to delete the unnecessary sentence. To help students talk it out, remind them to explore how each sentence should support the event described in the paragraph. By justifying their thinking, students take ownership of their decision to delete.

When ready, students compare their deletion choice with others in class, talking through their decisions together. The point here is for them to discuss WHY they made the choice. Share the author's original text by displaying **6.3 Invitation to Delete Unnecessary Information: Part II** for comparative analysis, using the reflective questions provided to facilitate a conversation about meaning and effect.

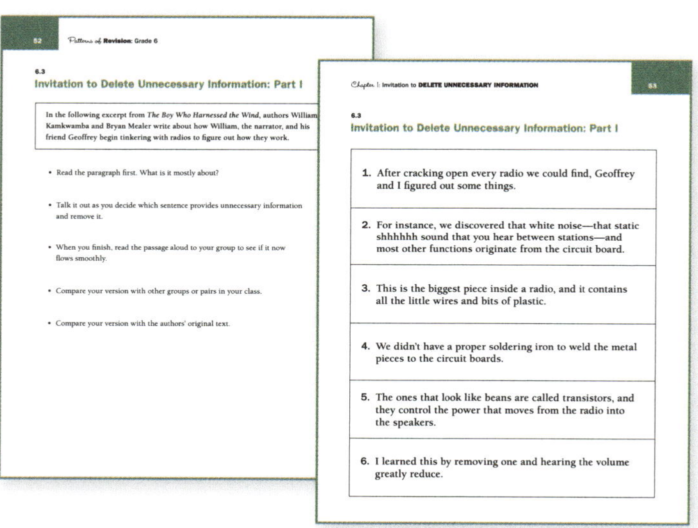

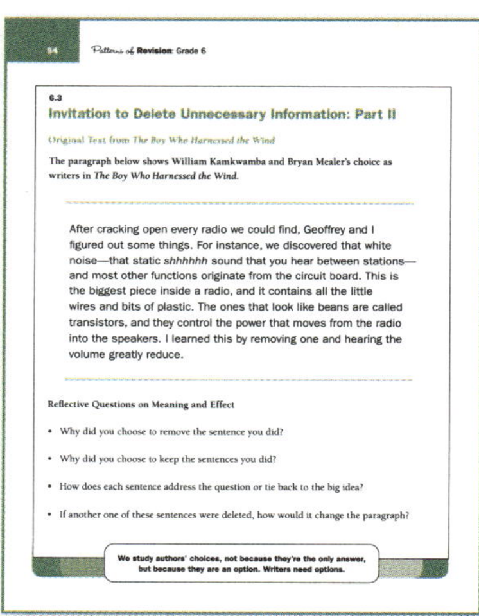

Quickwrite Opportunity (Optional)

1. Imagine you stumble upon an old radio from a different era. If tuning the dial transported you to a different era of time, what era would you travel to, and what kind of music would you hear?

2. Describe what your typical day would look like in a world where electricity doesn't exist. How would you wake up, prepare meals, study, or even entertain yourself?

Applying Revision

Students return to their own writing or their writer's notebooks and play with deleting unnecessary information and noticing the effect of the removal. If students are writing to a prompt, invite them to check each sentence in their entire piece to ensure that each one supports what the prompt is asking of them. Or, if working on another piece that's not prompt-driven, students may choose one section or paragraph to revise at a time. It often helps to talk things out with a partner when revising a piece of writing, so invite your writers to self-select into learning pairs if they think it would be helpful.

Sharing Results

Share and celebrate the revision writers did in this lesson. They may have chosen to delete a few words or phrases while others deleted entire sentences, or even paragraphs. Choose one or two students to share their revised selections with the class, naming how the writer effectively used the revision strategy: delete unnecessary information. If you've used sentence stems in either of the previous lessons, encourage students to use these stems as they talk with each other.

If time allows, this is also a great opportunity for students to participate in reflective practice around their learning and takeaways as writers from participating in the lessons in this chapter. Use any of the following prompts to support a more holistic reflection of learning across the three lessons in this chapter.

- What is one thing you've learned from the lessons about deleting that you want to use as a writer moving forward?
- What did you learn about yourself as a writer from our work with these revision lessons?
- What is your biggest takeaway about writing you gained from the authors we've studied in class?

6.3

Unnecessary Sentence: Part I

1. Since we didn't have electricity or television, the radio was our only link to the world outside our village.

2. The same was true in many other parts of Africa.

3. In most places you go, whether it's deep in the forest or in the city, you'll see people listening to small portable radios.

4. At the time, Malawi had two stations called Radio One and Radio Two, both run by the government.

5. Malawi is often called "The Warm Heart of Africa," which says nothing about its location, but everything about the people who call it home.

6. In addition to giving us the news and sports, they also played Malawian reggae music and American rhythm and blues, along with Chichewa gospel choirs and Sunday church sermons.

6.3

Unnecessary Sentence: Part II

The paragraph below is William Kamkwamba and Bryan Mealer's original version from *The Boy Who Harnessed the Wind.*

Since we didn't have electricity or television, the radio was our only link to the world outside our village. The same was true in many other parts of Africa. In most places you go, whether it's deep in the forest or in the city, you'll see people listening to small portable radios. At the time, Malawi had two stations called Radio One and Radio Two, both run by the government. In addition to giving us the news and sports, they also played Malawian reggae music and American rhythm and blues, along with Chichewa gospel choirs and Sunday church sermons.

Reflective Questions on Meaning and Effect

- Why did you choose to remove the sentence you did?

- Why did you choose to keep the sentences you did?

- How does each sentence address the question or tie back to the big idea?

- If another one of these sentences were deleted, how would it change the paragraph?

We study authors' choices, not because they're the only answer, but because they are an option. Writers need options.

6.3

Invitation to Delete Unnecessary Information: Part I

In the following excerpt from *The Boy Who Harnessed the Wind*, authors William Kamkwamba and Bryan Mealer write about how William, the narrator, and his friend Geoffrey begin tinkering with radios to figure out how they work.

- Read the paragraph first. What is it mostly about?

- Talk it out as you decide which sentence provides unnecessary information and remove it.

- When you finish, read the passage aloud to your group to see if it now flows smoothly.

- Compare your version with other groups or pairs in your class.

- Compare your version with the authors' original text.

6.3

Invitation to Delete Unnecessary Information: Part I

1. After cracking open every radio we could find, Geoffrey and I figured out some things.

2. For instance, we discovered that white noise—that static shhhhhh sound that you hear between stations—and most other functions originate from the circuit board.

3. This is the biggest piece inside a radio, and it contains all the little wires and bits of plastic.

4. We didn't have a proper soldering iron to weld the metal pieces to the circuit boards.

5. The ones that look like beans are called transistors, and they control the power that moves from the radio into the speakers.

6. I learned this by removing one and hearing the volume greatly reduce.

6.3

Invitation to Delete Unnecessary Information: Part II

Original Text from *The Boy Who Harnessed the Wind*

The paragraph below shows William Kamkwamba and Bryan Mealer's choice as writers in *The Boy Who Harnessed the Wind.*

After cracking open every radio we could find, Geoffrey and I figured out some things. For instance, we discovered that white noise—that static *shhhhhh* sound that you hear between stations—and most other functions originate from the circuit board. This is the biggest piece inside a radio, and it contains all the little wires and bits of plastic. The ones that look like beans are called transistors, and they control the power that moves from the radio into the speakers. I learned this by removing one and hearing the volume greatly reduce.

Reflective Questions on Meaning and Effect

- Why did you choose to remove the sentence you did?

- Why did you choose to keep the sentences you did?

- How does each sentence address the question or tie back to the big idea?

- If another one of these sentences were deleted, how would it change the paragraph?

We study authors' choices, not because they're the only answer, but because they are an option. Writers need options.

*I rearrange a sentence many times. . . . For me, the . . . process feels like a form of play,
like a puzzle that needs solving, and it's one of the most satisfying parts of writing.*

– Karen Thompson Walker

Interior designers move furniture and decorations around again and again. They continue adjusting until everything is in just the right place. Writers do this kind of design work as well. We can move words around. We can move phrases around. We can move sentences around. We can even move entire paragraphs around. Meaning and emphasis can change as we rearrange words.

a shower of meteors vs. a meteor shower

Since rearranging can often cause us to make meaning-driven additions and deletions, you'll see your writers calling on strategies they've learned in previous lessons—and dabbling with a few they'll study in future lessons—as they tease out possibilities across this lesson set. Notice how rearranging the preceding example caused us to delete the word *of*, which didn't really change the meaning—but did create a slightly different effect. This is a natural part of rearranging that occurs organically in the discussions you'll have with your writers.

We can move phrases and clauses, too, listening for the most effective options.

When I was little, I ate Spaghetti-Os. vs. I ate Spaghetti-Os when I was little.

Rearranging opens new possibilities and encourages revisers to play and experiment. Orally talking out arrangement choices and shuffling sequences can bring order out of chaos. Keep it light, keep it playful, and emphasize that rearranging is about stretching. If you aren't trying out things and discovering they don't work, you're likely not playing with the words or the order enough.

All the lessons in this chapter follow the same format. We share a paragraph with sentences arranged in an illogical or mixed-up order and then ask students to rearrange them in a way that makes sense. First, we try it out together, then writers try a different paragraph in small groups or with partners. We conclude each lesson by inviting students to go back to their own writing to consider how they have arranged their ideas and revise in places in which doing so would make their piece more effective. Even if they choose not to keep their revisions, we still encourage them to try a few versions, because we count it as a win any time we can spur students into revising multiple times, testing out and stretching with possibilities.

The **Rearrange chart** on page 56 can be used as a reference throughout the lessons and beyond. Students may keep a copy in their writing folder, glue a copy into their writing notebook, or access a copy hanging in your classroom.

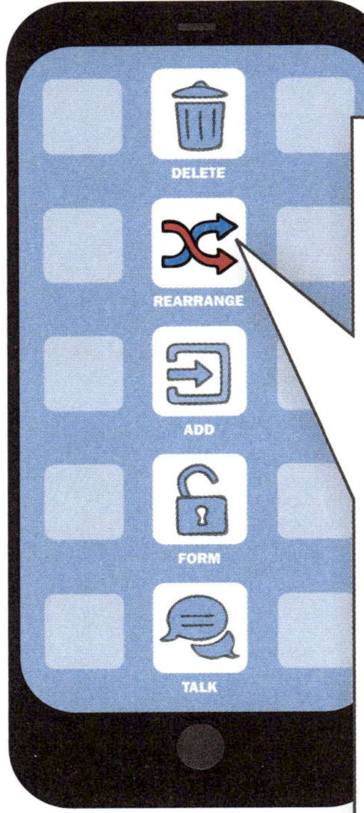

REARRANGE

Rearranging at the **Sentence** Level

Rearranging Words in a Sentence

The cat played with the ball of yarn gently.	to	The cat gently played with the ball of yarn.
Also, Travis plays basketball.	to	Travis also plays basketball.

Rearranging Phrases in a Sentence

Writers can take a phrase and move it to the beginning, in the middle, or at the end of the sentence. You might have to rearrange, add, or delete words or punctuation when you do this.

Phrases that show when	In the meantime, Jeff read a book. Jeff read a book in the meantime.
Phrases that show where	The parade lasted forever on the TV. The parade on the TV lasted forever.
Phrases that show action	Whitney was walking the dogs and saw a cat. While walking the dogs, Whitney saw a cat.

Rearranging Parts of Compound or Complex Sentences

Rearranging a compound sentence	At recess, I went down the slide, and I played with my friends. I played with my friends, and I went down the slide at recess.
Rearranging a complex sentence	While Summer played basketball at recess, Josie twirled on the monkey bars. Josie twirled on the monkey bars while Summer played basketball at recess.

Rearranging at the **Paragraph** Level

Writers can also look at each of the sentences in a paragraph to ensure they are ordered in a way that makes the most sense. Not sure if your sentences are in the best order? Try one of these ideas out:

Break it up!	Break the sentences in your paragraph apart and look at each one separately. Ask yourself if putting them in another order makes sense. If your original order makes the most sense to you, ask yourself why that is. Imagine you had to defend this order of sentences to a classmate or your teacher. What would you say? Talk yourself through why this order makes the most sense. If you notice moving one or more sentences around sounds better, you have the power to do it!
Find a friend	Get a friend or classmate to look at the sentences in one of your paragraphs separated out into individual sentences. Have them put the sentences back together in the order that makes sense to them. Then, have a discussion about why they chose the order they did. If their order is different from your original, you can either talk to your friend/classmate about why you chose a different order, or you can rearrange your sentences to this new order.

6.4 Finding the Ripest Order

Lesson Overview

Revision goal connected to standards:

Develop and strengthen writing by rearranging ideas to ensure a logical progression.

Model Text

Hello, Universe
- – Written by Erin Entrada Kelly
- – Illustrated by Isabel Roxas

Teacher Considerations

In addition to deleting unnecessary information, another important writing goal for our students is to compose pieces that are clear and connected with logically ordered ideas, sentences, and paragraphs. Share the **Rearrange chart** on page 56 with your students, so they can refer to it as they work across the upcoming lessons. You may decide to have them glue it into their notebooks for future reference. In this revision lesson, we focus on coherence as we invite students to consider places in their writing that may seem disconnected or illogical. We chose *Hello, Universe* by Erin Entrada Kelly as a focus for this lesson not only because it's a Newbery Award winner, but also because the characters in this story are so relatable to our students.

This lesson begins with the teacher reading an excerpt from the book. We then take part of that excerpt, present it out of order, and invite students to organize it in ways that make sense through conversations about meaning and effect. We especially encourage them to take time to visualize the text and discuss how sentence placement impacts mental images and logical order.

The second model in *Patterns of Power (6–8)* **Lesson 7.1** includes two complex sentences with *If* as the opener, showing conditional mood.

Setting the Context

You may decide to read part of this book aloud to your students, or you can share what the book is about and explain that today, we will learn more about the character Valencia as she shops with her mother at the Super Saver grocery store. To set up the reading, tell students Valencia's mother asks her to grab some avocados, and Valencia shares how she chooses the best ones. Then read aloud this section:

"Go get me three avocados," she says, like I'm her personal servant. Then she gestures toward the produce section, which is like five hundred aisles away. Great. Now I have to find the avocados, and I don't even like them.

Even though I think avocados are weird and gross, I'm excellent at choosing the perfect ones. You have to pick an avocado that is darker in color, not too green. Then you place it in the palm of your hand and squeeze—gently, real gently.

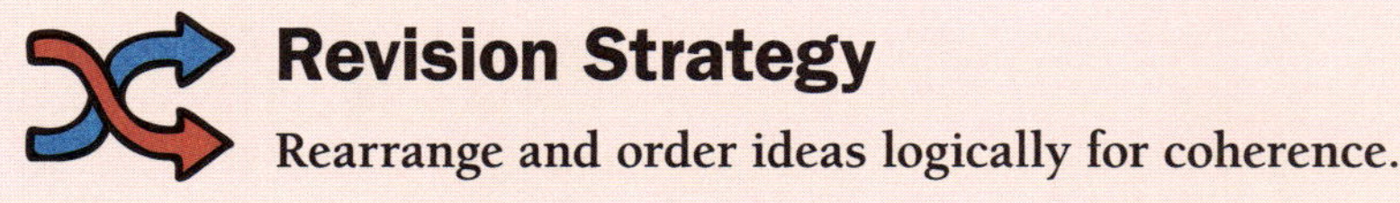

Revision Strategy

Rearrange and order ideas logically for coherence.

Modeling

Lift the sentences from **6.4 Modeled Sentence Shuffle: Part I,** and display them (e.g., on sentence strips, index cards, or electronically) face up in no particular order for all students to see. Invite students to consider the order of the sentences. "These sentences from part of the read-aloud are out of order." Think aloud as you model ordering the sentences in several different ways, stopping to discuss each order: "Does this make sense? Why or why not? How are things more or less effective this way?"

When the class feels like the order they chose is logical, revisit Erin Entrada Kelly's original version on the display page, **6.4 Modeled Sentence Shuffle: Part II**, comparing the author's order to that of the class, and discussing WHY they likely chose this order. It's important to note that this is not about finding the exact same order the author chose. The order the class chose may also be logical. Use this compare and contrast conversation to reinforce that writers have options.

You may choose to use the reflective questions as a guide:
- Why do you think the author put the sentences in this order?
- Is there another order that would be effective?
- Why do you think our order was different from or the same as the author's?

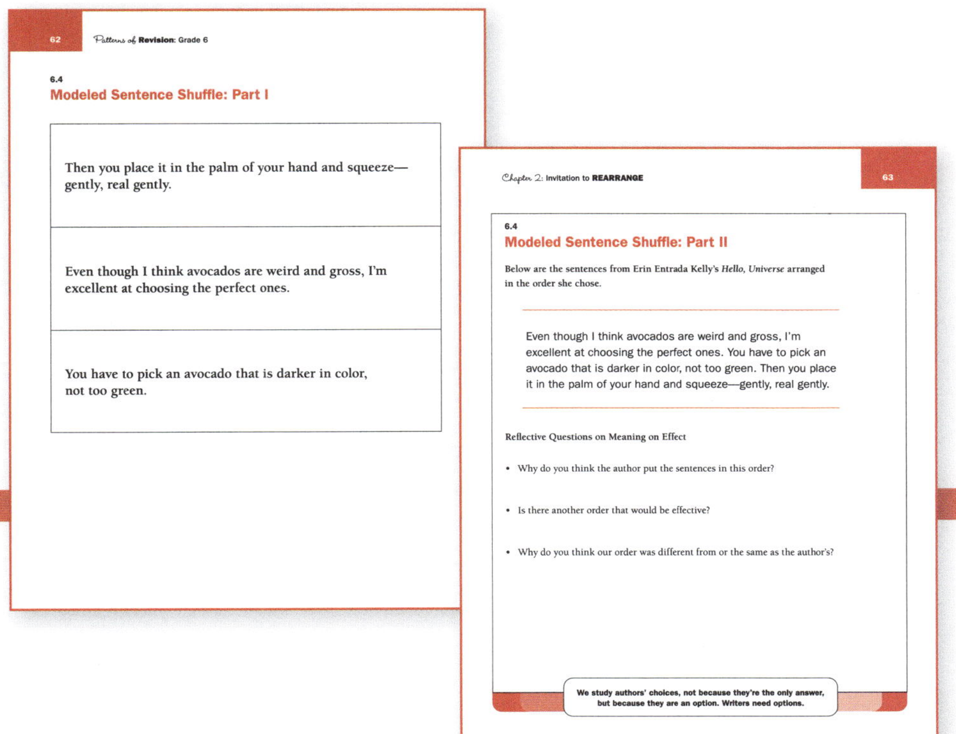

Collaborating Through Conversation

Distribute the sentences lifted from, **6.4 Invitation to Rearrange: Part I**, (e.g., on sentence strips, index cards, or electronically). In pairs or small groups, students collaborate through conversation to order the sentences in a way that makes sense and helps the reader visualize the action. As you move around the class to confer with pairs or groups, especially those struggling to find a logical order for the sentences, you might pose any of these questions to move the work forward:

- What does this group of sentences mostly seem to be about? What tipped you off to that?
- Which sentence or sentences make the most sense as a starting point for this paragraph? Why do you think that?
- Do you notice any sentences that would make sense to be arranged next to each other? What about their content makes you think that?

When ready, students compare their order with others in class, sharing their thought processes. Afterward, display **6.4 Invitation to Rearrange: Part II**, to share Erin Entrada Kelly's original text for comparative analysis. Use the reflective questions provided to facilitate a conversation about meaning and effect.

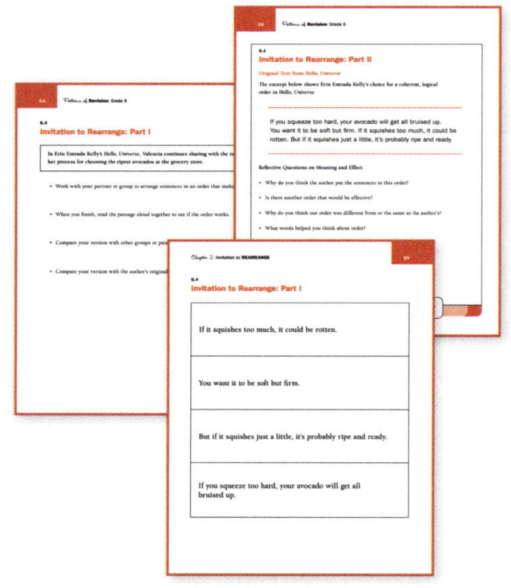

Figure 6.4

Students talk it out as they decide on the most effective paragraph order.

Quickwrite Opportunity (Optional)

1. Share your process for doing an everyday thing, like making your breakfast, putting on your shoes, or getting to school.
2. Share your process for doing something you're good at, like playing a specific sport, playing an instrument, cooking a favorite recipe, or getting an A on a test.

Applying Revision

Begin by modeling for students what this process looks like with your own writing. You may choose to highlight one paragraph on a document camera or digitally on your computer and begin talking through the order of each sentence in that paragraph. Ask the class questions like, "Is there another order that would be effective?", and elicit their feedback to move your possible revisions forward.

Students return to current or past drafts or their writer's notebook—or generate a quick draft to work from using the prompts above—and play with order, noticing effect and rearranging as needed. They may choose to focus on one section or paragraph at a time. Some writers may find that an entire paragraph needs to go to another place in the piece. It's all about meaning, effect, and what makes the most sense.

In this process, writers have options. They may choose to write the sentences from their chosen section on sticky notes or strips of paper to rearrange. They may also decide to look at the piece as a whole, making sure it flows smoothly, and asking a partner to help them. Remind them to use their **Rearrange chart** (page 56) as a guide. For narrative writing, invite students to act out their stories, checking to make sure they've included each detail in a logical order, or invite them to make a quick sketch to illustrate how they want their readers to visualize that part, like a page from a graphic novel. Then, have them go back to their draft to see if that selection shows the order in a way that's clear for their readers.

Sharing Results

Students number off in groups of four. Choose a number to begin, like number 3. The student who is number 3 in each group shares their revisions with the others in their group, and then number 4 shares next, celebrating order and coherence in their writing. Continue until everyone has had a chance to share in their small groups.

Modeled Sentence Shuffle: Part I

Then you place it in the palm of your hand and squeeze—
gently, real gently.

Even though I think avocados are weird and gross, I'm
excellent at choosing the perfect ones.

You have to pick an avocado that is darker in color,
not too green.

6.4

Modeled Sentence Shuffle: Part II

Below are the sentences from Erin Entrada Kelly's *Hello, Universe* arranged in the order she chose.

Even though I think avocados are weird and gross, I'm excellent at choosing the perfect ones. You have to pick an avocado that is darker in color, not too green. Then you place it in the palm of your hand and squeeze—gently, real gently.

Reflective Questions on Meaning on Effect

- Why do you think the author put the sentences in this order?

- Is there another order that would be effective?

- Why do you think our order was different from or the same as the author's?

We study authors' choices, not because they're the only answer,
but because they are an option. Writers need options.

6.4

Invitation to Rearrange: Part I

> In Erin Entrada Kelly's *Hello, Universe*, Valencia continues sharing with the reader her process for choosing the ripest avocados at the grocery store.

- Work with your partner or group to arrange sentences in an order that makes sense.

- When you finish, read the passage aloud together to see if the order works.

- Compare your version with other groups or pairs in your class.

- Compare your version with the author's original text.

6.4

Invitation to Rearrange: Part I

<table>
<tr><td>If it squishes too much, it could be rotten.</td></tr>
<tr><td>You want it to be soft but firm.</td></tr>
<tr><td>But if it squishes just a little, it's probably ripe and ready.</td></tr>
<tr><td>If you squeeze too hard, your avocado will get all bruised up.</td></tr>
</table>

6.4

Invitation to Rearrange: Part II

Original Text from *Hello, Universe*

The excerpt below shows Erin Entrada Kelly's choice for a coherent, logical order in *Hello, Universe*.

If you squeeze too hard, your avocado will get all bruised up. You want it to be soft but firm. If it squishes too much, it could be rotten. But if it squishes just a little, it's probably ripe and ready.

Reflective Questions on Meaning and Effect

- Why do you think the author put the sentences in this order?

- Is there another order that would be effective?

- Why do you think our order was different from or the same as the author's?

- What words helped you think about order?

We study authors' choices, not because they're the only answer, but because they are an option. Writers need options.

6.5 Kicking Around Sentence Order

Lesson Overview

Revision goal connected to standards:

Develop and strengthen writing by rearranging ideas to ensure a logical progression.

Model Text

The Big Book of Soccer
- Written by the writing team at Mundial
- Illustrated by Damien Weighill

Teacher Considerations

In this lesson focusing on the revision strategy of rearranging, we bring in a favorite nonfiction text to highlight the history of soccer around the world with *The Big Book of Soccer* by the team at Mundial. We chose this content to connect with not only the ever-growing fandom of soccer but also to share interesting facts with our students. We will again be looking at arranging sentences within a paragraph to maintain logical order from one sentence to the next. After strengthening our work with sentence-to-sentence connections at the paragraph level, the lesson that follows this (Lesson 6.6) will extend the challenge as we explore rearranging across multiple paragraphs.

Setting the Context

Begin this lesson by giving students a few minutes in partners or small groups to generate their shared understanding of the game of soccer, listing everything they can think of that they know (or think they know) about the sport. Offer space for student groups to share their understandings, building a class-wide foundational understanding of the sport of soccer. Then, read aloud the excerpt from *The Big Book of Soccer*:

Soccer hasn't always been on TV and watched by millions of people. But people have played soccer, or something very similar, for thousands of years. Here's how it all began and how over time it has changed and evolved into what we watch and play today.

It all started in China, over 2,000 years ago with a game called "Ts'u-chu." The ball was made of leather, and it was stuffed with animal hair and feathers. The goal was as tall as five grown-ups stood on each other's heads and as narrow as a child. As you can imagine, with a goal this shape, it was incredibly difficult to score, and it was a very skillful game.

Revision Strategy

Rearrange and order ideas logically for coherence.

Modeling

Display the sentences from **6.5 Modeled Sentence Shuffle: Part I** in no particular order for all students to see. Invite them to consider the order. "These sentences from part of the read-aloud are out of order." Think aloud as you model, reading through the sentences and deciding which one could start out the paragraph: "Which of these sentences might make the most sense to begin this paragraph? (After students give suggestions) What makes you say that?" Continue the discussion as you work together to organize the remaining sentences in a sensible order.

When the class feels like the order they chose is logical, revisit the team at Mundial's original version on the display page, **6.5 Modeled Sentence Shuffle: Part II**, comparing the authors' order to that of the class, and discussing WHY they likely chose this order. It's important to note that this is not about finding the exact same order the authors chose. The order the class chose may also be logical. Use this compare-and-contrast conversation to reinforce that writers have options.

You may choose to use the reflective questions as a guide:

- Why do you think the authors put the sentences in this order?
- Is there another order that would be effective?
- Why do you think our order was different from or the same as the authors'?

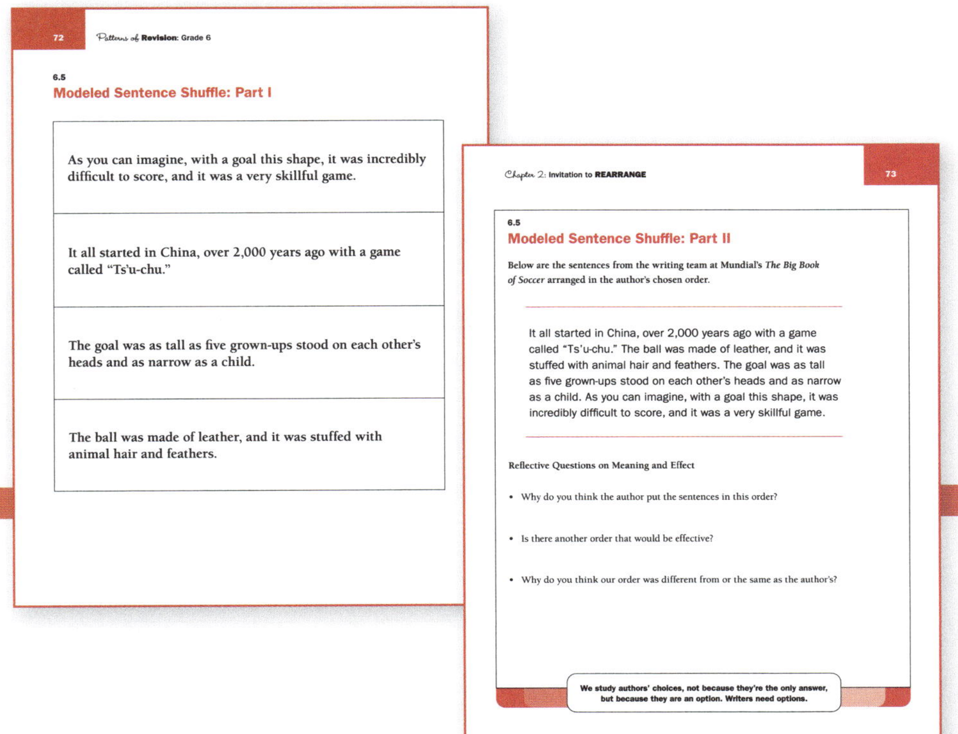

6.5

Modeled Sentence Shuffle: Part I

> As you can imagine, with a goal this shape, it was incredibly difficult to score, and it was a very skillful game.

> It all started in China, over 2,000 years ago with a game called "Ts'u-chu."

> The goal was as tall as five grown-ups stood on each other's heads and as narrow as a child.

> The ball was made of leather, and it was stuffed with animal hair and feathers.

6.5

Modeled Sentence Shuffle: Part II

Below are the sentences from the writing team at Mundial's *The Big Book of Soccer* arranged in the author's chosen order.

> It all started in China, over 2,000 years ago with a game called "Ts'u-chu." The ball was made of leather, and it was stuffed with animal hair and feathers. The goal was as tall as five grown-ups stood on each other's heads and as narrow as a child. As you can imagine, with a goal this shape, it was incredibly difficult to score, and it was a very skillful game.

Reflective Questions on Meaning and Effect

- Why do you think the author put the sentences in this order?

- Is there another order that would be effective?

- Why do you think our order was different from or the same as the author's?

> We study authors' choices, not because they're the only answer, but because they are an option. Writers need options.

Collaborating Through Conversation

Distribute the sentences lifted from, **6.5 Invitation to Rearrange: Part I**, in a format for students to easily interact with. Pairs or small groups of writers then collaborate through conversation to order the sentences in a way that makes sense. When groups are ready, they compare their order with others in class, sharing their thought processes for the choices they made. Afterwards, display **6.5 Invitation to Rearrange: Part II**, to share the original text for comparative analysis. Use the reflective questions provided to facilitate a conversation about meaning and effect.

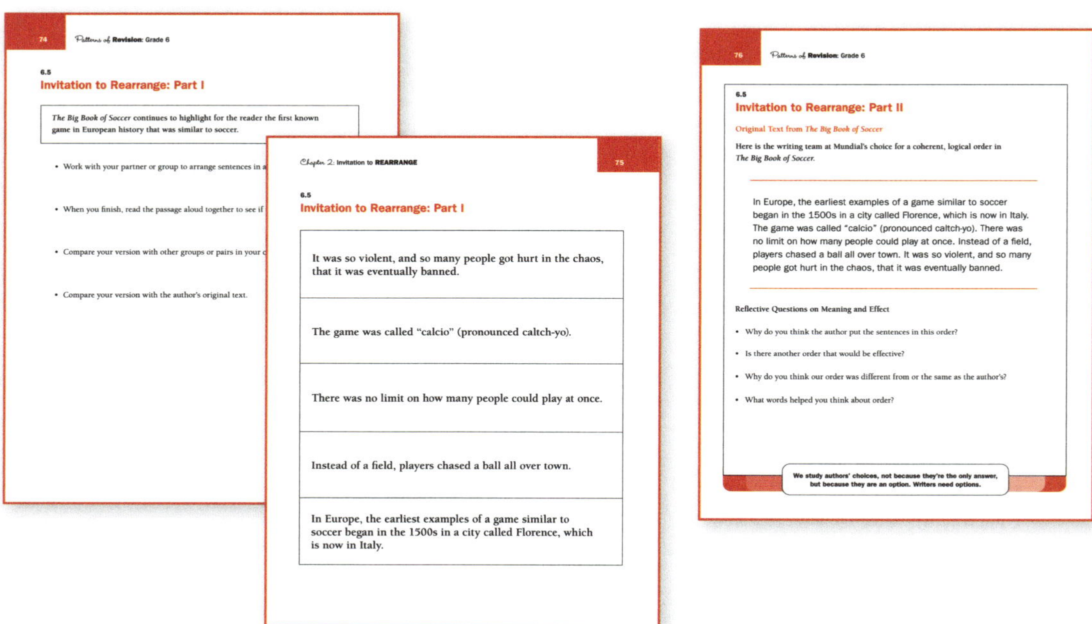

Quickwrite Opportunity (Optional)

1. Describe the sport or hobby you love the most. Explain some of its most basic rules you'd need to know to get started, what equipment you might need, how it's played, and why you enjoy it so much.
2. Write about a famous athlete or expert in your hobby who inspires you. What qualities do they possess that you admire, and how have they influenced your own approach to the activity?

Applying Revision

Prior to inviting students to apply the revision strategy from this lesson, you may choose to revise something from your own writing in a demonstration, eliciting support from students. Teacher modeling that incorporates student input will reinforce the idea that revision strategies apply to all writers and can strengthen all writing. Read your writing aloud to students and think through (or ask the class) options for rearranging ideas within the piece. Here are some options you could play with:

- Rearrange which paragraph starts (or ends) your writing piece (different from the current starting or ending paragraph).
- Rearrange the order of the sentences within a paragraph.
- Rearrange words within a sentence, such as switching the order of words in compound or complex sentences you may have written.

After deciding on a focus for revision, write it down on a sticky note. Then, either directly on your piece or on a separate page or notecard, try the revision. If the revision you create sounds less effective than the original, talk it through with the class. It's important for them to hear you process the effectiveness of your revision choices and to highlight that writers don't always use the revision choices they make.

Students return to current or past drafts or their writer's notebook and play with order, noticing effect and rearranging as needed. They may choose to focus on one section or paragraph at a time. Some writers may find that an entire paragraph needs to go to another place in the piece. It's all about meaning, effect, and what makes the most sense. Remind them to use their **Rearrange chart** (page 56) as a guide.

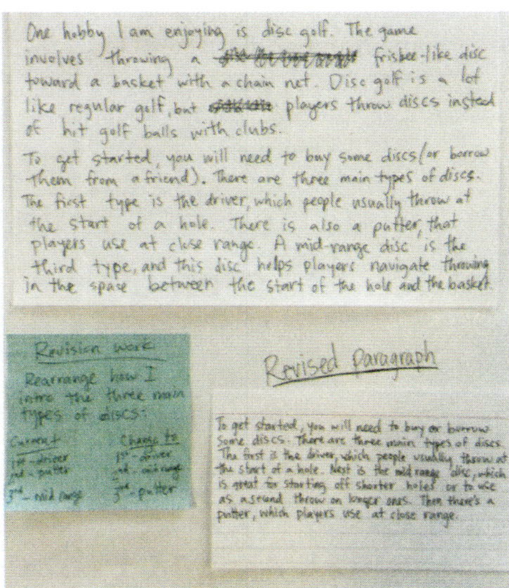

Figure 6.5

Here's an example of revision taken from writing drafted out of one of the lesson's writing prompts.

Sharing Results

Students rearrange their writing by passing it around their table to another classmate, passing it ahead or behind to a nearby student, or by standing, moving around the room, and exchanging their writing with one or more students. Classmates then read the writing in front of them, deciding on the most effective part of the piece they've read. Pass out one sticky note to each student, and then have students write on that sticky note which part of the writing they felt was most effective and what made it so effective to them as they read the piece.

6.5

Modeled Sentence Shuffle: Part I

As you can imagine, with a goal this shape, it was incredibly difficult to score, and it was a very skillful game.

It all started in China, over 2,000 years ago with a game called "Ts'u-chu."

The goal was as tall as five grown-ups stood on each other's heads and as narrow as a child.

The ball was made of leather, and it was stuffed with animal hair and feathers.

6.5

Modeled Sentence Shuffle: Part II

Below are the sentences from the writing team at Mundial's *The Big Book of Soccer* arranged in the author's chosen order.

It all started in China, over 2,000 years ago with a game called "Ts'u-chu." The ball was made of leather, and it was stuffed with animal hair and feathers. The goal was as tall as five grown-ups stood on each other's heads and as narrow as a child. As you can imagine, with a goal this shape, it was incredibly difficult to score, and it was a very skillful game.

Reflective Questions on Meaning and Effect

- Why do you think the author put the sentences in this order?

- Is there another order that would be effective?

- Why do you think our order was different from or the same as the author's?

We study authors' choices, not because they're the only answer, but because they are an option. Writers need options.

6.5

Invitation to Rearrange: Part I

> *The Big Book of Soccer* continues to highlight for the reader the first known game in European history that was similar to soccer.

- Work with your partner or group to arrange sentences in an order that makes sense.

- When you finish, read the passage aloud together to see if the order works.

- Compare your version with other groups or pairs in your class.

- Compare your version with the author's original text.

6.5

Invitation to Rearrange: Part I

It was so violent, and so many people got hurt in the chaos, that it was eventually banned.

The game was called "calcio" (pronounced caltch-yo).

There was no limit on how many people could play at once.

Instead of a field, players chased a ball all over town.

In Europe, the earliest examples of a game similar to soccer began in the 1500s in a city called Florence, which is now in Italy.

6.5

Invitation to Rearrange: Part II

Original Text from *The Big Book of Soccer*

Here is the writing team at Mundial's choice for a coherent, logical order in *The Big Book of Soccer.*

In Europe, the earliest examples of a game similar to soccer began in the 1500s in a city called Florence, which is now in Italy. The game was called "calcio" (pronounced caltch-yo). There was no limit on how many people could play at once. Instead of a field, players chased a ball all over town. It was so violent, and so many people got hurt in the chaos, that it was eventually banned.

Reflective Questions on Meaning and Effect

- Why do you think the author put the sentences in this order?

- Is there another order that would be effective?

- Why do you think our order was different from or the same as the author's?

- What words helped you think about order?

> **We study authors' choices, not because they're the only answer, but because they are an option. Writers need options.**

6.6 Itching to Rearrange

Lesson Overview

Revision goal connected to standards:

Develop and strengthen writing by rearranging ideas to ensure a logical progression.

Model Text

Itch! Everything You Didn't Want to Know About What Makes You Scratch
- Written by Anita Sanchez
- Illustrated by Gilbert Ford

Teacher Considerations

This lesson moves into more advanced revision strategy work: rearranging and organizing sentences into multiple paragraphs. In both sections, we have curated sentences from two separate paragraphs that logically flow from one to the next. Teacher demonstration and guided discussion in the model lesson will be critical to building student confidence as they move into the second part of the lesson.

For this lesson, we chose sentences from *Itch! Everything You Didn't Want to Know About What Makes You Scratch* by Anita Sanchez. Sanchez deftly weaves together heavy informational content with humor, as she highlights the shock value found in what makes us all itch. We focus both parts of this lesson on her chapter about skin.

Setting the Context

We've found it engaging to begin this lesson by asking students to make a list of what makes them itch. Common answers usually include things like mosquitoes, sunburn, dry skin, or allergies. This is a great segue to highlight that we'll be talking about the book *Itch! Everything You Didn't Want to Know About What Makes You Scratch* by Anita Sanchez. Read aloud this excerpt from the text, which we'll pull sentences from for our model lesson.

Everything you are—all your thoughts, dreams, fears—every breath you take—your heart, your brain, your blood—it's all contained inside your skin. But you probably never give skin a thought—until it gets itchy.

Skin is like a bag holding you together. But it isn't like a plastic bag, airtight and waterproof. Things can get on, or under, or into your skin, and can give you a big itch.

Your skin isn't the same all over. On top of your head, it grows lots of hair. On your palms, there's no hair at all. Your skin is paper-thin and delicate around your eyes, much thicker on the bottom of your feet. So some parts of it are more likely to get itchy.

Revision Strategy

Rearrange and order ideas logically for coherence.

Modeling

Display the sentences from **6.6 Modeled Sentence Shuffle: Part I** in no particular order for all students to see. Invite students to consider the order of the sentences. "These sentences from part of the read-aloud are out of order. Something new we're going to look at today is how to reorder these sentences and organize them into two paragraphs. Let's read these sentences first and see if we can decide two big things they are mostly about, so we can organize them into two sections." Read aloud each sentence for the class or allow students time to read silently before eliciting responses. When students generate two different focus topics to sort the sentences into, notate those two topics somewhere where they can see them, either on the printable or on a board in your classroom. Then model, starting with the first group of sentences: "Let's look at this group of sentences first. Which sentence makes sense to start the paragraph with? Why do you say that?" Continue exploring order as you talk through which sentences would come next in the paragraph until you've had a chance to consider each sentence. Repeat the demonstration with the second set of sentences.

When the class feels like the order they chose for both paragraphs is logical and organized, revisit Anita Sanchez's original version on the display page, **6.6 Modeled Sentence Shuffle: Part II**, comparing the author's decisions to those of the class, and discussing WHY she likely chose the sentence grouping and order. It's important to note that this is not about finding the exact result as the author. The order the class chose may also be logical. Use this compare-and-contrast conversation to reinforce that writers have options.

You may choose to use the reflective questions as a guide:

- Why do you think the author put the sentences in this order?
- Is there another order that would be effective?
- Why do you think our order was different from or the same as the author's?

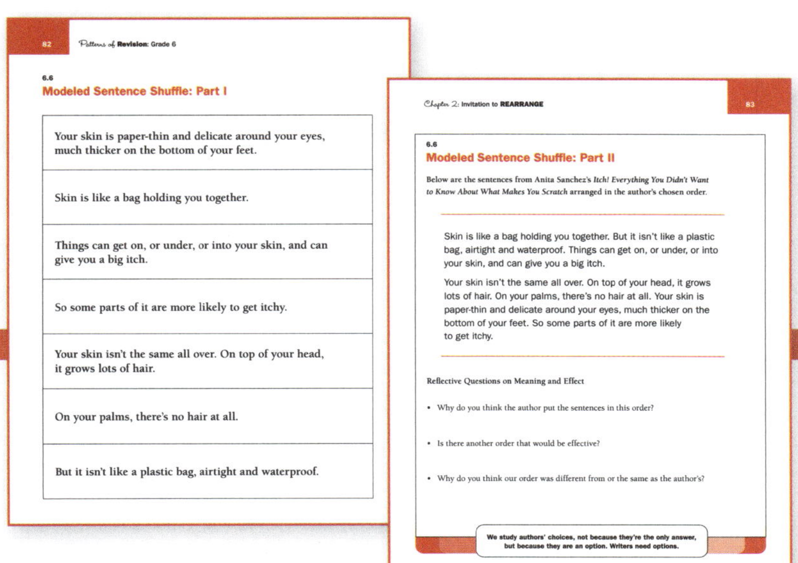

6.6

Modeled Sentence Shuffle: Part I

Your skin is paper-thin and delicate around your eyes, much thicker on the bottom of your feet.
Skin is like a bag holding you together.
Things can get on, or under, or into your skin, and can give you a big itch.
So some parts of it are more likely to get itchy.
Your skin isn't the same all over. On top of your head, it grows lots of hair.
On your palms, there's no hair at all.
But it isn't like a plastic bag, airtight and waterproof.

6.6

Modeled Sentence Shuffle: Part II

Below are the sentences from Anita Sanchez's *Itch! Everything You Didn't Want to Know About What Makes You Scratch* arranged in the author's chosen order.

Skin is like a bag holding you together. But it isn't like a plastic bag, airtight and waterproof. Things can get on, or under, or into your skin, and can give you a big itch.

Your skin isn't the same all over. On top of your head, it grows lots of hair. On your palms, there's no hair at all. Your skin is paper-thin and delicate around your eyes, much thicker on the bottom of your feet. So some parts of it are more likely to get itchy.

Reflective Questions on Meaning and Effect

- Why do you think the author put the sentences in this order?
- Is there another order that would be effective?
- Why do you think our order was different from or the same as the author's?

We study authors' choices, not because they're the only answer, but because they are an option. Writers need options.

Collaborating Through Conversation

Distribute the sentences lifted from, **6.6 Invitation to Rearrange: Part I**, (e.g., on sentence strips, index cards, or electronically). In pairs or small groups, students collaborate through conversation to order the sentences in a way that makes sense, grouping them into two separate paragraphs and thinking about the most effective sentence order in both. After partners or groups are ready, have them share with at least one other group before revealing the author's original. Next, display **6.6 Invitation to Rearrange: Part II**, to share Anita Sanchez's original text for comparative analysis. Use the reflective questions provided to facilitate a conversation about meaning and effect.

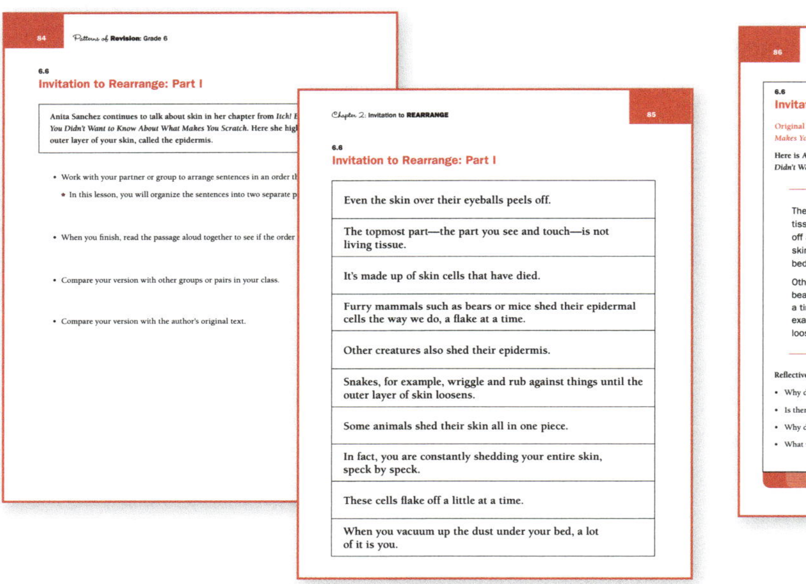

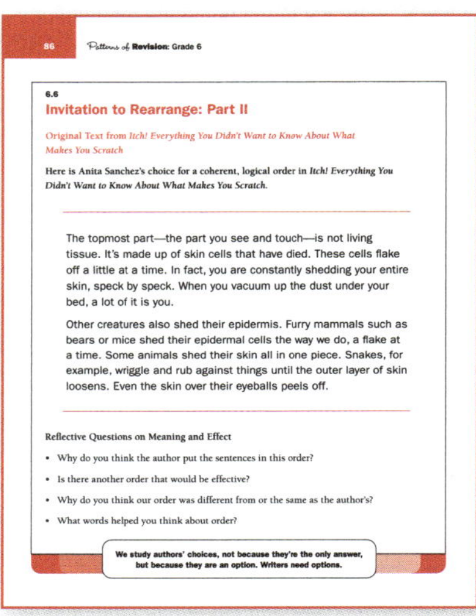

Quickwrite Opportunity (Optional)

1. In the book, allergies are explored as one of the causes of itching. Develop a scene where the protagonist discovers they have developed an unusual allergic reaction to something unexpected.
2. Develop a scene about a creature whose touch induces unbearable itching. Describe its appearance, origins, and the effects of its itch-inducing powers. Explain how characters in your story attempt to cope with or defeat this creature.

Applying Revision

For application of this lesson, students will need access to a multi-paragraph written piece (either a current draft or some quick, prompted writing). Prior to inviting students to apply the revision strategy from this lesson, you may choose to revise something from your own writing as a demonstration, eliciting support from students. Using the text you're revising, model with a similar conversation as you had with the students during the model lesson, focusing on deciding on the topic of each paragraph before revisiting them to ensure the order of sentences makes sense. Students may decide to rearrange words, sentences, or even whole paragraphs within their written piece. If students find they need to add something additional, they may use this time to add new content to their written piece.

In this process, writers have options. They may choose to write the sentences from their chosen section on sticky notes or strips of paper to rearrange. They may also decide to look at the piece as whole, making sure it flows smoothly, asking a partner to help them. Remind them to use their **Rearrange chart** (page 56) as a guide.

Figure 6.6

This student thinks through application after practicing rearranging.

Sharing Results

Set up a digital whiteboard for your class to post a revised section of their writing or a section of their writing they feel is most effective. This could be a sentence, a paragraph, or even multiple paragraphs (we suggest a maximum of two). After students add their writing to the digital whiteboard, have them go back to read the writing of their classmates. Give them a specific focus and prompt for leaving feedback when reading their classmates' writing. Here are some prompt options you could use:

- Find one sentence that you think is an effective use of description (or action). Explain why it is effective.
- Find one sentence that is particularly effective and give your partner feedback on why you think it is effective.
- What do you think works well in your partner's writing? What is one thing you would suggest to make it even better?

6.6

Modeled Sentence Shuffle: Part I

Your skin is paper-thin and delicate around your eyes, much thicker on the bottom of your feet.

Skin is like a bag holding you together.

Things can get on, or under, or into your skin, and can give you a big itch.

So some parts of it are more likely to get itchy.

Your skin isn't the same all over. On top of your head, it grows lots of hair.

On your palms, there's no hair at all.

But it isn't like a plastic bag, airtight and waterproof.

6.6

Modeled Sentence Shuffle: Part II

Below are the sentences from Anita Sanchez's *Itch! Everything You Didn't Want to Know About What Makes You Scratch* arranged in the author's chosen order.

Skin is like a bag holding you together. But it isn't like a plastic bag, airtight and waterproof. Things can get on, or under, or into your skin, and can give you a big itch.

Your skin isn't the same all over. On top of your head, it grows lots of hair. On your palms, there's no hair at all. Your skin is paper-thin and delicate around your eyes, much thicker on the bottom of your feet. So some parts of it are more likely to get itchy.

Reflective Questions on Meaning and Effect

- Why do you think the author put the sentences in this order?

- Is there another order that would be effective?

- Why do you think our order was different from or the same as the author's?

> We study authors' choices, not because they're the only answer, but because they are an option. Writers need options.

6.6

Invitation to Rearrange: Part I

Anita Sanchez continues to talk about skin in her chapter from *Itch! Everything You Didn't Want to Know About What Makes You Scratch*. Here she highlights the outer layer of your skin, called the epidermis.

- Work with your partner or group to arrange sentences in an order that makes sense.

  ★ In this lesson, you will organize the sentences into two separate paragraphs as well.

- When you finish, read the passage aloud together to see if the order works.

- Compare your version with other groups or pairs in your class.

- Compare your version with the author's original text.

Invitation to Rearrange: Part I

Even the skin over their eyeballs peels off.
The topmost part—the part you see and touch—is not living tissue.
It's made up of skin cells that have died.
Furry mammals such as bears or mice shed their epidermal cells the way we do, a flake at a time.
Other creatures also shed their epidermis.
Snakes, for example, wriggle and rub against things until the outer layer of skin loosens.
Some animals shed their skin all in one piece.
In fact, you are constantly shedding your entire skin, speck by speck.
These cells flake off a little at a time.
When you vacuum up the dust under your bed, a lot of it is you.

6.6

Invitation to Rearrange: Part II

Original Text from Itch! Everything You Didn't Want to Know About What Makes You Scratch

Here is Anita Sanchez's choice for a coherent, logical order in *Itch! Everything You Didn't Want to Know About What Makes You Scratch.*

The topmost part—the part you see and touch—is not living tissue. It's made up of skin cells that have died. These cells flake off a little at a time. In fact, you are constantly shedding your entire skin, speck by speck. When you vacuum up the dust under your bed, a lot of it is you.

Other creatures also shed their epidermis. Furry mammals such as bears or mice shed their epidermal cells the way we do, a flake at a time. Some animals shed their skin all in one piece. Snakes, for example, wriggle and rub against things until the outer layer of skin loosens. Even the skin over their eyeballs peels off.

Reflective Questions on Meaning and Effect

- Why do you think the author put the sentences in this order?

- Is there another order that would be effective?

- Why do you think our order was different from or the same as the author's?

- What words helped you think about order?

> We study authors' choices, not because they're the only answer, but because they are an option. Writers need options.

*We are wired for connection. But the key is that, in any given moment of it,
it has to be real.*

– Brené Brown

E. M. Forster wrote, "Only connect." Connectors are the glue that holds our writing together, shifting from one idea to the next, helping our reader move through the text. When a writer is combining sentences, connectors are a fabulous friend. Consider how these connectors help transition or link ideas and help define the relationship between and among ideas:

- *And*
- *Or*
- *But*
- *So*
- *Although*
- *When*
- *While*

Connectors may also include phrases that writers add to join ideas and make their message clearer:

- *In other words,*
- *For example,*
- *When ____________, ____________*
- *Like ____________, ____________*
- *If ____________, ____________*

Middle graders often have a flurry of ideas, drafting sentence after sentence to get it all on the page before they forget. If you see that writers include too many short, choppy sentences or are struggling with repetition in their writing, a need for more connectors may be the culprit. You'll immediately notice an elevation in your students' writing as they learn to add in connectors such as transitional words, conjunctions, punctuation, or sentences to help connect their ideas, making their message more coherent for the reader.

Tip

Connectors aren't limited just to words and phrases. Punctuation marks are essential connectors as well. And, while all punctuation separates, notice how these punctuation marks also connect or join ideas or sentence and their purpose and effect:

- Comma
- Colon
- Dash
- Semicolon

Connectors are primarily thought of as punctuation marks or words, especially conjunctions and relative pronouns. (For more information on connector words and punctuation, please refer to the **Connectors chart** located on page 90, which can be kept in a student's writer's notebook, binder, or a folder—digital or analog.) To support the concept of adding connectors for middle-grade revisers, this chapter of lessons explores how adding transitional or additive ideas within a paragraph helps writers to give their writing clarity, deepening readers' sequential understanding, adding needed details to connect one idea to the next, and maintaining focus. As always, we try the process out together first, then writers try a different example in small groups or with partners. We conclude the lesson by inviting students to return to their own writing to add connecting ideas whether with sentences, phrases, or words that might help clarify the writer's message or purpose.

Building this awareness that writers use connectors to link their ideas is crucial to the development of adolescent writers and readers. As writers, they begin to see the options and effects in our numerous discussions. As readers, they become more likely to notice shifts in ideas, aiding in comprehension.

The reciprocal nature of reading, writing, and grammar are not lost during revision.

ADD

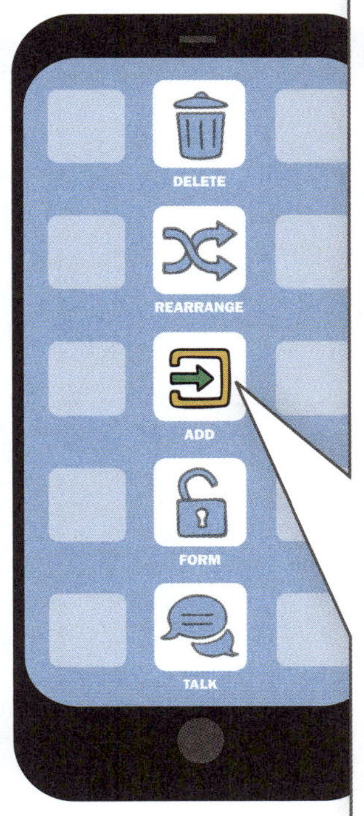

Adding Connectors at the Sentence Level

Prepositions	Adding a preposition (or a prepositional phrase) grounds the reader in time and place. They can also introduce examples, contrasts, or comparisons. *Without a glass of milk, cookies aren't as delicious.*
Conjunctions	Subordinating conjunctions show relationships between ideas, sometimes making one idea more or less important than another. They are used within complex sentences. *When I bake cookies, a delicious aroma fills the air.* Coordinating conjunctions make connections that are equal to each other. They can join sentences to create compound sentences, and they can also show a relationship between a pair or a list. *I like to bake cookies, but I will only eat them with a glass of milk.*
Relative Pronouns	Introduces or links additional information to the noun before it. *Cookies that have large chocolate chunks in them are better than plain chocolate chip cookies.*
Punctuation	Combines, introduces, and encloses information within a sentence. *Cookies, for example, are best when dipped in milk.*

Adding Connectors at the Paragraph Level

Add a sentence (or even a paragraph or more) . . .

- to the beginning of a paragraph to introduce the new main idea, or to transition to a new idea.
- to transition from one idea to the next.
- to add important information to the sentence before.
- to move the reader through time.

The Connectors

Prepositions

What do they do? *They show time and place as well as introduce examples, contrasts, or comparisons.*

Function	Example
Time	*at, in, on*
Extended Time	*by, during, for, from, since, to, until, with(in)*
Direction	*in, into, on, onto, to, toward*
Location	*above, across, against, ahead of, along, among, around, at, behind, below, beneath, beside, between, by, from, in, inside, near, of, off, on, out, over, through, toward, under, within*
Introduce Examples and Comparisons or Contrasts	*as, despite, except, for, like, of, per, than, with, without*

Subordinating Conjunctions (AAAWWUBBIS)

Although
As
After
While
When
Until
Because
Before
If
Since

What do they do? *They show relationships, sometimes making one idea more or less important.*

Function	Example
Time	*after, before, during, since, until, when, whenever, while*
Cause-Effect	*as, because, since, so*
Opposition	*although, even though, though, whatever, while*
Condition	*as long as, if, in order to, unless, until, whatever*

Relative Pronouns

What do they do? *Introduce and link additional information to the noun before it.*

Function	Example
Link **ideas and things** to more detail	*that, what, which*
Link **people** to more detail	*who, whoever, whom, whose*

Connector Punctuation

What do they do? *They combine, introduce, and enclose information.*

Combines	Introduces	Encloses
Comma ,		Comma ,
Dash —	Dash —	Dash —
Semicolon ;	Colon :	Parentheses ( )
		Quotation Marks " "

Coordinating Conjunctions (FANBOYS)

For
And
Nor
But
Or
Yet
So

What do they do? *They make connections that are equal to each other. They join sentences (thereby making compound sentences), and they can show a relationship between a pair or a list.*

Function	Example
Combine	*and*
Opposition	*but, nor, yet*
Cause-Effect	*for, so*
Choice	*or*

6.7 Connecting Ideas with a Flash of Brilliance

Lesson Overview

Revision goal connected to standards:

Develop and strengthen writing by adding information and ideas for coherence and clarity.

Model Text

The Miscalculations of Lightning Girl
— Written by Stacy McAnulty

Teacher Considerations

In the next few revision lessons, students will focus on the A in the DRAFT mnemonic: Add Connectors. When revising, writers check for coherence (making sure each idea connects to the next) and clarity (making sure the ideas include clarifying information). We use this lesson to focus on coherence by adding a sentence that connects one idea within a paragraph to the next.

We share Stacy McAnulty's *The Miscalculations of Lightning Girl* as a mentor because it begins with action and intrigue: the main character is struck by lightning and gains the powers of super math calculation. It's also a sweet coming-of-age story about navigating middle school.

When students revise their own writing, they will check to make sure all of their ideas are tightly connected, adding sentences, phrases, and/or words where needed. Hanging the **Add chart** (page 89) in your classroom or inviting students to glue it into their writing notebooks along with **The Connectors chart** (page 90) will provide writers with a reference when needed.

Setting the Context

The book *The Miscalculations of Lightning Girl* by Stacy McAnulty begins by introducing us to the main character Lucille Callahan and her friend Cecelia, who are both playing outside one day when they notice a nearby thunderstorm. Lucille climbs a chain link fence to watch the storm roll in, while Cecelia stands next to her. When a bolt of lightning strikes, Lucille is knocked out and Cecelia runs for help. Explain this to your students before sharing the following scene that happens afterwards:

A week later, Nana and I were watching TV, and a commercial came on for a used-car dealership. The man was screaming, so I had to pay attention.

"That's $359 a month for 48 months, folks." He was really loud. "Nobody beats Frank Fontana. Nobody."

I yelled back, "17,232."

"What?" Nana asked.

"That's how much the car costs," I said.

"Did you read it on the TV?"

"I just know. 359 times 48 is 17,232."

Sum up the read aloud by sharing that Nana goes and gets a calculator and punches in 359 times 48. "Let's read the next few sentences together to see what happens next."

Revision Strategy

Add a connector, a sentence, or sentences to connect information for your reader.

Modeling

Display **6.7 Something's Missing: Part I**, which has the model selection that shows where a connecting sentence needs to be inserted. "The writer of this paragraph needs to revise by adding a sentence that will connect one idea to the next. Let's look at this paragraph in which something's missing." Discuss the author's message in the existing parts around the blank. Possible questions to prompt discussion are:

- "What is the author saying in the first sentence? What about the sentence after the blank?"
- "What is the author's message in this paragraph?"
- "What do you notice about the writing before/after the blank space?"

Invite students to consider which of the four starred sentence choices could be added to the author's writing. Model trying out one of the sentences, reading it in the paragraph, and discussing WHY this option works or doesn't seem to work well. Continue to model with the other two starred options or invite students to try it out and discuss in pairs or small groups. Remind students that their conversations should focus on WHY the author might choose or not choose to add the sentence rather than trying to select the right answer. After some time for conversation about the meaning and effect of each choice, reveal Stacy McAnulty's original version with the display page, **6.7 Something's Missing: Part II**. Use the reflective questions to guide a comparative analysis discussion.

- Why do you think the author used this sentence?
- Do any of the other starred sentence options work? Why or why not?
- Why do you think your choice was different from or the same as the author's?

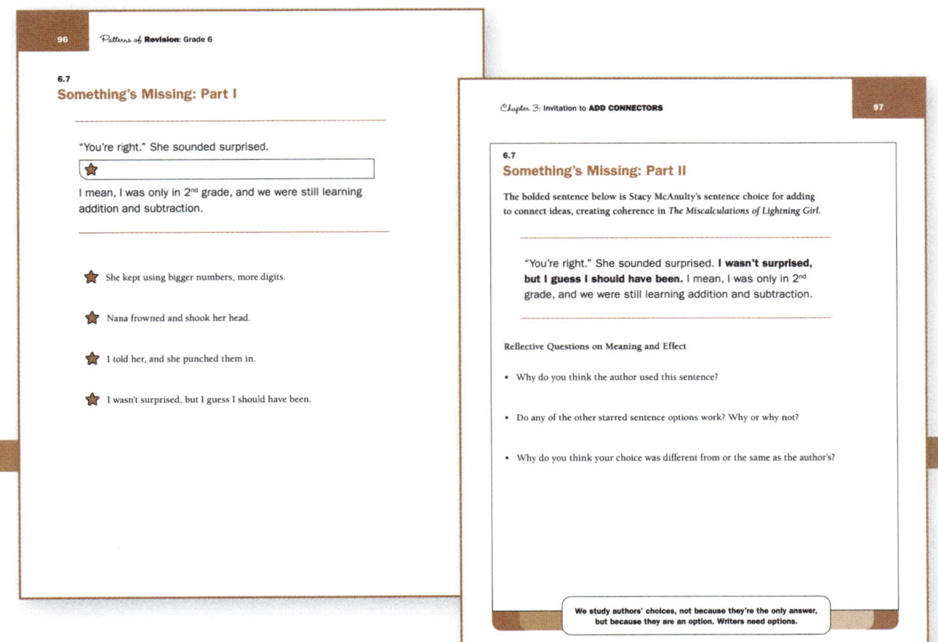

Collaborating Through Conversation

Display **6.7 Invitation to Add Connectors: Part I**. In pairs or small groups, students collaborate through conversation to select the sentence they think best connects ideas for the reader. As students work, remind them to focus on meaning and effect: what works, what doesn't, and why. When students are ready, they compare their revisions with others in class, discussing why they made their choices. Display **6.7 Invitation to Add Connectors Part II** to facilitate further discussion and display the author's original text for comparison.

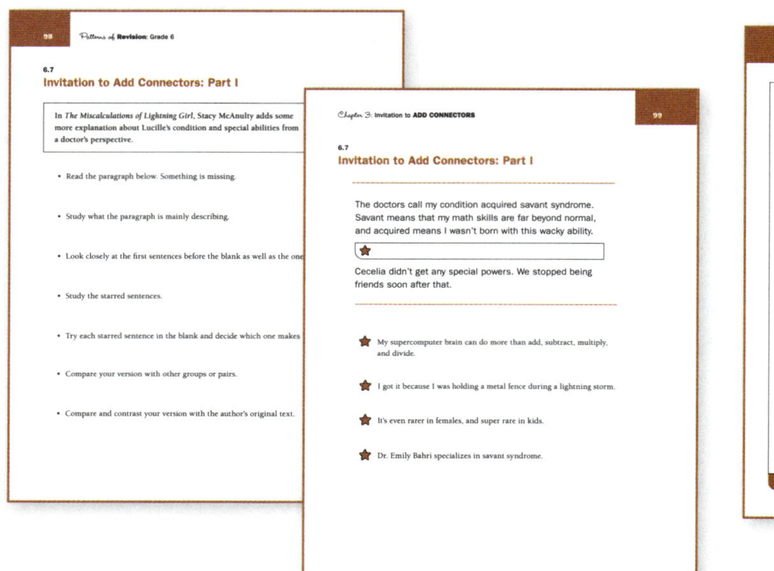

Quickwrite Opportunity (Optional)

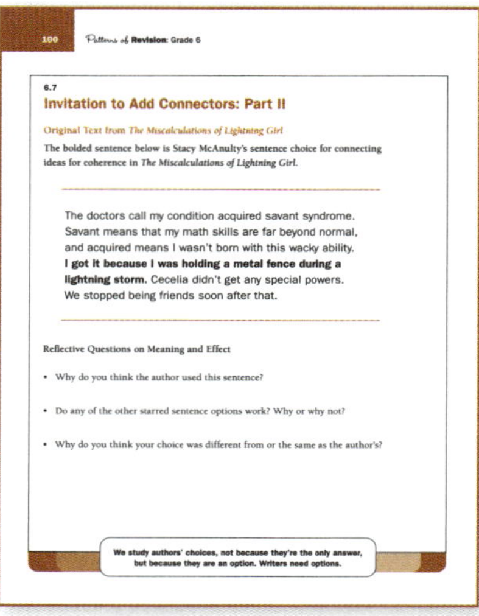

1. Imagine you were to gain a superpower. What would that superpower be? Write a scene about how you gained this superpower.
2. Describe a time when you first realized you had a particular skill or talent. What was the experience like, and how did you feel when you discovered this skill? Explain how you've improved this skill or talent since then.

Applying Revision

Students return to a piece of writing they have drafted, or writing they've recently generated connected to one of the prompts in this lesson and consider how they might add details to connect their ideas. You may have them start with a partner, sharing their goal for the piece: "As a reader, I want you to understand or get ______________ from this piece." They then read their selection and ask their partner to help find a part that might be a little confusing or needs additional connecting information. Some questions their partner may ask include:

- What are you saying in the first sentence?
- What is your message in this part?
- What do you want your reader to know here?

After this conference with a partner, the writer can decide how they will insert a sentence or more to connect information or clear up any confusion. They may choose to write their additions on sticky notes, jot them on strips of paper, or insert the information directly onto their page with a caret. If time permits, invite them to meet back with their partner for another check with the revisions in place.

Sharing Results

Partner Pitch: If partners worked together in Applying Revision, have them connect with another group. Each partner takes turns pitching to the other group what revision their partner made and why that revision makes their writing more effective. Having pairs pitch the effectiveness of their partner's revision challenges students to not only be active participants in their partner's revision process, but also be able to paraphrase their partner's process of revision in a concise way.

6.7

Something's Missing: Part I

"You're right." She sounded surprised.

I mean, I was only in 2nd grade, and we were still learning addition and subtraction.

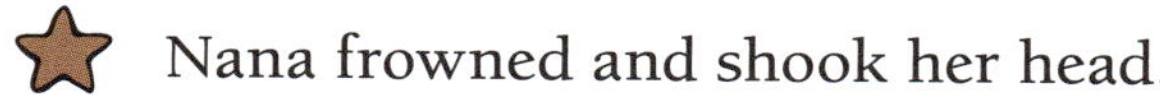

⭐ She kept using bigger numbers, more digits.

⭐ Nana frowned and shook her head.

⭐ I told her, and she punched them in.

⭐ I wasn't surprised, but I guess I should have been.

6.7

Something's Missing: Part II

The bolded sentence below is Stacy McAnulty's sentence choice for adding to connect ideas, creating coherence in *The Miscalculations of Lightning Girl*.

"You're right." She sounded surprised. **I wasn't surprised, but I guess I should have been.** I mean, I was only in 2nd grade, and we were still learning addition and subtraction.

Reflective Questions on Meaning and Effect

- Why do you think the author used this sentence?

- Do any of the other starred sentence options work? Why or why not?

- Why do you think your choice was different from or the same as the author's?

We study authors' choices, not because they're the only answer, but because they are an option. Writers need options.

6.7

Invitation to Add Connectors: Part I

In *The Miscalculations of Lightning Girl*, Stacy McAnulty adds some
more explanation about Lucille's condition and special abilities from
a doctor's perspective.

- Read the paragraph below. Something is missing.

- Study what the paragraph is mainly describing.

- Look closely at the first sentences before the blank as well as the ones after the blank.

- Study the starred sentences.

- Try each starred sentence in the blank and decide which one makes the most sense.

- Compare your version with other groups or pairs.

- Compare and contrast your version with the author's original text.

6.7

Invitation to Add Connectors: Part I

The doctors call my condition acquired savant syndrome. Savant means that my math skills are far beyond normal, and acquired means I wasn't born with this wacky ability.

Cecelia didn't get any special powers. We stopped being friends soon after that.

 My supercomputer brain can do more than add, subtract, multiply, and divide.

 I got it because I was holding a metal fence during a lightning storm.

 It's even rarer in females, and super rare in kids.

 Dr. Emily Bahri specializes in savant syndrome.

6.7

Invitation to Add Connectors: Part II

Original Text from *The Miscalculations of Lightning Girl*

The bolded sentence below is Stacy McAnulty's sentence choice for connecting ideas for coherence in *The Miscalculations of Lightning Girl*.

The doctors call my condition acquired savant syndrome. Savant means that my math skills are far beyond normal, and acquired means I wasn't born with this wacky ability. **I got it because I was holding a metal fence during a lightning storm.** Cecelia didn't get any special powers. We stopped being friends soon after that.

Reflective Questions on Meaning and Effect

- Why do you think the author used this sentence?

- Do any of the other starred sentence options work? Why or why not?

- Why do you think your choice was different from or the same as the author's?

We study authors' choices, not because they're the only answer, but because they are an option. Writers need options.

6.8 **Adding an Extra Dash of Connection**

Lesson Overview

Revision goal connected to standards:

Develop and strengthen writing by adding information and ideas for coherence and clarity.

Model Text

The Complete Cookbook for Young Chefs: 100+ Recipes that You'll Love to Cook and Eat
— Written by America's Test Kitchen Kids

Teacher Considerations

When revising, writers check for coherence (making sure each idea connects to the next) and clarity (making sure the ideas include clarifying information). In this lesson, we continue to focus on coherence by adding a sentence that connects one idea within a paragraph to the next.

We chose *The Complete Cookbook for Young Chefs* as a mentor because of the authors' use of informational text, procedural text, and a variety of text features including a flow chart. You might want to be cautious about completing this lesson right before lunch, since it's about food, and we know what happens when we talk about food right before lunch!

Although we've chosen to use a nonfiction text for this lesson, keep in mind that this revision strategy, like the others, can be applied to any form of writing. When students revise their own writing, they will check to make sure all of their ideas are tightly connected, adding sentences, phrases, and/or words where needed. Hanging the **Add chart** (page 89) in your classroom or inviting students to glue it into their writing notebooks along with **The Connectors chart** (page 90) will provide writers with a reference when needed.

Setting the Context

To engage students in the topic of cooking, have them discuss experiences with cooking in partners, small groups, or the whole group. You'll be reading with your students from *The Complete Cookbook for Young Chefs*, learning a little bit about herbs and how to use them in cooking. Read aloud the following excerpt on page 53 about cilantro, one of the amazing herbs used in cooking, keeping in mind that we've intentionally taken away a sentence (but don't tell your students that).

Cilantro is used in many Mexican, Asian, and Mediterranean dishes. Its flavor is lemony and even a bit flowery. If you're in this camp, use parsley in its place. Cilantro stems are tender and flavorful, so it's fine if you chop them up with the leaves.

Invite students to consider how this paragraph is written and the meaning within it. "Yes, this paragraph is all about the herb cilantro, but guess what? A sentence is missing from this paragraph. Did you notice? Some of these ideas are not tightly connected. Where do you see some disconnect?"

When the conversation warrants, share what writers do to connect their ideas for coherence: "Writers will often add details to connect one idea to the next, helping their readers to fully comprehend the main idea."

Revision Strategy

Add a connector, a sentence, or sentences to connect information for your reader.

Modeling

Display **6.8 Something's Missing: Part I**, which has the previous mentor paragraph that shows where a connecting sentence needs to be inserted. "The writers of this paragraph need to revise by adding a sentence that will connect one idea to the next. Let's look at this paragraph in which something's missing." Discuss the authors' message in the existing parts around the blank. Possible questions to prompt discussion:

- What are the authors saying in the sentence before the blank? What about the sentence after the blank?
- What do you notice about the writing before/after the blank space?
- What is the authors' message in this paragraph?

Invite students to consider which of the four starred sentence choices could be added to the authors' writing. Model trying out one of the sentences, reading it in the paragraph, and discussing WHY this option works or doesn't seem to work well. Continue to model with the other starred options or invite students to try it out and discuss in pairs or small groups. Remind them that their conversations should focus on WHY the authors might choose or not choose to add the sentence rather than trying to select the right answer. After some time for conversations about the meaning and effect of each choice, reveal the original version with the display page, **6.8 Something's Missing: Part II**. Use the reflective questions to guide a comparative analysis discussion.

- Why do you think the author used this sentence?
- Do any of the other starred sentence options work? Why or why not?
- Why do you think your choice was different from or the same as the authors'?

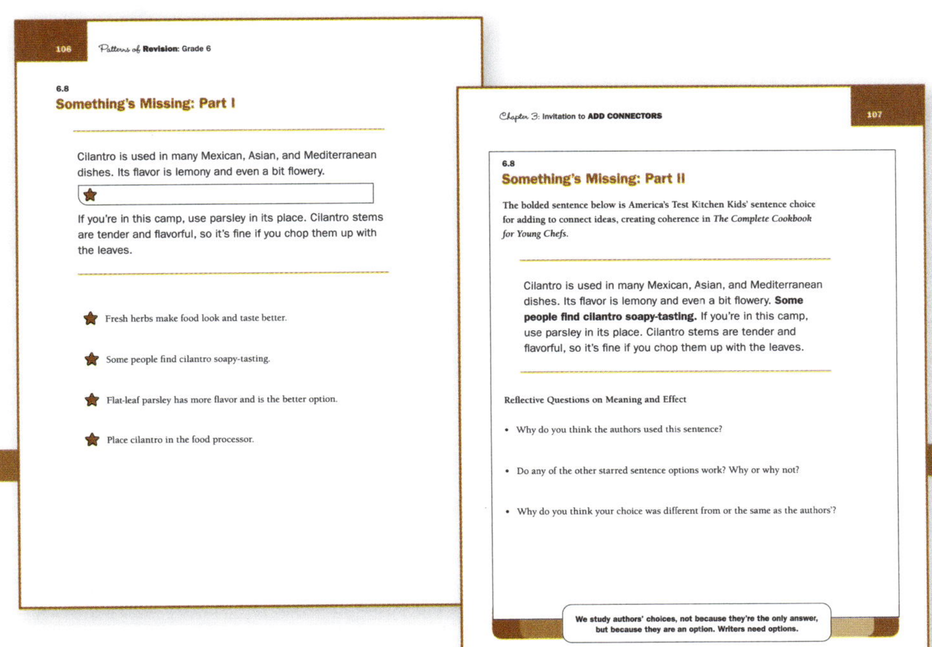

Collaborating Through Conversation

Display **6.8 Invitation to Add Connectors: Part I**. In pairs or small groups, students collaborate through conversations to select the sentence they think best connects ideas for the reader. While working, remind students to focus their conversations on meaning and effect: what works, what doesn't, and why. When ready, students compare their revision with others in class, discussing WHY they made their choices. To close the discussion, display **6.8 Invitation to Add Connectors Part II** to show the original text for comparative analysis and use the reflective questions to facilitate a further conversation about meaning and effect.

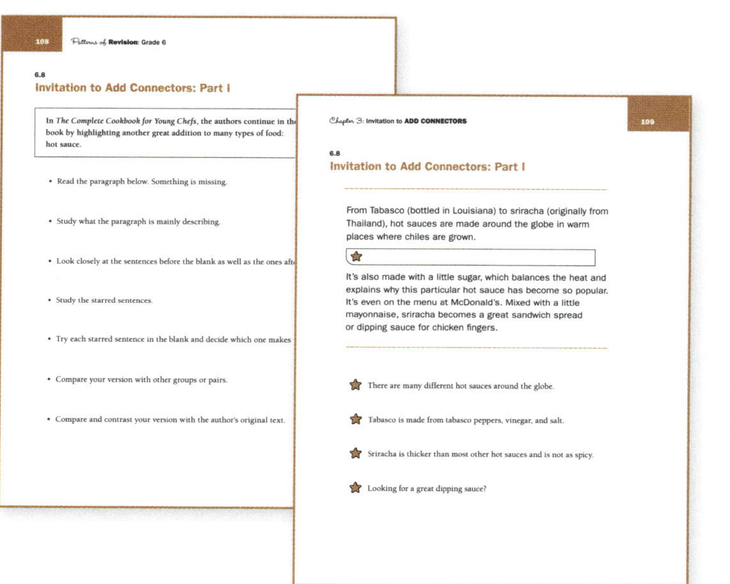

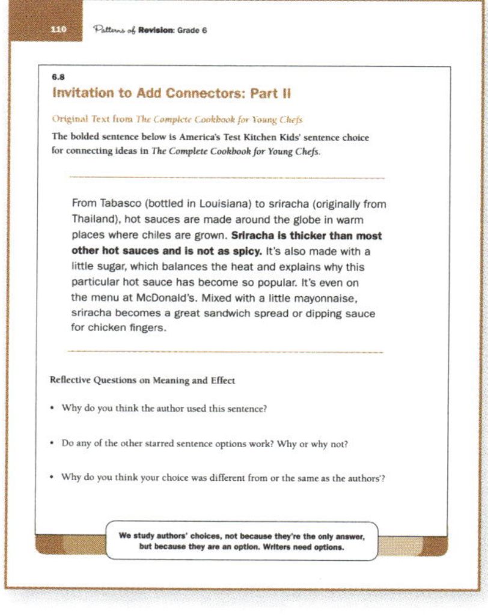

Quickwrite Opportunity (Optional)

1. Write a familiar scene from your kitchen. Explain who is in the kitchen and what they are doing.

2. Think about something you know how to do well. Write a short "how to" to give a classmate steps on successfully doing something you're good at, like making a grilled cheese sandwich or shooting a free throw.

Applying Revision

Begin with a demonstration and elicit input from your students as you showcase how to go back to your own writing to consider places where details could be added to connect and clarify. Here are some guiding questions that can be displayed in the classroom for students to reference:

- What am I saying in the first sentence?
- What is my message in this part?
- What do you think my reader needs to know here?

Your students will then move into their own pieces of writing to do this same work, choosing places where clarifying details could be added, using the guided questions to help them. They may also decide to work with a partner as needed.

Sharing Results

Have students rewrite their best revision on a notecard. Then pair them with partners to share their revision. Have everyone rotate to new partners and repeat the process as time allows. Finally, create a space in the classroom for students to attach their notecards up on the wall, displaying their revision work so the rest of the class—and other classes—can check it out throughout the day.

6.8

Something's Missing: Part I

Cilantro is used in many Mexican, Asian, and Mediterranean dishes. Its flavor is lemony and even a bit flowery.

If you're in this camp, use parsley in its place. Cilantro stems are tender and flavorful, so it's fine if you chop them up with the leaves.

 Fresh herbs make food look and taste better.

 Some people find cilantro soapy-tasting.

 Flat-leaf parsley has more flavor and is the better option.

Place cilantro in the food processor.

6.8
Something's Missing: Part II

The bolded sentence below is America's Test Kitchen Kids' sentence choice for adding to connect ideas, creating coherence in *The Complete Cookbook for Young Chefs*.

Cilantro is used in many Mexican, Asian, and Mediterranean dishes. Its flavor is lemony and even a bit flowery. **Some people find cilantro soapy-tasting.** If you're in this camp, use parsley in its place. Cilantro stems are tender and flavorful, so it's fine if you chop them up with the leaves.

Reflective Questions on Meaning and Effect

- Why do you think the authors used this sentence?

- Do any of the other starred sentence options work? Why or why not?

- Why do you think your choice was different from or the same as the authors'?

We study authors' choices, not because they're the only answer, but because they are an option. Writers need options.

6.8

Invitation to Add Connectors: Part I

> In *The Complete Cookbook for Young Chefs*, the authors continue in the book by highlighting another great addition to many types of food: hot sauce.

- Read the paragraph below. Something is missing.

- Study what the paragraph is mainly describing.

- Look closely at the sentences before the blank as well as the ones after the blank.

- Study the starred sentences.

- Try each starred sentence in the blank and decide which one makes the most sense.

- Compare your version with other groups or pairs.

- Compare and contrast your version with the author's original text.

6.8

Invitation to Add Connectors: Part I

From Tabasco (bottled in Louisiana) to sriracha (originally from Thailand), hot sauces are made around the globe in warm places where chiles are grown.

It's also made with a little sugar, which balances the heat and explains why this particular hot sauce has become so popular. It's even on the menu at McDonald's. Mixed with a little mayonnaise, sriracha becomes a great sandwich spread or dipping sauce for chicken fingers.

 There are many different hot sauces around the globe.

 Tabasco is made from tabasco peppers, vinegar, and salt.

 Sriracha is thicker than most other hot sauces and is not as spicy.

 Looking for a great dipping sauce?

6.8

Invitation to Add Connectors: Part II

Original Text from *The Complete Cookbook for Young Chefs*

The bolded sentence below is America's Test Kitchen Kids' sentence choice for connecting ideas in *The Complete Cookbook for Young Chefs*.

From Tabasco (bottled in Louisiana) to sriracha (originally from Thailand), hot sauces are made around the globe in warm places where chiles are grown. **Sriracha is thicker than most other hot sauces and is not as spicy.** It's also made with a little sugar, which balances the heat and explains why this particular hot sauce has become so popular. It's even on the menu at McDonald's. Mixed with a little mayonnaise, sriracha becomes a great sandwich spread or dipping sauce for chicken fingers.

Reflective Questions on Meaning and Effect

- Why do you think the author used this sentence?

- Do any of the other starred sentence options work? Why or why not?

- Why do you think your choice was different from or the same as the authors'?

We study authors' choices, not because they're the only answer, but because they are an option. Writers need options.

6.9 Inventing Connections to Link Sentences

Lesson Overview

Revision goal connected to standards:

Develop and strengthen writing by adding information and ideas for coherence and clarity.

Model Text

Girls Think of Everything: Stories of Ingenious Inventions by Women
- Written by Catherine Thimmesh
- Illustrated by Melissa Sweet

Teacher Considerations

We use this lesson to consider how we can use transition words to act as connectors when moving from one idea to the next within a paragraph. The chart on page 112 (**Writers Connect Ideas and Link to the Next with Transitions**) shows some common transition words and phrases writers might use for this work. We suggest students use this chart as a starting place or a guide, and then think beyond it as they start to collect transitions that can best show the connection between their ideas and why. The options are endless!

Patterns of Power (6–8) Lesson 13.5 invites writers to discover how conjunctive adverbs connect two related sentences.

Writers Connect Ideas and Link to the Next with Transitions

Words and Phrases You Might Use

To Show Time or Order		To Show Location	
first	meanwhile	beyond	by
soon	now	on top of	inside
after	later	throughout	within

To Compare Ideas		To Contrast Ideas	
in the same way	like	however	unlike
similarly	also	instead	bigger than
likewise	accordingly	although	on the other hand

To Emphasize an Idea		To Provide More Information	
indeed	in fact	additionally	for example
specifically	with this in mind	also	another
again	anyway	furthermore	and

To Summarize Ideas

in conclusion	as a result	therefore	consequently

Setting the Context

In *Girls Think of Everything*, Catherine Thimmesh highlights the contributions of numerous female inventors: "Whether in medicine or science, household products or high-tech gadgets, women and girls invent—and their inventions surround us and affect our everyday lives." In this lesson, the focus is on one specific inventor, Mary Anderson, and her invention of the windshield wiper. Share this information with your students, and then read aloud the following excerpt (with a sentence missing) from *Girls Think of Everything*:

> It was a dreadful day, weather-wise. Snow and sleet pelted the pavement, and people burrowed deep within their coats. Hoping to catch the sights and escape the blustery cold, Mary Anderson of Birmingham, Alabama, climbed aboard a New York City street car. The year was 1902. It turned out to be a ride she would never forget, but not because of the scenery. And simply because she felt sorry for the streetcar driver, who struggled to see through the glass.

Invite students to consider how this paragraph is written and the meaning within it. "Guess what? A sentence is missing from this paragraph. Did you notice? Are you left wondering anything? Does anything seem unclear?"

When the conversation warrants, share what writers do to clear up confusion for readers: "Writers add sentences, as connectors, to show a transition for their readers."

Revision Strategy

Add a connector, a transitional sentence to guide your reader.

Modeling

Display **6.9 Something's Missing: Part I**, which includes the paragraph you just shared and shows where a new transitional sentence needs to be inserted. "The writer of this paragraph needs to revise by adding a sentence that will connect ideas with a transition for the reader. Let's look at this paragraph in which something's missing." Discuss the author's message in the existing parts around the blank. Consider using her first name to show she's a writer just like your students. Possible questions to prompt discussion:

- What is Catherine saying in the sentences before the blank? What about the sentence after the blank?
- What is Catherine's message in this paragraph?
- What do you notice about the writing right before and after the blank space?
- What idea or ideas might best connect these two sentences together?

Model trying out one of the starred sentence choices, reading it in the paragraph, and think aloud as to WHY this option works or doesn't seem to work well. Invite your students to help you think through the addition of the other starred sentence choices. Rather than trying to select the right answer, keep the conversation focused on WHY the author might choose or not choose to add the sentence. After some time for conversations about the meaning and effect of each choice, reveal Catherine Thimmesh's original version with the display page, **6.9 Something's Missing: Part II**. Use the reflective questions to guide a comparative analysis discussion.

- Why do you think Catherine used this sentence?
- Do any of the other starred sentence options work? Why or why not?
- Why do you think your choice was different from or the same as Catherine's?

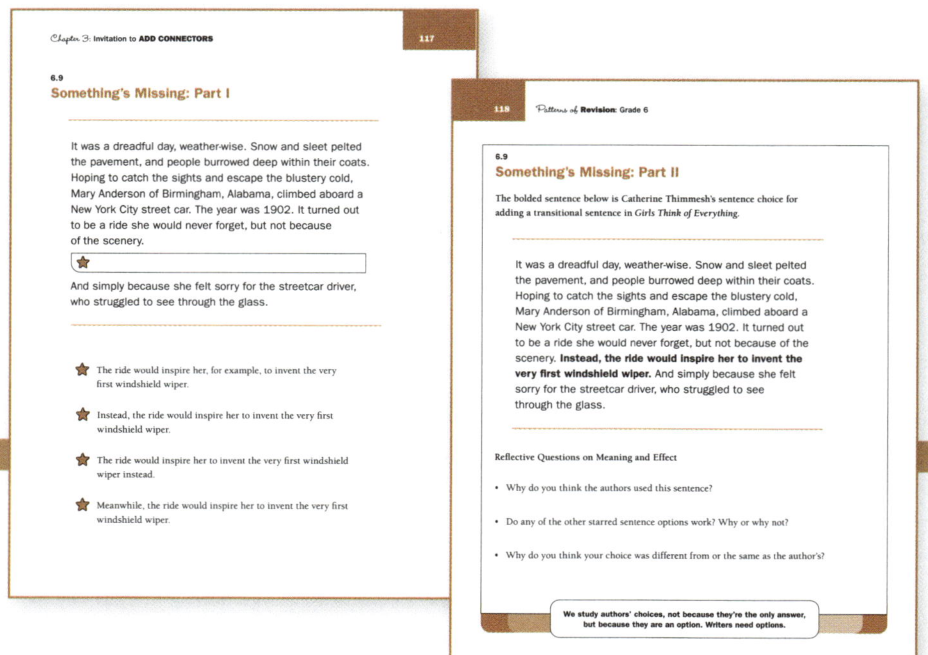

Collaborating Through Conversation

Display **6.9 Invitation to Add Connectors: Part I**. Students work in pairs or small groups to select the sentence that best connects the information for the reader, paying close attention to meaning and effect: what works, what doesn't, and why. Once they are finished revising, they compare their revisions with others in class, discussing WHY they made their choices. The author's original text is shown for comparative analysis in **6.9 Invitation to Add Connectors Part II**, and the reflective questions facilitate further discussion on meaning and effect.

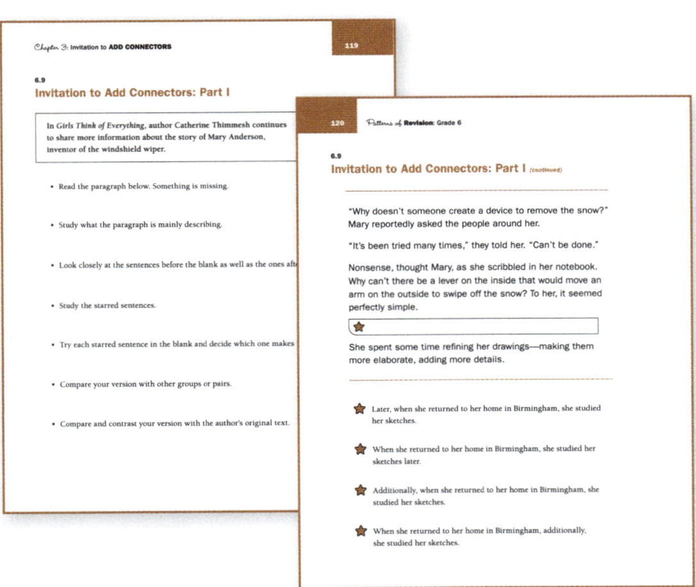

Chapter 3: Invitation to **ADD CONNECTORS**   119

6.9
Invitation to Add Connectors: Part I

In *Girls Think of Everything*, author Catherine Thimmesh continues to share more information about the story of Mary Anderson, inventor of the windshield wiper.

- Read the paragraph below. Something is missing.
- Study what the paragraph is mainly describing.
- Look closely at the sentences before the blank as well as the ones after.
- Study the starred sentences.
- Try each starred sentence in the blank and decide which one makes.
- Compare your version with other groups or pairs.
- Compare and contrast your version with the author's original text.

120   *Patterns of* **Revision**: Grade 6

6.9
Invitation to Add Connectors: Part I *(continued)*

"Why doesn't someone create a device to remove the snow?" Mary reportedly asked the people around her.

"It's been tried many times," they told her. "Can't be done."

Nonsense, thought Mary, as she scribbled in her notebook. Why can't there be a lever on the inside that would move an arm on the outside to swipe off the snow? To her, it seemed perfectly simple.

☆ ____________________

She spent some time refining her drawings—making them more elaborate, adding more details.

☆ Later, when she returned to her home in Birmingham, she studied her sketches.

☆ When she returned to her home in Birmingham, she studied her sketches later.

☆ Additionally, when she returned to her home in Birmingham, she studied her sketches.

☆ When she returned to her home in Birmingham, additionally, she studied her sketches.

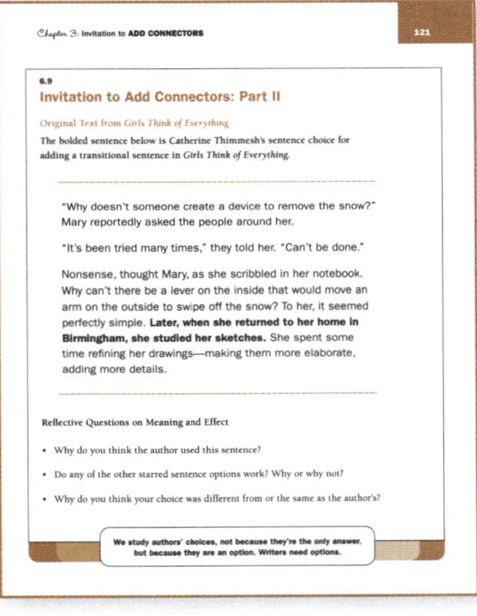

Chapter 3: Invitation to **ADD CONNECTORS**   121

6.9
Invitation to Add Connectors: Part II

Original Text from Girls Think of Everything

The bolded sentence below is Catherine Thimmesh's sentence choice for adding a transitional sentence in *Girls Think of Everything*.

"Why doesn't someone create a device to remove the snow?" Mary reportedly asked the people around her.

"It's been tried many times," they told her. "Can't be done."

Nonsense, thought Mary, as she scribbled in her notebook. Why can't there be a lever on the inside that would move an arm on the outside to swipe off the snow? To her, it seemed perfectly simple. **Later, when she returned to her home in Birmingham, she studied her sketches.** She spent some time refining her drawings—making them more elaborate, adding more details.

Reflective Questions on Meaning and Effect

- Why do you think the author used this sentence?
- Do any of the other starred sentence options work? Why or why not?
- Why do you think your choice was different from or the same as the author's?

We study authors' choices, not because they're the only answer, but because they are an option. Writers need options.

Quickwrite Opportunity (Optional)

1. What is something about your everyday life that you think could be improved? What idea(s) do you have for creating something that could improve it?
2. What qualities do you think make successful inventors? Write about any of those qualities that you also have and make a case for why you think you might or might not be a good inventor.

Applying Revision

Students return to a piece of writing and consider where they may need to add information. To help this process, invite them to use sticky notes to form a quick outline of their writing (or a piece they are planning). Students can sketch each scene on a separate sticky note or write separate ideas on each sticky note. On their own or partnering up to discuss their thinking, students consider how they could transition from one part of their outline to the next.

Sharing Results

Set up four choices for students to pick a favorite from, such as seasons of the year (winter, spring, summer, fall) and attach a sign for each one in the four corners of the room. Invite students to pick their favorite and walk to that corner of the room with their writing. Once gathered, each corner group member takes turns sharing their revisions with their group mates. If time allows, volunteers from each of the four corners share their revisions with the class.

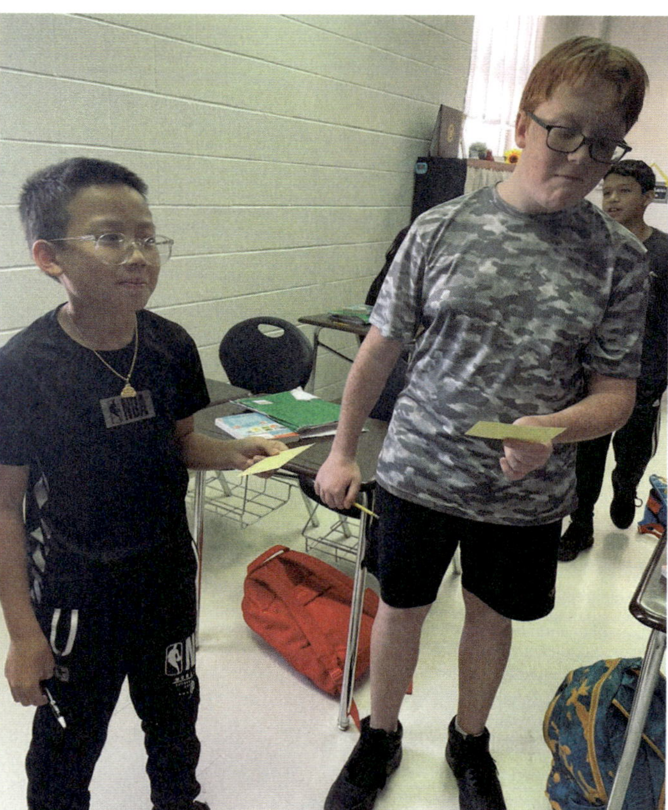

Figure 6.9

A group of students share their revision work with each other.

6.9

Something's Missing: Part I

It was a dreadful day, weather-wise. Snow and sleet pelted the pavement, and people burrowed deep within their coats. Hoping to catch the sights and escape the blustery cold, Mary Anderson of Birmingham, Alabama, climbed aboard a New York City street car. The year was 1902. It turned out to be a ride she would never forget, but not because of the scenery.

And simply because she felt sorry for the streetcar driver, who struggled to see through the glass.

 The ride would inspire her, for example, to invent the very first windshield wiper.

 Instead, the ride would inspire her to invent the very first windshield wiper.

 The ride would inspire her to invent the very first windshield wiper instead.

 Meanwhile, the ride would inspire her to invent the very first windshield wiper.

6.9

Something's Missing: Part II

The bolded sentence below is Catherine Thimmesh's sentence choice for adding a transitional sentence in *Girls Think of Everything*.

It was a dreadful day, weather-wise. Snow and sleet pelted the pavement, and people burrowed deep within their coats. Hoping to catch the sights and escape the blustery cold, Mary Anderson of Birmingham, Alabama, climbed aboard a New York City street car. The year was 1902. It turned out to be a ride she would never forget, but not because of the scenery. **Instead, the ride would inspire her to invent the very first windshield wiper.** And simply because she felt sorry for the streetcar driver, who struggled to see through the glass.

Reflective Questions on Meaning and Effect

- Why do you think the authors used this sentence?

- Do any of the other starred sentence options work? Why or why not?

- Why do you think your choice was different from or the same as the author's?

> We study authors' choices, not because they're the only answer, but because they are an option. Writers need options.

6.9

Invitation to Add Connectors: Part I

> In *Girls Think of Everything*, author Catherine Thimmesh continues
> to share more information about the story of Mary Anderson,
> inventor of the windshield wiper.

- Read the paragraph below. Something is missing.

- Study what the paragraph is mainly describing.

- Look closely at the sentences before the blank as well as the ones after the blank.

- Study the starred sentences.

- Try each starred sentence in the blank and decide which one makes the most sense.

- Compare your version with other groups or pairs.

- Compare and contrast your version with the author's original text.

Invitation to Add Connectors: Part I *(continued)*

"Why doesn't someone create a device to remove the snow?" Mary reportedly asked the people around her.

"It's been tried many times," they told her. "Can't be done."

Nonsense, thought Mary, as she scribbled in her notebook. Why can't there be a lever on the inside that would move an arm on the outside to swipe off the snow? To her, it seemed perfectly simple.

She spent some time refining her drawings—making them more elaborate, adding more details.

 Later, when she returned to her home in Birmingham, she studied her sketches.

 When she returned to her home in Birmingham, she studied her sketches later.

 Additionally, when she returned to her home in Birmingham, she studied her sketches.

 When she returned to her home in Birmingham, additionally, she studied her sketches.

6.9

Invitation to Add Connectors: Part II

Original Text from *Girls Think of Everything*

The bolded sentence below is Catherine Thimmesh's sentence choice for adding a transitional sentence in *Girls Think of Everything*.

"Why doesn't someone create a device to remove the snow?" Mary reportedly asked the people around her.

"It's been tried many times," they told her. "Can't be done."

Nonsense, thought Mary, as she scribbled in her notebook. Why can't there be a lever on the inside that would move an arm on the outside to swipe off the snow? To her, it seemed perfectly simple. **Later, when she returned to her home in Birmingham, she studied her sketches.** She spent some time refining her drawings—making them more elaborate, adding more details.

Reflective Questions on Meaning and Effect

- Why do you think the author used this sentence?

- Do any of the other starred sentence options work? Why or why not?

- Why do you think your choice was different from or the same as the author's?

We study authors' choices, not because they're the only answer, but because they are an option. Writers need options.

4

Invitation to

FORM NEW VERBS

The verb is the heartthrob of the sentence.

– Karen Elizabeth Gordon

In language, verbs are where the action is. Wielding them effectively requires a certain degree of finesse. When combining sentences or ideas, writers will sometimes need to change the verb endings or form new verbs to match the structure of the revised sentence. Without *verbs*, nothing happens. Sentences don't live without verbs. In short, we need verbs to activate our writing. So when revising, don't forget the ever-powerful verb as a place to look for possible enhancements. The lessons in this chapter embrace three specific ways we can revise verbs to improve our writing:

- The Infinitive
- The Participle
- The Active Voice

Sometimes when writers are applying revision strategies of deleting, rearranging, or adding connectors, they will see opportunities to form new verbs. To be sure, writers won't always need to change their verbs during revision, but it's definitely an option to consider.

Tip

Revision Strategies Don't Always Work

Writers have options on what and how they revise. In fact, writing and revising are all about making choices and trying different strategies to see which works best for purposes of meaning and effect. If your students find their revision doesn't quite make sense, encourage them to try another verb or another strategy completely. Writers have to try things out to see how they sound to the ear. They take risks as they play with a variety of moves, but ground those risks in an ultimate consideration of meaning and effect.

The Infinitive

The *Chicago Manual of Style* says, "infinitives are the basic form of the verb, the one mentioned in the dictionary entries (260)." Infinitives most often have the word *to* in front of them. An infinitive is easy **to spot** because of the **to + verb** stem. Changing a verb to an infinitive changes how it operates in a sentence. Infinitives often act as different parts of speech within a sentence: nouns, adjectives, or adverbs. Why might writers choose to use infinitives? Here are some ways infinitives can enhance your writing:

Infinitives help writers express what someone wants to do or the purpose behind an action.

She went to the store **to buy** a birthday card for her cousin.

This purpose uses infinitives as adverbs, enhancing the verb in the sentence and telling us why the subject of the sentence did or is something.

Infinitives can be used to give directions, suggestions, or advice.

To make a birthday card, you need construction paper and colorful writing utensils.

This purpose makes infinitives the subject of the sentence, acting as a noun.
Infinitives can be used to modify nouns, giving the reader more detail and clarity about it.

His desire **to craft** a birthday card from scratch is admirable.

This purpose shows more about the specifics of the noun *desire* making *to craft* act as an adjective.

Let's check back in with Tae Keller's work *When You Trap a Tiger* to see an example of her deftly using infinitives to enhance her writing.

The steam dances and floats up to kiss her face, but she doesn't notice.

Keller could have just as easily written *The steam dances and floats up, but she doesn't notice.* So, what is this extra information, the infinitive phrase *to kiss her face*, adding to the sentence? One thought is that it modifies the verb *floats* to express to the reader how that steam moves. To kiss is a delicate action, and Keller's addition of this infinitive helps the reader to see the delicate nature of the steam's movement.

The Participle

Participles are one of the forms of any verb and can be presented either in present tense, by adding -ing, or past tense, by adding either -ed, -d, -t, or -en to the end of the verb. According to the *Chicago Manual of Style,* "a participle is used as a modifier or as part of a verb phrase." Modifying often elicits the idea of adding to something. If we are looking to include more descriptive details and depth to sentences, adding a participle (or participial phrase) is a choice writers have to do the trick. Jeff noted in *Revision Decisions* a finding about participial phrases discussed by Francis Christensen in her book *Notes Toward a New Rhetoric* that still rings just as true for us today: "Francis Christensen (2007) said sentences with participial phrases tumbling off the end are one of the most used patterns in modern writing and one of the easiest for novice writers to navigate."

Let's take a look at a sentence from Tae Keller's *When You Trap a Tiger* and explore how her use of a participle helps to modify the sentence:

An instinctive kind of fear twists in my stomach, making me carsick.

The phrase *making me carsick* is a participial phrase that starts with the present participle *making*. Adding this phrase gives the reader insight into the consequence of the fear that is twisting in the speaker's stomach. As a result of the fear, the body reacts physically by feeling carsick.

The Active Voice

According to the *Chicago Manual of Style*, "voice shows whether the subject acts (active voice) or is acted on (passive voice) — that is, whether the subject performs or receives the action of the verb (264)." Readers, in general, prefer the *active voice*. Middle graders are likely to prefer the active voice as well, but first, they have to be shown the contrast between active and passive voice to wrap their minds around the concept. Basically, active voice is not complicated if you remember these two enduring truths:

- In the **active voice**, the *subject performs* the action: Students *write*.
- In the **passive voice**, the *subject* is acted upon: The writing *is being completed* by the students.

Here are a few reasons why active voice is an effective choice for writers to make:

Being Direct: Active voice tends to be clearer and more direct. It clearly identifies the person who performs the action and what the action is. Use active voice when you want your writing to be straightforward and easy to understand.

> Active: "The student wrote a beautiful poem."
> Passive: "The beautiful poem was written by the student."

Focusing on the Subject: Active voice emphasizes the person performing the action. It highlights the agent of the action and gives them prominence in the sentence.

> Active: "The teacher shared her writing with the class."
> Passive: "Her writing was shared with the class by the teacher."

Being Concise: By using active voice, writers can often convey the same information with less words.

> Active: "He solved the problem quickly."
> Passive: "The problem was solved quickly by him."

The lessons in this chapter will highlight each of the options for forming new verbs: creating infinitives, creating participles, and shifting writing from passive to active voice. You will notice that we've shifted in this chapter from focusing revision work at the paragraph level to focusing on sentence-level revision. This will be a great transition for you and your students as we move into sentence combining in the following chapter. The **Form New Verbs** chart on page 126 can be used as a reference throughout this chapter's lessons and in the following chapter's sentence combining lessons.

Tip

Though writing in passive voice isn't incorrect, this form often isn't the most economical or direct way to share your message with your reader. There are writing occasions where passive voice can be an effective choice. One example is in scientific writing, where the action or process is often more important to know about than the person performing the action. Another example is in journalism, where the person doing the action (like committing a crime) can be unknown.

FORM NEW VERBS

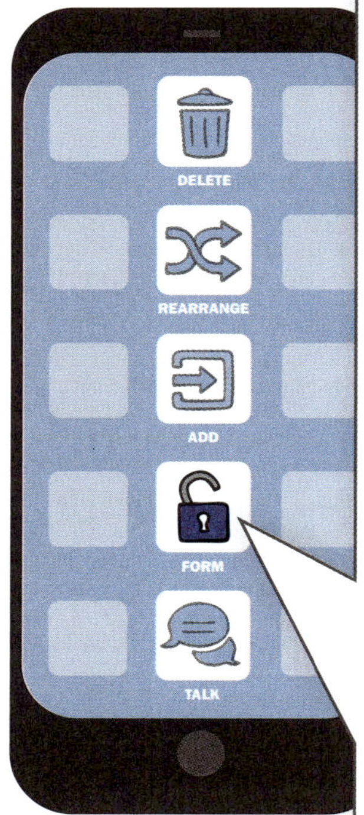

Possibilities for Forming New Verbs

Unrevised Text First Attempts	 to	Revised Text
Regular Past Tense Verb My puppy **wagged** her tail as she met my friends for the first time.	 to	**Infinitives** (revise VS to *revise*) My puppy had **to wag** her tail as she met my friends for the first time.
Repetitious I show my dog love. **I play** games with her like hide-and-seek. **I also play** fetch with her. **I play** games with her whenever she gets restless or bored.	 to	**Participles** (-*ing* verbs) I show my dog love, **playing** games with her like hide-and-seek or fetch whenever she gets restless or bored.
Passive (The action is being done by the subject) Going for a walk together is always done before dinner by my dog and me.	 to	**Active** (The subject is doing the action) We always go for a walk together before dinner.

Forming New Verb Revision Process

- Underline any verbs.
- Think about the meaning of the sentence(s).
- Search for ways to connect related ideas with participles, active verbs, or infinitives.
- See if you can try to compress repetition by changing at least one verb form.

Though verb form most often deals with tense, such as past, present, and future, here we know that would change the meaning significantly. Unless we need to shift text for style reasons, **we don't get tense about tense**. We only change tense to aid agreement in a piece of text.

6.10 The Remarkable Journey of Forming New Verbs

Lesson Overview

Revision goal connected to standards:

Develop and strengthen writing by forming new verbs to compress repetition, connect ideas, and improve clarity.

Model Text

The Remarkable Journey of Coyote Sunrise
– Written by Dan Gemeinhart

Teacher Considerations

The lessons in this chapter begin the shift from doing revision work at the paragraph level to revising at the sentence level. Familiarize yourself with the **Form New Verbs** chart on page 126. You'll find it helpful if students can check out this reference throughout the lessons presented in this chapter. To explore the different ways we can **Form New Verbs,** we focus the first lesson in this chapter on talking students through forming infinitives and participles.

The author's originals include participial phrases, which are organized in both instances as closers—coming at the end, after what could be a standalone sentence, closing it out. As closers, the author uses a comma to separate the participial phrase from the rest of the sentence. This could be an important talking point with students as you do comparative analysis with the author's original writing: that writers connect a participial phrase to a sentence using a comma. If you don't want to get students hung up in the academic language, you might instead call it *a phrase that starts with an -ing verb.* For more visual support on the pattern of this type of sentence, as well as how writers punctuate sentences with participial phrase openers, check out Figure 6.10 in this lesson for a visual that you can share with students.

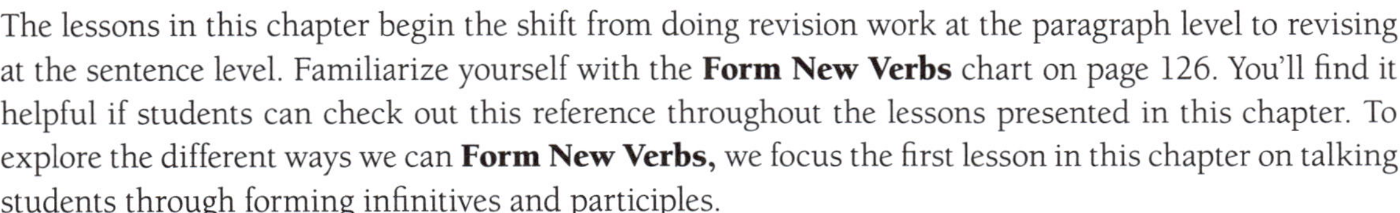

Figure 6.10 Sentence pattern: participial phrases.

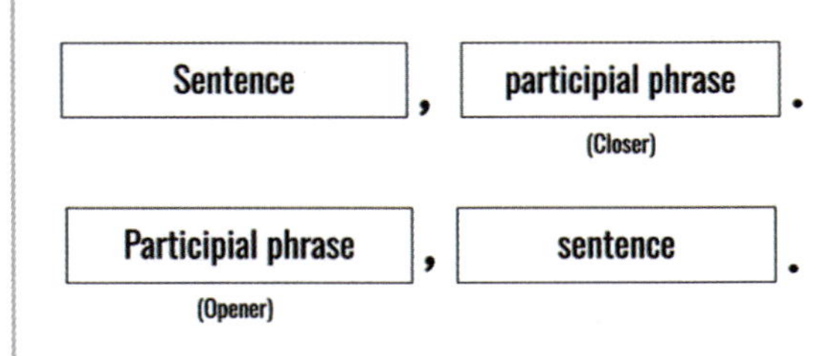

Patterns of Power (6–8), Lesson 7.4 or 9.1: These lessons focus on participial phrases, so students experiencing either lesson set will come away with a stronger mastery of applying participles in their writing. (You don't have to call them participles in this lesson. Students will still get the concept.)

Setting the Context

The Remarkable Journey of Coyote Sunrise is a story about a father named Rodeo and his daughter named Coyote Sunrise who travel across the country together in a big old school bus. In this part of the story, Coyote and her father have stopped at a campground in Turquoise Lake, Colorado. While Coyote explores the campground with her cat, Ivan, she makes fast friends with another girl named Fiona, who invites her over to her family's campsite for dinner. Read the excerpt below to give students more context about the story.

The girl's name was Fiona, and even though she gave me a look when I told her I went by Coyote, she didn't make a big deal out of it–always a good sign in a human being.

We spent the afternoon mostly at her family's site, playing with Ivan and comparing favorite books and avoiding her little brothers.

Her family was her mom and her dad and her two little brothers, Alex and Avery, who were kinda annoying but mostly cute, and Fiona was right: Tofu sausages, if you put enough ketchup on 'em, aren't half bad.

You'll continue into the model lesson with students, picking up on the story right after the excerpt you've read aloud.

Revision Strategy
Form new verbs to compress repetition, connect ideas, and improve clarity.

Tip

Remember, though the lessons in this chapter will have writers calling on all the revision strategies they've worked on so far, you'll focus your instructional lens to prioritize the role verbs, specifically, play in this work.

Modeling

Display **6.10 Verb Form Shuffle: Part I** to explore a group of sentences that you will merge into one. "There are four sentences here that need to be revised down to one. First, let's read aloud the sentences."

After dinner her dad took the boys down to the lake to burn off some energy.

It was just me and Fiona.   We sat around the table.   We talked.

Modeling *(continued)*

"Let's start by looking at what you already know about revision. Do we see any repeated words or groups of words here that can be Deleted? I notice the word *we* is repeated in sentences three and four. Let's look at *who* the word *we* is referring to." Students talk about this repetition and share their thinking with the class. "So, the *we* in sentences three and four refers to Coyote and her new friend Fiona. Let's think about how we might connect these ideas in sentences three and four to sentence two. If we look at the **Form New Verbs Chart,** I notice one way would be to turn the *verbs* into *infinitives*. Let's see what that might look like:

It was just me and Fiona, to sit around the table and to talk.

"Talk about how our revision choices sound as we read them aloud and to each other. This sounds pretty strange to me. Let's look back at the chart and see what else we can do. Another option would be to add -ing to these verbs and attach them to sentence two. Let's try a few options."

It was just me and Fiona, **sitting** around the table, talking.

It was just me and Fiona, **sitting** around the table and talking.

It was just me and Fiona. We were **sitting** around the table and talking.

Which of these versions is the most effective to you? Why do you say that?" Students discuss and choose the most effective option. You may choose to have a student or group defend each choice as the most effective, explaining their thinking to the class.

"Now we need to connect the first sentence (*After dinner her dad took the boys down to the lake to burn off some energy.*) to the revised portion we just created. We can Add a Connector. The connector can be a word, a phrase, or even punctuation. Let's try a few options." Write a few options on the board for students to see.

After dinner her dad took the boys down to the lake to burn off some energy, so it was just me and Fiona, sitting around the table, talking.

After dinner her dad took the boys down to the lake to burn off some energy, and it was just me and Fiona, sitting around the table and talking.

After dinner her dad took the boys down to the lake to burn off some energy; it was just me and Fiona, sitting around the table and talking.

Modeling *(continued)*

Students suggest any other options for connecting these sentences and then come to a consensus on the one they think is most effective. After finishing this discussion, reveal the author's original sentence as displayed in **6.10 Verb Form Shuffle: Part II**, prompting things along with the following reflective questions as necessary.

- Why do you think Dan combined the sentences this way?
- Is there another combination that would be effective?
- Why do you think your combination was different from or the same as the author's?
- If your combination was different from Gemeinhart's, which do you prefer now, and why?

Throughout this discussion, be sure to reiterate that the comparing-and-contrasting conversation about the various versions of the revised sentence is about discussing choices and their effects as opposed to choosing one right version.

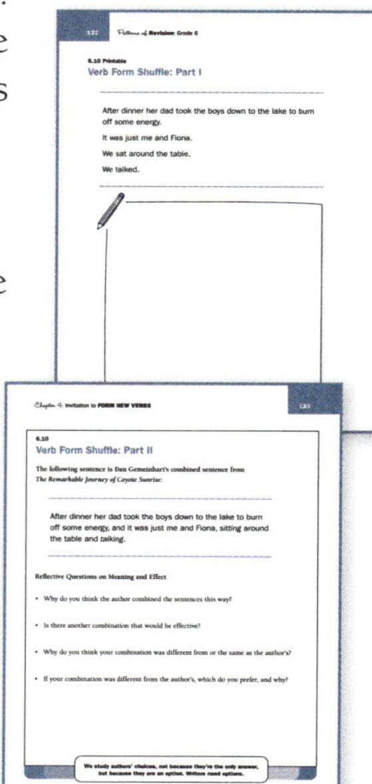

Collaborating Through Conversation

Provide each student with the printable, **6.10 Invitation to Form New Verbs: Part I**. To form new verbs, follow the directions included in the printable and use the **Form New Verbs chart** on page 126. You can display the printable so students can follow along. Invite students to combine sentences through conversations with at least one classmate. The sentences provided will most likely lead your students to discover a few possible combinations. Use the space provided on the printable, notebooks, or digital space to record their possibilities.

The students then make comparisons between their choices and those of other groups or partnerships. Focus class conversations on the effectiveness of combinations rather than getting the right answer, as in previous lessons. For comparative analysis, display **6.10 Invitation to Form New Verbs: Part II** on page 136 to share the author's original text. Discussions of meaning and effect can be facilitated by the reflective questions at the bottom of the sheet.

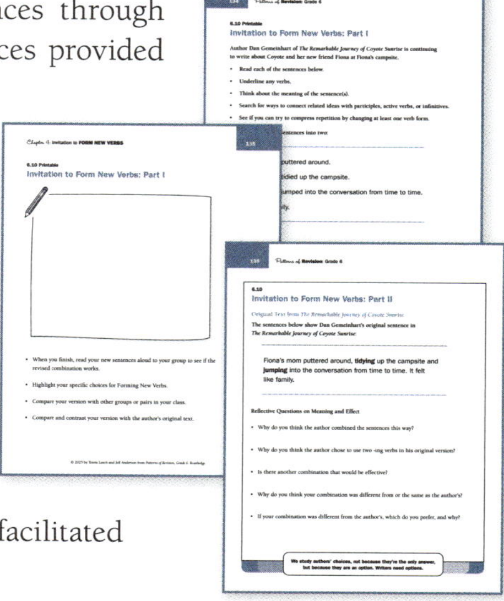

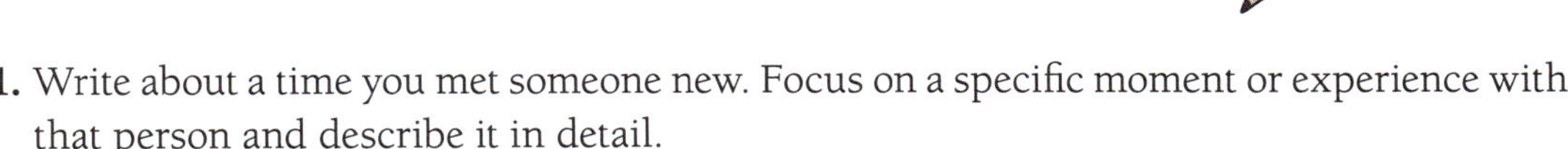

1. Write about a time you met someone new. Focus on a specific moment or experience with that person and describe it in detail.
2. Where is your favorite place to visit or explore? It can be someplace in your neighborhood, close to home, or far away. Describe what you do or have done when visiting this place.

Applying Revision

Each student selects a piece of writing to revisit. This can be something written in a previous class period or writing generated in class connected to one of the writing prompts. Model this revision process with your own writing to support student clarity. Display your writing, talking through your process for finding a place to revise. A great starting point is focusing on the *verbs* you've used within your sentences and paragraphs. During your model revision, explain why you made the choices you did and why you think they led to more effective writing.

Students return to their own writing to play with different revision possibilities. Invite them to focus on one section or paragraph. **Forming New Verbs** is the main objective of this lesson, but students will likely need to apply other revision techniques they have already learned, such as Deleting, Rearranging, or Adding Connectors. Welcome this natural extension. Offering numerous entry points into revision enhances the likelihood that students see this process as applicable to the different writing pieces they will be interacting with across the classroom.

Sharing Results

Circling and Sharing: Group students so there is an inner and outer circle of the same number of students, with each student in the inner circle facing a student in the outer circle. If one or more classes have an odd number of students, you may choose to stand in to partner with a student to even out the numbers.

- Students in the inner circle share part or all of their revised writing (or discuss the revision they're going to do) with their partner in the outer circle.
- Students in the outer circle then share with their partner in the inner circle.
- After both groups share, have the students in the inner circle stay put, while students in the outer circle move one person (or two people) to their left (or right).
- New partnerships now repeat the sharing process above.
- Repeat as often as time allows.

6.10 Printable

Verb Form Shuffle: Part I

After dinner her dad took the boys down to the lake to burn off some energy.

It was just me and Fiona.

We sat around the table.

We talked.

6.10

Verb Form Shuffle: Part II

The following sentence is Dan Gemeinhart's combined sentence from
The Remarkable Journey of Coyote Sunrise:

After dinner her dad took the boys down to the lake to burn off some energy, and it was just me and Fiona, *sitting* around the table and *talking*.

Reflective Questions on Meaning and Effect

- Why do you think the author combined the sentences this way?

- Is there another combination that would be effective?

- Why do you think your combination was different from or the same as the author's?

- If your combination was different from the author's, which do you prefer, and why?

We study authors' choices, not because they're the only answer,
but because they are an option. Writers need options.

6.10 Printable

Invitation to Form New Verbs: Part I

Author Dan Gemeinhart of *The Remarkable Journey of Coyote Sunrise* is continuing to write about Coyote and her new friend Fiona at Fiona's campsite.

- Read each of the sentences below.

- Underline any verbs.

- Think about the meaning of the sentence(s).

- Search for ways to connect related ideas with participles, active verbs, or infinitives.

- See if you can try to compress repetition by changing at least one verb form.

Combine these four sentences into two:

____

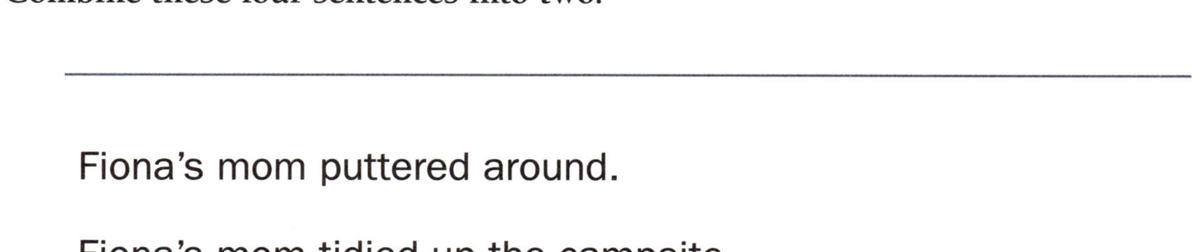

____

6.10 Printable

Invitation to Form New Verbs: Part I

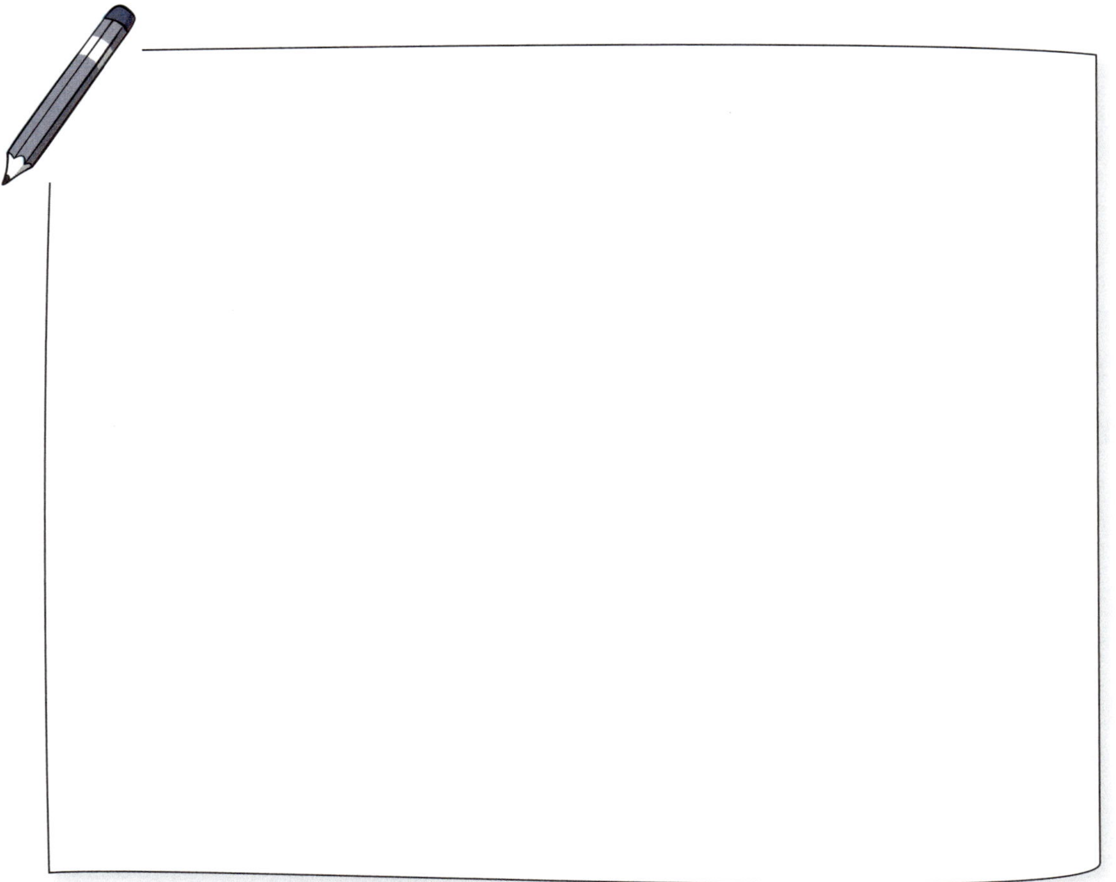

- When you finish, read your new sentences aloud to your group to see if the revised combination works.

- Highlight your specific choices for Forming New Verbs.

- Compare your version with other groups or pairs in your class.

- Compare and contrast your version with the author's original text.

6.10

Invitation to Form New Verbs: Part II

Original Text from *The Remarkable Journey of Coyote Sunrise*

The sentences below show Dan Gemeinhart's original sentence in
The Remarkable Journey of Coyote Sunrise:

Fiona's mom puttered around, **tidying** up the campsite and
jumping into the conversation from time to time. It felt
like family.

Reflective Questions on Meaning and Effect

- Why do you think the author combined the sentences this way?

- Why do you think the author chose to use two -ing verbs in his original version?

- Is there another combination that would be effective?

- Why do you think your combination was different from or the same as the author's?

- If your combination was different from the author's, which do you prefer, and why?

We study authors' choices, not because they're the only answer,
but because they are an option. Writers need options.

6.11 **Trading Voice**

Lesson Overview

Revision goal connected to standards:

Develop and strengthen writing by forming new verbs to compress repetition, connect ideas, and improve clarity.

Model Text

The Season of Styx Malone
- Written by Kekla Magoon

Teacher Considerations

The sentence level work in this lesson focuses on *passive voice* and encourages writers to revise their writing to make it more *active*. Both its model stage and the collaborating through conversation stage introduce the option of changing at least one sentence in the group from *passive* to *active voice*.

Patterns of Power (6–8), **Lesson 8.1** highlights active and passive voice and includes helpful tips and charts to support students in understanding the difference between the two.

Setting the Context

In *The Season of Styx Malone* by Kekla Magoon, the character Caleb Franklin, who is also the narrator, goes to a party with his brother Bobby Gene and their father. They are tasked with watching their one-year-old sister, Suzie. As they head outside to find other kids at the party, they walk into an interesting scene. Read this excerpt from the book to set the stage for the lesson.

Cory Cormier stood on one of the picnic tables, alongside the largest gunnysack I had ever seen. It could have held my entire body. Maybe even Bobby Gene's. Everyone—literally every kid in attendance, twenty or thirty of them—was gathered around, shouting and bidding on the goods inside.

Cory reached into the bag and extracted a rocket-style firework the size of his forearm. He held it aloft . . . the boy on the table and the bag in his hands loomed larger than life up there.

As it turned out, Cory Cormier had always wanted a little sister, and we had one to spare.

Engage students in a discussion by focusing on the trade implied in the excerpt: "A little sister for a gunnysack full of fireworks. Does that seem like a fair trade? What about if the boys' sister had a dirty diaper? That's exactly what they find as they trade her to Cory Cormier for the sack of fireworks. Let's check out some more of this story and think through how we might revise the next sentences."

Revision Strategy

Form new verbs to compress repetition, connect ideas, and improve clarity.

Modeling

Use printable **6.11 Verb Form Shuffle: Part I** on page 142 to explore the three sentences that will be revised to one. "There are three sentences here that need to be revised down to one. First, let's read aloud the sentences."

The diaper bag was run for by Bobby Gene.

The fireworks were defended by me.

Our former sister was cooed and cuddled by Cory.

Modeling (continued)

"When I read these sentences, they sound strange—not like I would write or say them. Look at the **Form New Verbs chart**. Notice that one option for revision is changing sentences written in *passive voice* to *active voice*. But what is passive voice? Let's look at the first sentence to figure that out."

The diaper bag was run for by Bobby Gene.

"Who is this sentence about? Is it about the diaper bag or about Bobby Gene? These sentences are a little confusing. Bobby Gene is located at the end of the sentence. What is Bobby Gene running for? The thing he's running for, the diaper bag, is at the beginning. This is an example of passive voice. The emphasis in this sentence is on the object, the diaper bag, instead of the *subject* of the *sentence*, Bobby Gene. Let's revise it to active voice.

- First, I'll start with the subject: *Bobby Gene.*
- Next, I'll explain what he's doing.
- Because our reading was in past tense, I'll match that here: Bobby Gene *ran.*
- Now, what is the *object* he ran to get? Let's piece it all together."

Bobby Gene ran for the diaper bag.

"Just like that, we've revised the sentence from passive voice to active voice." Repeat this process with the other two sentences (both are in passive voice). Model the revising process, or as students are ready, organize them into groups and give them time to talk out revision work together.

"The last thing we need to do is **Add Connectors** to connect these sentences. We can use words, punctuation, or both to connect these ideas. If we have three ideas that we want to put together, almost like a list of things that happened, how might we connect them?"

After discussing several possible versions, reveal the author's original sentence. Reiterate that the conversation comparing and contrasting the students' final choice option, next to the author's original, is meant to be about meaning and effect as opposed to right or wrong. Share **6.11 Verb Form Shuffle: Part II** on page 143, prompting students' thinking with the following reflective questions as necessary:

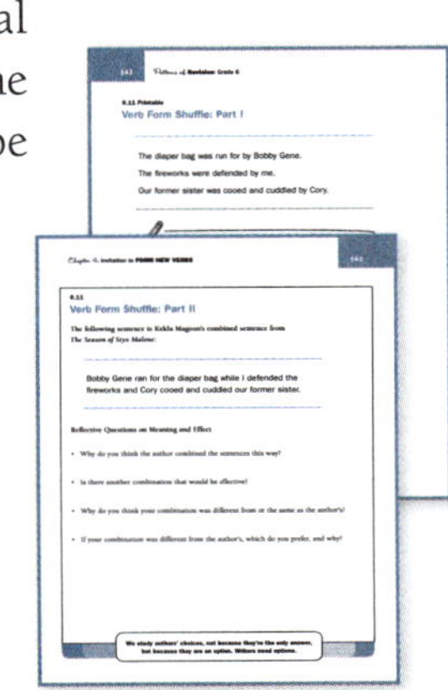

- Why do you think Kekla combined the sentences in this way?
- Is there another combination that would be effective?
- Why do you think your combination was different from or the same as the author's?
- If your combination was different from Magoon's, which do you prefer, and why?

Collaborating Through Conversation

Distribute the printable, **6.11 Invitation to Form New Verbs: Part I** on page 144, to each student. Following the directions on the printable and using the **Form New Verbs chart**, students collaborate through conversation with one or more classmates to combine the sentences into one. While **Forming New Verbs** is the priority focus of this lesson, students will most likely naturally discover other elements of **DRAFT** for combining the sentences. Celebrate this, inviting students to record their possibilities on the lines provided on the printable, in their notebooks, or in a digital space.

When ready, writers compare their choices with other partnerships or groups. Then, groups discuss the similarities and differences of their choices with the author's original text, found in **6.11 Invitation to Form New Verbs: Part II** on page 146. Reflective questions at the bottom of the page can support prompting effective discussions about meaning and effect.

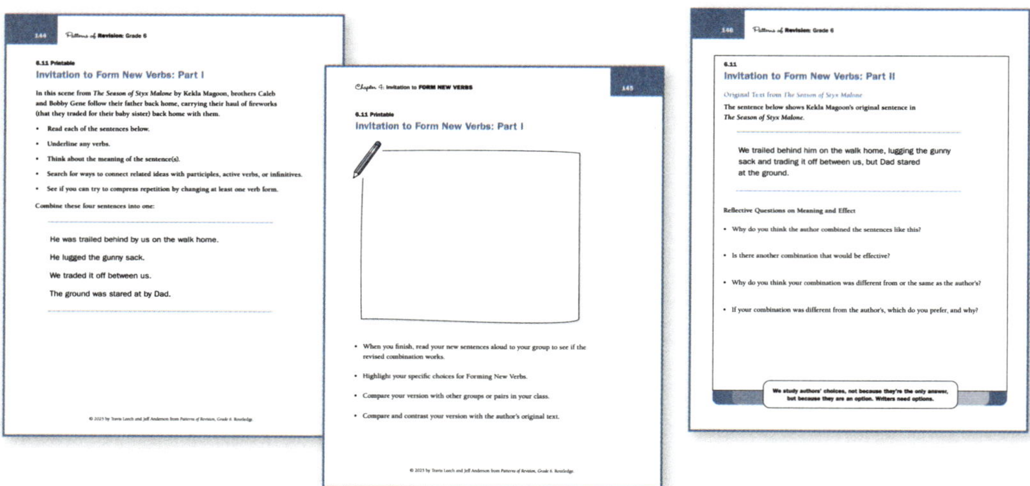

Quickwrite Opportunity (Optional)

1. Recall a moment of laughter or mischief shared with a sibling, family member, or close friend. What was the situation, and how did it bring you both closer?
2. Write about a funny or embarrassing moment that you and a sibling, family member, or close friend shared. How did you handle the situation, and what lasting memory did it create?

Applying Revision

Students choose a piece of writing to revisit. This can be something written in a previous class period or writing generated in class connected to one of the writing prompts. Set students up for success by modeling how you revise your writing to **Form New Verbs**. You may purposely include a sentence in passive voice so you can model changing it to active voice, or you may naturally find another way to connect ideas by changing a verb to a new form. For instance, a sentence from an initial draft of writing connected to a prompt above could have been in passive voice and said, "The ball was kicked onto the roof by my brother," which can be changed to the active voice by instead writing, "My brother kicked the ball onto the roof." After revising, talk out the choices you made and explain why you think the change creates more effective writing.

Students return to their own writing, playing with different revision possibilities. Remind students to reference the **Form New Verbs chart** on page 126 for a reminder of options for revision.

Sharing Results

Pair Square: This sharing strategy will get students moving around the classroom and allow them to hear revisions of multiple classmates.

- Pair students and have them discuss the work they did to revise their piece.
- After partners finish sharing, invite them to pair up with another group, forming a foursome.
- All four share one revision they made.
- The group votes on the revision that they liked best or feel is the most effective to share with the whole class.
- Throughout the sharing, encourage students to evaluate why they made the revision they did and how they think it has enhanced their writing.

6.11 Printable

Verb Form Shuffle: Part I

The diaper bag was run for by Bobby Gene.

The fireworks were defended by me.

Our former sister was cooed and cuddled by Cory.

6.11

Verb Form Shuffle: Part II

The following sentence is Kekla Magoon's combined sentence from
The Season of Styx Malone:

Bobby Gene ran for the diaper bag while I defended the
fireworks and Cory cooed and cuddled our former sister.

Reflective Questions on Meaning and Effect

- Why do you think the author combined the sentences this way?

- Is there another combination that would be effective?

- Why do you think your combination was different from or the same as the author's?

- If your combination was different from the author's, which do you prefer, and why?

We study authors' choices, not because they're the only answer,
but because they are an option. Writers need options.

6.11 Printable

Invitation to Form New Verbs: Part I

In this scene from *The Season of Styx Malone* by Kekla Magoon, brothers Caleb and Bobby Gene follow their father back home, carrying their haul of fireworks (that they traded for their baby sister) back home with them.

- Read each of the sentences below.

- Underline any verbs.

- Think about the meaning of the sentence(s).

- Search for ways to connect related ideas with participles, active verbs, or infinitives.

- See if you can try to compress repetition by changing at least one verb form.

Combine these four sentences into one:

He was trailed behind by us on the walk home.

He lugged the gunny sack.

We traded it off between us.

The ground was stared at by Dad.

6.11 Printable

Invitation to Form New Verbs: Part I

- When you finish, read your new sentences aloud to your group to see if the revised combination works.

- Highlight your specific choices for Forming New Verbs.

- Compare your version with other groups or pairs in your class.

- Compare and contrast your version with the author's original text.

6.11

Invitation to Form New Verbs: Part II

Original Text from *The Season of Styx Malone*

The sentence below shows Kekla Magoon's original sentence in
The Season of Styx Malone.

We trailed behind him on the walk home, lugging the gunny
sack and trading it off between us, but Dad stared
at the ground.

Reflective Questions on Meaning and Effect

- Why do you think the author combined the sentences like this?

- Is there another combination that would be effective?

- Why do you think your combination was different from or the same as the author's?

- If your combination was different from the author's, which do you prefer, and why?

We study authors' choices, not because they're the only answer,
but because they are an option. Writers need options.

6.12 **We're Popping and Locking with Verbs**

Lesson Overview

Revision goal connected to standards:

Develop and strengthen writing by forming new verbs to compress repetition, connect ideas, and improve clarity.

Model Text

"The Definition of Cool" from *Black Boy Joy*
- Written by Varian Johnson
- Edited by Kwame Mbalia

Teacher Considerations

In this lesson, we're upping the rigor a bit for students, pulling in multiple elements of **DRAFT**, while continuing to focus on **Forming New Verbs** within each sentence. Students will need to **Delete**, **Rearrange**, and **Add Connectors**. In the mentor text, the author uses dashes to enclose information in the model sentence, so we've highlighted a lesson set from *Patterns of Power* that will help students master this punctuation move. The author also uses complex sentences, so subordinating conjunctions (AAAWWUBBIS!) will be an additional focal point of the lesson. We've included two possible lesson suggestions from *Patterns of Power* that will highlight the complex sentence pattern used in the excerpted text.

Patterns of Power (6–8), Lesson 10.6: helps students understand that dashes can be used to set off the addition of extra information, which is how the author includes extra information within the sentence in the model lesson.

Patterns of Power (6–8), Lesson 6.1 or 6.6: because both of the author's original sentences are complex sentences that include dependent clause openers, either lesson will support students in better understanding this complex sentence pattern.

Setting the Context

In Varian Johnson's story "The Definition of Cool," the narrator, Desmond, prepares for a concert. He and his brother, Roosevelt, are going to see their favorite band: The Juice Box Squad. Read aloud the excerpt below to set the context.

I pull the pink-and-peach Hawaiian shirt over my head, then check myself out in the mirror. The colors don't exactly match, and my shorts are a little too baggy, but otherwise, I look just like DJ Amplified from the Juice Box Squad. I had been planning this outfit for six months—ever since we bought the tickets to the concert. JBS— that's what us superfans call them—always picked people from the crowd to show on the jumbotron during their concerts. This outfit was guaranteed to get their attention.

As a brief introduction to dashes, display this paragraph for students to see as you read it. After reading, ask students what they notice about the punctuation in this paragraph. This is a great way to gauge students' background knowledge of the dash and will help you assess how in-depth a possible mini-lesson in dash usage might need to be.

Revision Strategy

Form new verbs to compress repetition, connect ideas, and improve clarity.

Tip Dashes are used to set off an amplifying or explanatory element and in that sense can function as an alternative to parentheses, commas, or a colon— especially when an abrupt break in thought is called for.

—*The Chicago Manual of Style*

Modeling

Use printable **6.12 Verb Form Shuffle: Part I** to explore the five sentences that will be revised down to one. "We're now picking up the story where everyone's at the concert and DJ Amplified asks the crowd if they want to get on the Jumbotron. Let's read these sentences."

I am on my feet.   My eyes are closed.   My shoulders wiggle.

I do my best interpretations of the King Cobra.

This all happens before I know it.

Modeling *(continued)*

"For quick reference, the King Cobra is a dance move that Desmond's dad taught him. That should help us better understand sentence four. To revise these five sentences down to one, let's revisit all of the strategies we know so far."

- Delete
- Rearrange
- Add Connectors
- Form New Verbs

"Let's start by looking for any repeated information. I notice the words *I* and *my* are both repeated in different sentences. I'm going to mark those to come back to later. The next strategy is to Rearrange. As I read the last sentence, *This all happens before I know it*, it makes me think that maybe this sentence belongs somewhere else. I would usually say *Before I know it* to introduce what's next when I tell a story to someone, so I am going to move this sentence to the front and delete *This all happens* from the front of this sentence.

Next, we'll see if we can Add Connectors to combine sentences. If we're starting with *Before I know it*, I'm going to want to connect it to the next sentence with a comma."

Before I know it, I am on my feet.

"When I think back to the read aloud, I remember the author put extra information in between dashes. I think I want to try that out, but what can go within the dashes? How about the next two sentences? Let's try revising to connect them in a few ways."

Before I know it, I am on my feet—my eyes are closed and my shoulders wiggle—I do my best interpretations of the King Cobra.

Before I know it, I am on my feet—to close my eyes and to wiggle my shoulders—and I do my best interpretations of the King Cobra.

Before I know it, I am on my feet—my eyes closed and my shoulders wiggling—doing my best interpretations of the King Cobra.

"I tried out our next revision strategy, **Form New Verbs**, with some of my revisions. First, I tried to turn the verbs in one option into infinitives. That one doesn't quite sound right to me. I also tried to create participles, and those sound better when I read them aloud and to myself."

Modeling *(continued)*

Share with students the author's original, found in **6.12 Verb Form Shuffle: Part II**, prompting discussion using any of these questions:

- Why do you think Varian combined his ideas like this?
- Is there another combination that would be effective?
- If your combination was different from Johnson's, which do you prefer, and why?

Throughout this discussion, be sure to reiterate that the comparing-and-contrasting conversation about the various versions of the revised sentence is about discussing choices and their effects as opposed to choosing one right version.

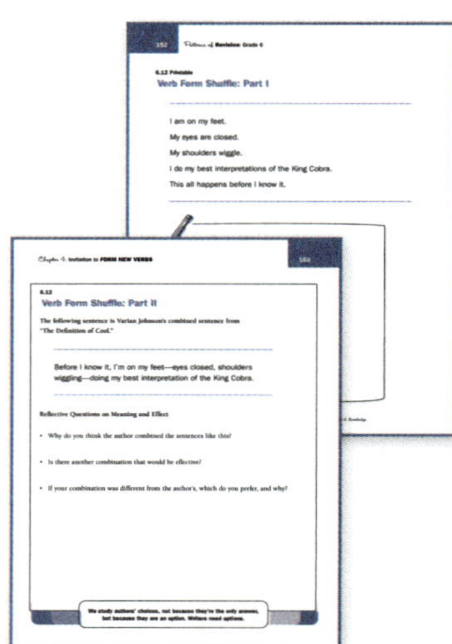

Collaborating Through Conversation

Distribute the printable, **6.12 Invitation to Form New Verbs: Part I** (page 154), to each student. Following the directions on the printable and using the **Form New Verbs chart** (page 126), students work together to follow the directions and complete the activity. While **Forming New Verbs** is a focus of this lesson, remind students it's okay to find other possibilities for combining the sentences using **DRAFT**. Ensure that partners or groups have decided on an appropriate place to write out their revision work.

When students are ready, display **6.12 Invitation to Form New Verbs: Part II** (page 156) to share the author's original text, allowing students time to check their revision work against the author's original. Highlight the reflective questions at the bottom for students to use to facilitate a conversation about meaning and effect.

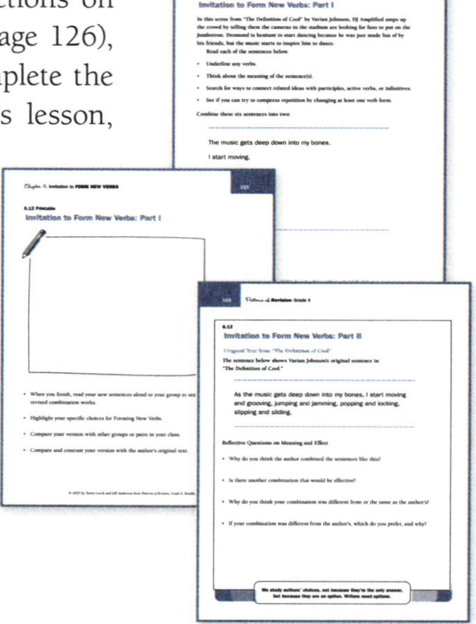

Quickwrite Opportunity (Optional)

1. Explore the impact your favorite musical artist has had on your life. How has their music influenced your emotions, decisions, or perspective? Write a letter to them expressing your gratitude for their artistry and what their work means to you.

2. Imagine you win a backstage pass to meet your favorite musical artist before their concert. Write about the experience of meeting them in person, the conversation you have, and the memories you create behind the scenes.

Applying Revision

Students choose a piece of writing to revisit. This can be something written in a previous class period or a piece generated in class connected to one of the writing prompts. Set students up for success by modeling how you revise your writing to **Form New Verbs**. After revising, talk out the choice you made and explain why you think it creates more effective writing.

Students revise their own writing to explore different revision possibilities. Invite them to choose a section or paragraph to focus on. When you move around the classroom and help writers identify revision points, remember that all the revision strategies we've covered can be fair game. If there is a section in a student's piece that highlights the need for another revision strategy (Deleting, Rearranging, or Adding Connectors), don't shy away from sharing that as an option for revision with each writer. It is more likely that students will find revision meaningful when there are many entry points into the process.

Sharing Results

Students highlight one sentence or paragraph they've revised and retype that in a shared digital space. After retyping their revised sentence or paragraph, each student reads their classmates' revisions and comments on one or two revisions they find the most effective (either digitally or verbally).

6.12 Printable

Verb Form Shuffle: Part I

I am on my feet.

My eyes are closed.

My shoulders wiggle.

I do my best interpretations of the King Cobra.

This all happens before I know it.

6.12

Verb Form Shuffle: Part II

The following sentence is Varian Johnson's combined sentence from
"The Definition of Cool."

Before I know it, I'm on my feet—eyes closed, shoulders
wiggling—doing my best interpretation of the King Cobra.

Reflective Questions on Meaning and Effect

- Why do you think the author combined the sentences like this?

- Is there another combination that would be effective?

- If your combination was different from the author's, which do you prefer, and why?

We study authors' choices, not because they're the only answer,
but because they are an option. Writers need options.

6.12 Printable

Invitation to Form New Verbs: Part I

In this scene from "The Definition of Cool" by Varian Johnson, DJ Amplified amps up the crowd by telling them the cameras in the stadium are looking for fans to put on the Jumbotron. Desmond is hesitant to start dancing because he was just made fun of by his friends, but the music starts to inspire him to dance.

Read each of the sentences below.

- Underline any verbs.

- Think about the meaning of the sentence(s).

- Search for ways to connect related ideas with participles, active verbs, or infinitives.

- See if you can try to compress repetition by changing at least one verb form.

Combine these six sentences into two:

____

The music gets deep down into my bones.

I start moving.

I also start grooving.

I jump and jam.

I pop and lock.

I slip and slide.

____

6.12 Printable

Invitation to Form New Verbs: Part I

- When you finish, read your new sentences aloud to your group to see if the revised combination works.

- Highlight your specific choices for Forming New Verbs.

- Compare your version with other groups or pairs in your class.

- Compare and contrast your version with the author's original text.

6.12

Invitation to Form New Verbs: Part II

Original Text from "The Definition of Cool"

The sentence below shows Varian Johnson's original sentence in "The Definition of Cool."

As the music gets deep down into my bones, I start moving and grooving, jumping and jamming, popping and locking, slipping and sliding.

Reflective Questions on Meaning and Effect

- Why do you think the author combined the sentences like this?

- Is there another combination that would be effective?

- Why do you think your combination was different from or the same as the author's?

- If your combination was different from the author's, which do you prefer, and why?

We study authors' choices, not because they're the only answer, but because they are an option. Writers need options.

REVISION
Through Sentence
COMBINING

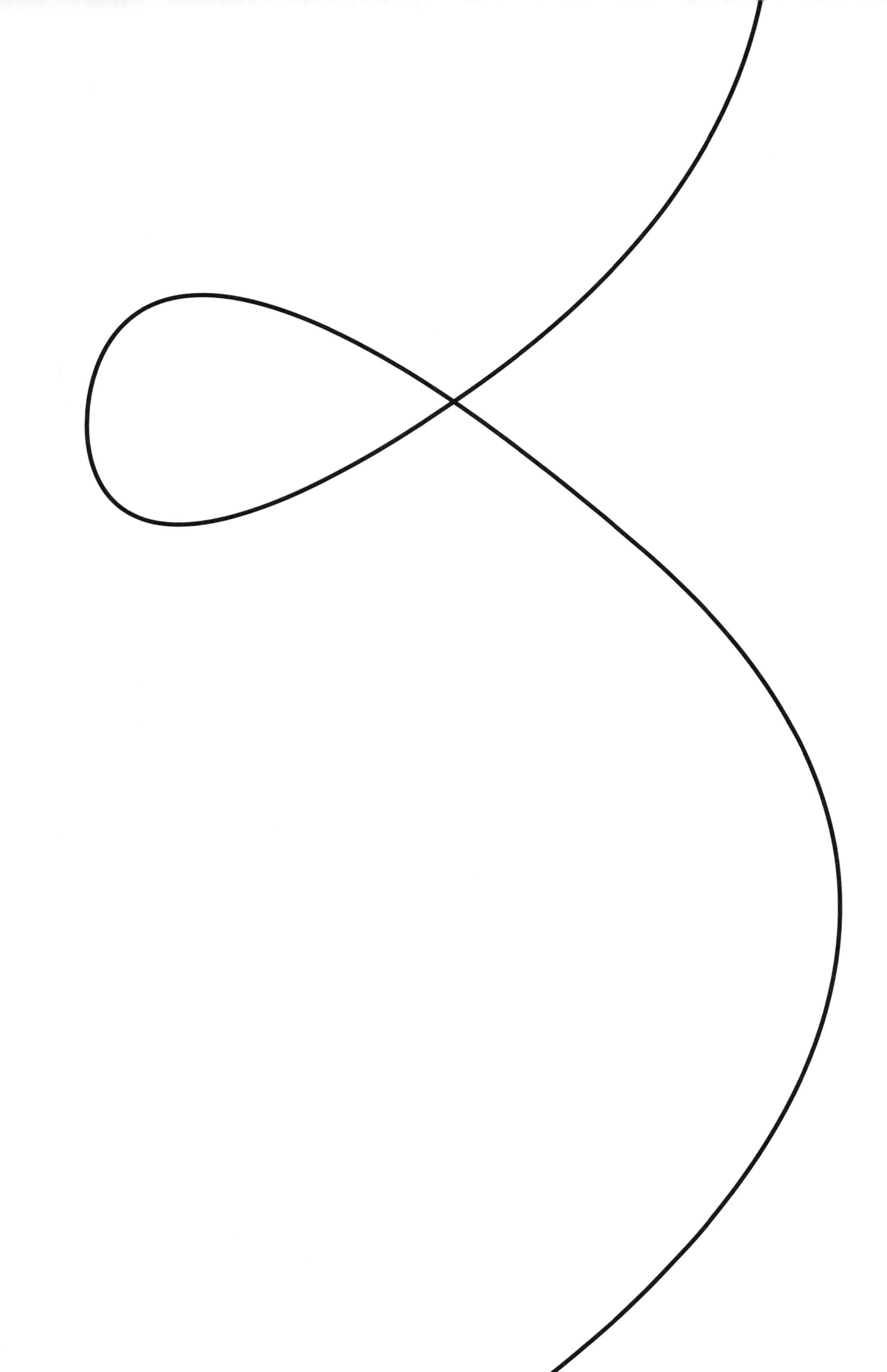

Part 2
Putting **DRAFT** Together

eachers are often told to teach writing strategies, including those regarding revision, within context. But what does that mean exactly?

In the context of literacy, our students need to write, read, talk, and think. In Part 2, students continue learning what writers do by exploring and examining texts written by published authors—texts they are already reading or want to read. But, at this point, we're ready to level up those conversations as students try out the moves they've learned in earlier lessons in a cumulative way, combining ideas, sentences, words, and phrases, while considering the best revisions for the message they are trying to convey. And, as they've done in every lesson up to this point, students will continue to talk through their choices with each other as they think about meaning and effect in their writing.

The lessons in Part 2 offer a culmination of all the revision strategies we've introduced so far and are grounded in a powerful mnemonic—**DRAFT** (delete, rearrange, add connectors, form new verbs, and talk it out) (page 162)—to remind intermediate writers of their options when revising. Notice, in this mnemonic, how the critical conversations we've centered student learning on across the lessons so far find a prominent placement, rounding things out as the final component—**T** for *talk*. The eight sentence-combining lessons that follow give middle school writers additional application opportunities through larger, more open, interpretive experimentation to apply both what they intuitively know and the *Patterns of Revision* targeted structures they've encountered in earlier lessons.

As you move into the second part of this book and its lessons, recognize that—at least initially—things could get messy. Take a close look at children who play with something for the first time—a toy, a video game, something that has to be put together. They mess around with it, trying it out in different ways to see what works. They learn to use the toy effectively, learn to play the game effectively, learn to build the model effectively. But this all comes after several starts and stops, messy mistakes, and realizations that only come with hands-on exploration.

Through this play, this trial and error, comes effectiveness.

And, in this same way, our writers will find effect through the play they do with revision. Remember, writing is a process. Revision is part of that process. The most important thing we can do when teaching students to combine sentences is to resist the urge to fix and, instead, embrace the play involved in revising, helping students see the choices they have as writers. We celebrate the experimentation, the discovery, and the approximations that may or may not also come with errors.

> **66** We celebrate the experimentation, the discovery, and the approximations that may or may not also come with errors. **99**

As we always say, "Mistakes are a sign of growth." When learning something new, we have to try it out and even fail a few times before we get comfortable with it. It's not always correct, but it gets better and more effective over time. Inviting students to try combining sentences in multiple ways allows for them to discover how some decisions make more meaning and have a stronger effect on the reader than others. This creates a flexible mindset, space for risk taking, and a pathway to a stronger craft of writing. So as students play with the choices they have as writers, relax. Breathe in the value in what they are doing. Trust where it will lead them.

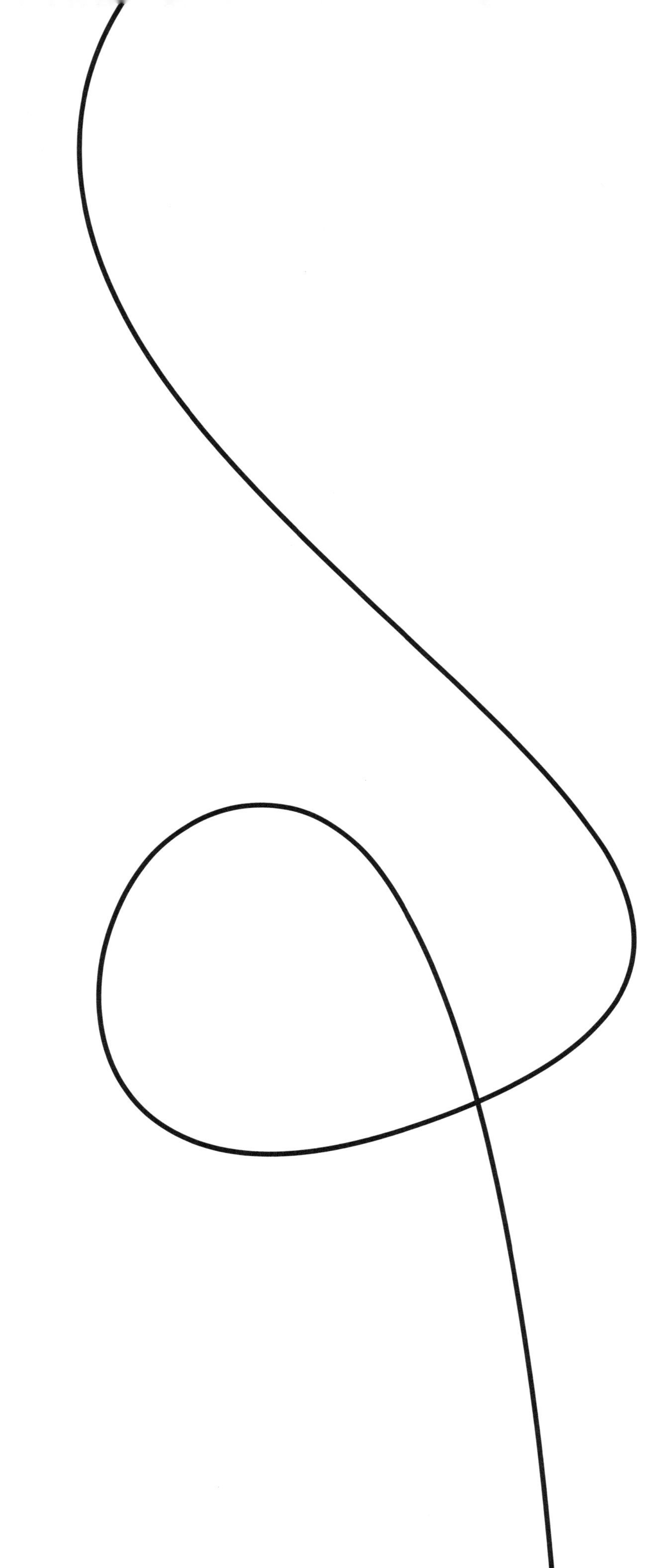

Read, read, read. Read everything . . . classics, good and bad, and see how they do it.
Just like a carpenter who works as an apprentice and studies the master. Read! You'll absorb it.
Then write. If it's good, you'll find out. If it's not, throw it out of the window.

— William Faulkner

now that students have been introduced to the revision strategies of **DRAFT**: *deleting, rearranging, adding, forming new verbs,* and *talking it out,* and forming new verbs, we use the largest of the lesson sets in this final chapter to give them practice applying the **DRAFT** mnemonic as a cumulative process to support sentence combining to revise. (See the **Reviser's DRAFTboard** printable on page 162).

The sentence combining lessons in this chapter are fertile ground for students to refine their skill of making choices and then evaluating them for effect. Expect students to do a lot of *talking it out* in every lesson in this chapter, like all the ones before it. More options can lead to more sharing, which in turn exposes writers to more possibilities and their effects. By this time, students know there isn't one right answer but, rather, options that work better (or not).

All the lessons in this chapter follow the same format. We share several sentences that have been pulled by deconstructing the model sentence into separate pieces. First, we use **DRAFT** to discuss how we could combine the ideas together into one sentence, then writers try out a different set of sentences in small groups or with partners. As with other lessons in this book, we conclude each interaction by inviting students to go back to their own writing, this time considering how they could combine some ideas to make their piece more concise and effective. And, as always, we encourage lots of time for sharing out loud and celebrating others' versions to deepen the students' understanding.

Reviser's DRAFTboard

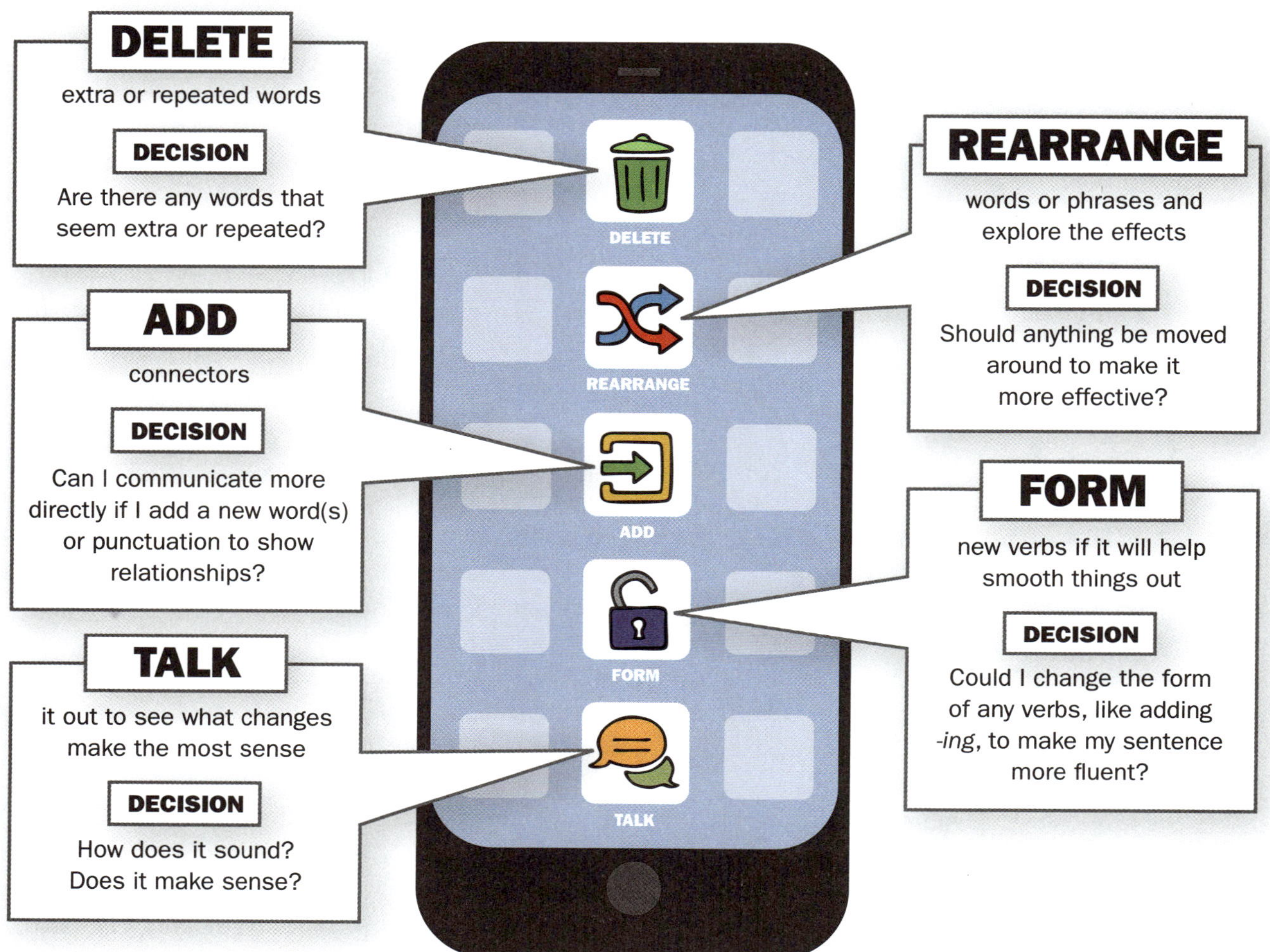

6.13 Saving The Best Content

Lesson Overview

Revision goal connected to standards:

Develop and strengthen writing by combining ideas to avoid redundancy, add clarity, and improve fluency.

Model Text

"The Save," from *The Hero Next Door*
- Written by Joseph Bruchac
- Edited by Olugbemisola Rhuday-Perkovich

Teacher Considerations

This lesson begins the chapter where we put all of the skills we've learned in previous chapters together and focus on revision at the sentence level. To support students in this work, we've lifted single sentences from Joseph Bruchac's short story "The Save" from the We Need Diverse Books anthology, *The Hero Next Door*, and deconstructed them into multiple sentences for students to piece back together through revision. In both opportunities for revision work, we'll focus on a different character in the story and arrange the description of each character into fewer sentences, using our revision tools we've learned in previous chapters.

This lesson provides a great opportunity to introduce **DRAFT**, the mnemonic we use for combining sentences, in its complete form. Throughout the lesson, refer to the **Reviser's DRAFTboard** as a visual touchstone for students. You may choose to display this chart in your classroom or have your students glue it into their notebooks. (See chart on page 162.)

Because this is the first lesson with this work, we've included more teacher talk and modeling prompts to support your work. Students will pick up the shift from paragraph-level focus to sentence-level focus pretty quickly if you intentionally model and think aloud while sharing your process. As always, providing time and space for students to talk out their ideas is an essential part of the work.

Finally, we want to share that students will come up with a whole host of different possible options that may or may not match the author's original. That's okay! This process helps to solidify the idea that writers make choices and there are often numerous effective options that could be made.

Patterns of Power (6–8), **Lesson 6.5** elevates understanding for students on how to add extra detail about a character using the relative pronoun *who*.

Setting the Context

In "The Save," author Joseph Bruchac writes about the Onondaga tribe's boys' lacrosse team, with the reader joining the main character Oren mid game against the Buffalo Bulls. Even though Oren's team is winning 14–2, he's still nervous while playing goalie. Set the context for students, and then read aloud this section:

Oren shifted the stick from one hand to the other. Usually that was no big deal. Right now it felt heavy as a sledgehammer. Even with the mask on his face, his padding, and his gloves, he was feeling naked. The goal behind him was the standard six feet by six feet, but it seemed as big as a barn door now that he was the one guarding it.

In front of him in their various positions ranged nine other Onondaga boys on their team.

Then share with your students, "The author, Joseph Bruchac, continues to share about some of Oren's other teammates. We're going to look at the sentences describing these characters, using our revision skills to think through how we might combine ideas to be more efficient and clearer for the reader."

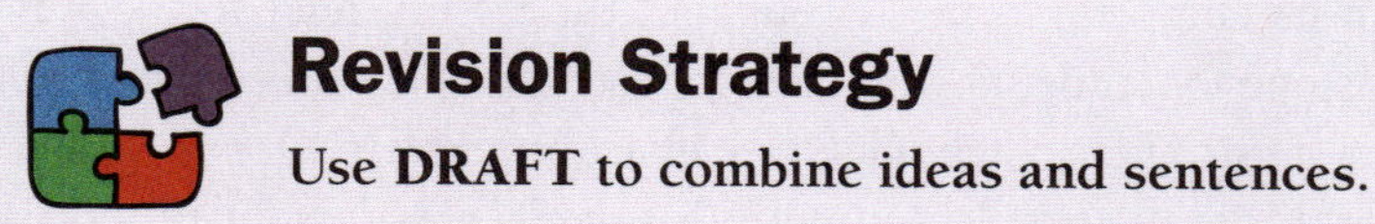

Revision Strategy
Use **DRAFT** to combine ideas and sentences.

Modeling

Display the **Reviser's DRAFTboard** or invite students to refer to it in their notebooks if they have it glued or taped inside. Then display printable **6.13 Modeled Sentence Combo: Part I** on page 168 and invite students to explore the three sentences that we will work on combining into one. "There are three sentences here. Let's play with what we know about revision to see if we can make these three sentences into one while describing one of Oren's teammates. First, let's read aloud the sentences":

Paul Hemlock was to his right.   Paul had the wingspan of an eagle.

Paul was even taller than their coach.

Let's spend some time talking out ways we could combine these sentences, remembering that we can use any of the **DRAFT** strategies that help reduce the sentences to one." Model how to combine the sentences, saying things like, "I see the name Paul three times. I'm sure I can combine this, deleting a few so his name is used only once. What else could we use so that readers know we're describing Paul? What if we used a pronoun like *he*? How might we connect these sentences to make one sentence? What connectors might we add if the descriptions in the second and third sentences are describing Paul?"

You may choose to write parts of the sentences on index cards, sticky notes, or on the whiteboard to show how the words or phrases could physically be rearranged. Guide your students through a conversation about the possibilities, thinking aloud as you go. Try a few different combinations, possibly rearranging words and phrases in a variety of ways to discuss which one is more effective and why. One of the combinations you create might not make sense. That's okay! Record it in the workspace provided on the printable and engage in conversation about why this wouldn't be effective. Writers make mistakes and reflect on them.

Once the class feels like they have an effective combination, reveal Joseph Bruchac's original sentence. Invite students to compare and contrast their version with his using **6.13 Modeled Sentence Combo: Part II**, prompting things along with the following reflective questions as necessary:

- Why do you think Joseph combined the sentences in this way?
- Is there another combination that would be effective?
- If your combination was different from Bruchac's, which do you prefer, and why?

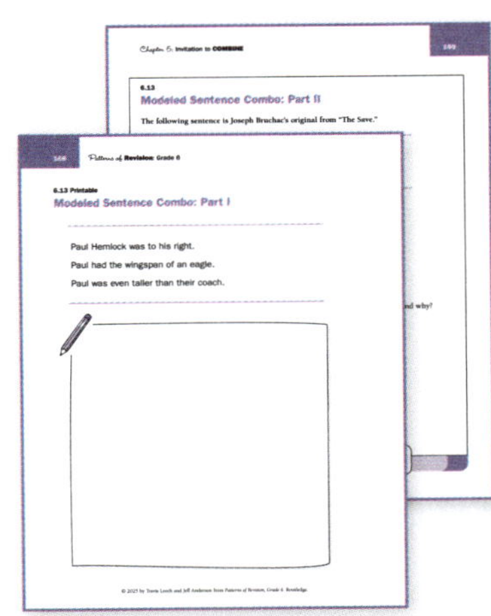

Collaborating Through Conversation

Distribute the printable, **6.13 Invitation to Combine: Part I** (on page 170), to each student. Following the directions on the printable and using **DRAFT**, students collaborate with one or more classmates to combine the sentences into one. They may decide to follow your modeling and write the parts of the sentences on index cards, sticky notes, or whiteboard space so they can be easily rearranged. Invite them to record their possibilities on the lines provided on the printable or their writer's notebooks. When ready, students compare their choices with other partnerships or groups. For comparative analysis, use the printable, **6.13 Invitation to Combine: Part II**, to share the author's original text. Use the reflective questions at the bottom of the printable to facilitate a conversation about meaning and effect.

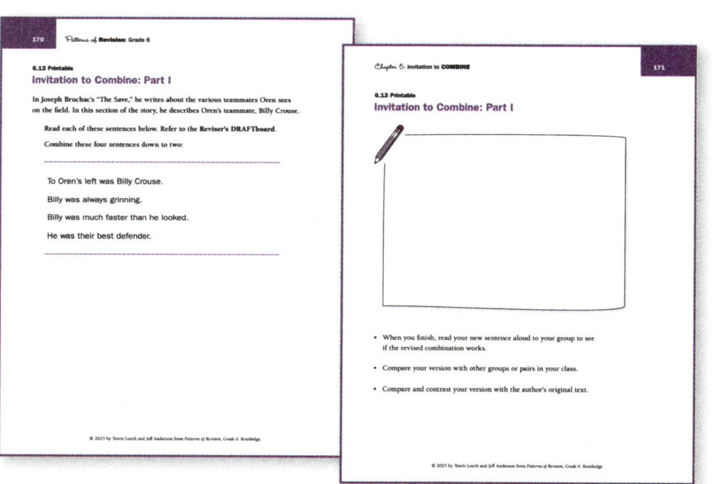
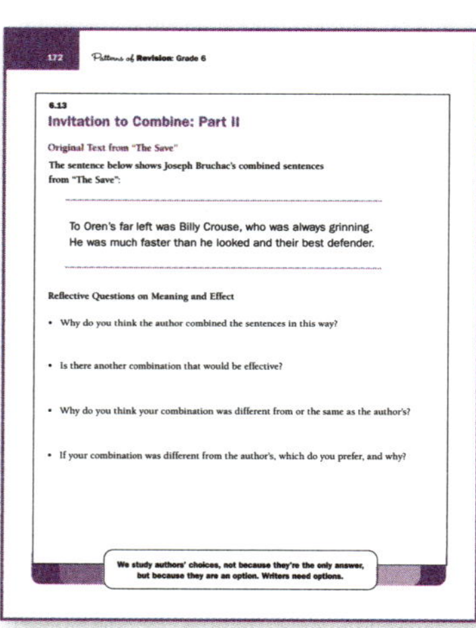

Quickwrite Opportunity (Optional)

1. Reflect on a specific event or competition that stands out in your mind. Describe the location, the atmosphere, and the people involved with as much detail as you can.
2. Describe a moment when you were completely in the zone during a sport or hobby you participate in. What did it feel like, and how did it enhance your performance?

Applying Revision

Students return to their own writing or their writer's notebook to play with different sentence combos, using the **DRAFT** strategies. If students don't have writing they can easily revisit for this application, have them respond to one of the prompts above to generate a draft to revise.

If students have a hard time finding sentences in their own writing to combine, bring them back to the work done together so far in this lesson. In both models, students looked at extra details being developed about Oren's teammates using the "comma who" to introduce that extra description. One possible focus for students could be looking at characters in their writing, even if they are the character, and thinking about how they could add more description about that character, using a comma and who to introduce that extra description.

Sharing Results

Students share their revisions in small groups, explaining the parts of **DRAFT** they chose to use. As a group, students discuss how their revisions made their writing more effective. Use the following guiding questions as needed:

- Did you choose to delete anything? Why or why not?
- Did you choose to rearrange anything? Why or why not?
- What connectors did you choose to add? Why?
- What made you decide to combine those ideas into one sentence?
- What was the best revision you made today? Why do you think so?

6.13 Printable

Modeled Sentence Combo: Part I

Paul Hemlock was to his right.

Paul had the wingspan of an eagle.

Paul was even taller than their coach.

6.13

Modeled Sentence Combo: Part II

The following sentence is Joseph Bruchac's original from "The Save."

Paul Hemlock, who had the wingspan of an eagle and who was even taller than their coach, was to his right.

Reflective Questions on Meaning and Effect

- Why do you think the author combined the sentences in this way?

- Is there another combination that would be effective?

- If your combination was different from the author's, which do you prefer, and why?

> We study authors' choices, not because they're the only answer, but because they are an option. Writers need options.

6.13 Printable

Invitation to Combine: Part I

In Joseph Bruchac's "The Save," he writes about the various teammates Oren sees on the field. In this section of the story, he describes Oren's teammate, Billy Crouse.

Read each of these sentences below. Refer to the **Reviser's DRAFTboard**.

Combine these four sentences down to two:

To Oren's left was Billy Crouse.

Billy was always grinning.

Billy was much faster than he looked.

He was their best defender.

6.13 Printable

Invitation to Combine: Part I

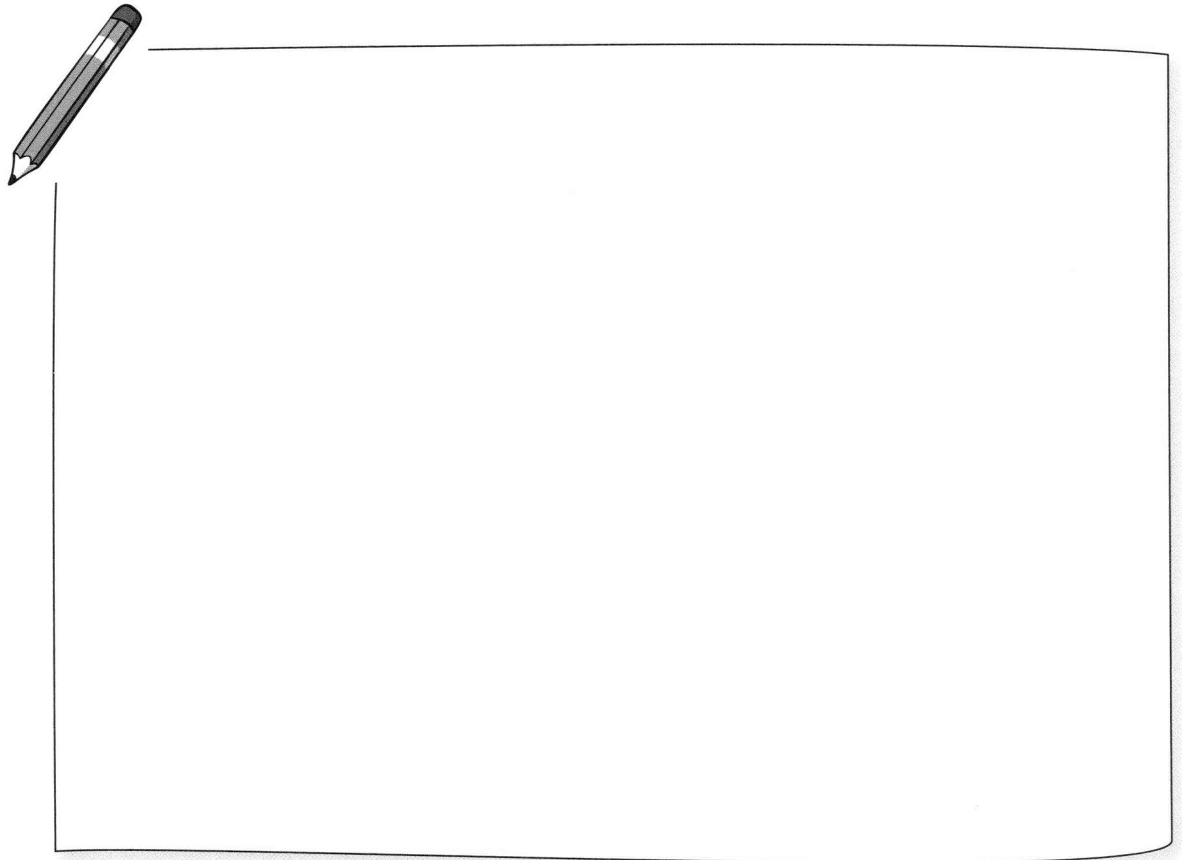

- When you finish, read your new sentence aloud to your group to see if the revised combination works.

- Compare your version with other groups or pairs in your class.

- Compare and contrast your version with the author's original text.

6.13

Invitation to Combine: Part II

Original Text from "The Save"

The sentence below shows Joseph Bruchac's combined sentences from "The Save":

To Oren's far left was Billy Crouse, who was always grinning. He was much faster than he looked and their best defender.

Reflective Questions on Meaning and Effect

- Why do you think the author combined the sentences in this way?

- Is there another combination that would be effective?

- Why do you think your combination was different from or the same as the author's?

- If your combination was different from the author's, which do you prefer, and why?

We study authors' choices, not because they're the only answer, but because they are an option. Writers need options.

6.14 Combining Isn't as Tough as My Sister

Lesson Overview

Revision goal connected to standards:

Develop and strengthen writing by combining ideas to avoid redundancy, add clarity, and improve fluency.

Model Text

Time Villains
 – Written by Victor Piñeiro

Teacher Considerations

In this lesson we continue our focus on sentence-level work using **DRAFT** to revise our writing for efficiency and effectiveness. We've chosen the book *Time Villains* by Victor Piñeiro because of its humor and the development of characters that are relatable to middle school students. In the model section, there are opportunities for students to Delete repeated information, Rearrange an idea to place it at the front of the revised sentence, as well as to Add a Connector in the form of a coordinating conjunction and punctuation to connect a series of three ideas.

In the collaborating through conversation section, the author's original sentence includes **Adding a Connector** to create a complex sentence, as well as **Forming New Verbs** to make a participle (-ing).

If students need support with creating a compound sentence or with how to punctuate items in a series, check out the suggested connections to *Patterns of Power* for possible instructional connections.

The model section in *Patterns of Power (6–8)*, **Lesson 5.2** explores connecting sentences using a comma and *and*.

Patterns of Power (6–8), **Lesson 10.1** supports student understanding of the pattern of connecting three or more items or ideas using commas.

Patterns of Power (6–8), **Lesson 6.1** students look at adding the connector *When* to create a complex sentence, following the author's original in the Collaborating Through Conversation section.

Setting the Context

In *Time Villains* by Victor Piñeiro, we are introduced to the Santiago family as they are shopping for antiques. We begin with Javi Santiago (the narrator) and his friend Will "Wiki" Green arguing while his dad and sister Brady shop close by. Read this brief excerpt to students to set the context for the lesson.

"A hot dog is actually a sandwich. Hear me out. It's got bread on two sides and meat and toppings in the middle."

"Not your sandwich theory again," Wiki said, shaking his head. "Can't we agree to disagree? A hot dog is definitely not a sandwich. For so many reasons!" . . .

"Guys. Enough. Don't make me break you," Brady said, like she was some action hero.

Continue by setting the stage for the work today: "The narrator goes on to tell us more about his sister, Brady. Just like the author may have done, let's take a look at how to combine the details about the sister into fewer sentences."

Revision Strategy

Use **DRAFT** to combine ideas and sentences.

Modeling

Use the **Reviser's DRAFTboard** along with printable, **6.14 Modeled Sentence Combo: Part I**, to explore the five sentences that need to be combined. "There are five sentences here about Javi's sister, Brady. Let's see if we can use **DRAFT** to help us combine these five sentences into two. First let's read aloud the sentences."

Her life goal is to become the president's bodyguard.

Another life goal of hers is to be a professional vigilante.

Another life goal of hers is to be a warrior empress of the world.

Modeling *(continued)*

I think she'll probably end up doing all three.

She's in third grade.

"Let's spend some time talking out ways we could combine these sentences, using any of the **DRAFT** strategies that help." Return to the **Reviser's DRAFTboard** and work through its mnemonic as you review how to use **DRAFT** as a guide to combine the sentences. "D means Delete repetitive words. Let's look for any repetition we can find across sentences. For example, in sentences one, two, and three, we see the words *life goal* repeated. I notice there are three life goals that Brady has. How might we combine these three ideas? Discuss with a partner how you might revise these sentences to make them one and delete repeated words."

"After looking at the last sentence in this group, I'm not sure how I feel about it being the last bit of information in this sentence. Is there any other place that might be rearranged to be more effective?" Model moving the sentence *She's in third grade* to the front of the sentence and ask students to discuss what they think about it being rearranged there.

"I'm thinking of keeping the sentence *She's in third grade* at the front of this sentence, but now I need to **Add a Connector** to connect this idea to the next sentence. What are some possible options we have available to us?" Write out some of the possibilities in the workspace provided on the printable or on the whiteboard. After each one, read it aloud and orally share your thinking process as you continue to play some more.

Once the class feels like they have an effective combination, reveal the author's original sentence. Keeping in mind that the conversation is meant to be about meaning and effect as opposed to right or wrong, invite students to compare and contrast their version with Victor Piñeiro's using **6.14 Modeled Sentence Combo: Part II**, prompting things along with the following reflective

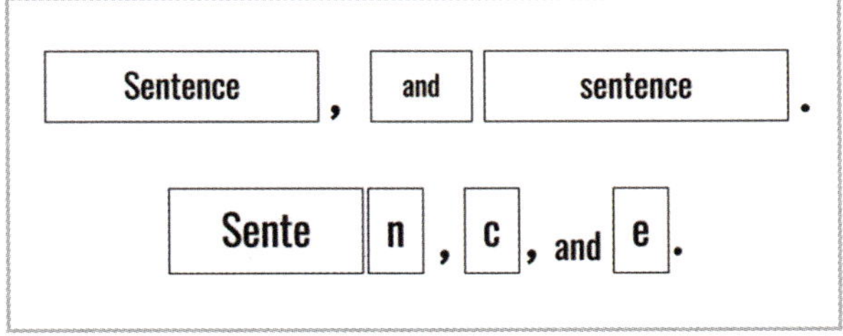

Figure 6.14
Sentence patterns: compound & list of items.

questions as necessary:

- Why do you think Victor combined the sentences in this way?
- Is there another combination that would be effective?
- Why do you think your combination was different from or the same as the author's?
- If your combination was different from Piñeiro's, which do you prefer, and why?

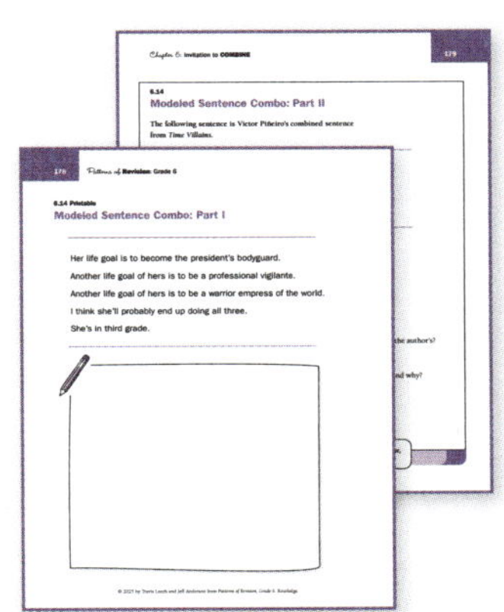

Collaborating Through Conversation

Distribute the printable, **6.14 Invitation to Combine: Part I**, to the class. Pair classmates and lead the pairs through a first read of the directions. As partners work together to combine ideas, they will most likely discover a couple of possibilities for combining the sentences provided. Invite them to decide on an appropriate space to record their combinations.

When the class is ready, display **6.14 Invitation to Combine: Part II** to share the author's original text. Prompt students to use the reflective questions at the bottom of the page to facilitate a conversation about meaning and effect.

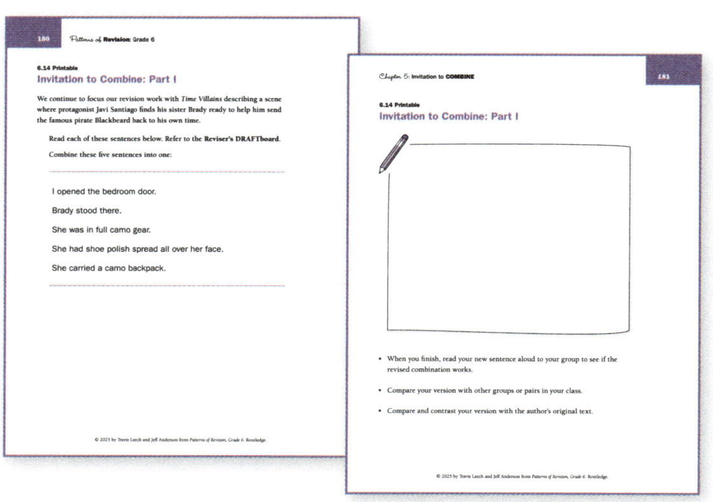
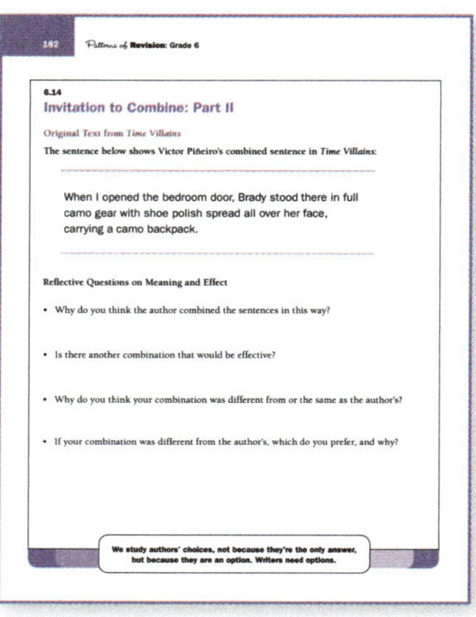

Quickwrite Opportunity (Optional)

1. Write about a person in your life or someone famous you admire. Highlight one or more things about them you admire or use a brief story about them to explain why you admire them.
2. What is something you are passionate about? Explain the main reasons why you're passionate about it.

Applying Revision

Begin by modeling this process with your own writing. Display your writing for students to easily see, then begin talking through your process for finding a place to revise. When focusing on an aspect of your writing to revise, you may choose to refer back to the work you did with either of the models in this lesson, such as **Adding** a new or different connector word or punctuation to connect multiple sentences or ideas. After revising, talk out the choice you made and explain why you think it creates more effective writing.

Students then return to their own writing, using the **DRAFT** strategies to try different revision options. One possible entry point to prompt students toward is to add more information about a character, setting, or idea in their writing, separating that information between commas if it becomes three or more ideas. Another point of entry might be looking at connections between sentences and deciding on whether a different connector word might be more effective.

Sharing Results

Students share their revisions with a shoulder partner or with their table group. Choose one to three students to share with the class, letting them display their writing and explain their revision choices and how they have enhanced the revised piece.

6.14 Printable

Modeled Sentence Combo: Part I

Her life goal is to become the president's bodyguard.

Another life goal of hers is to be a professional vigilante.

Another life goal of hers is to be a warrior empress of the world.

I think she'll probably end up doing all three.

She's in third grade.

6.14
Modeled Sentence Combo: Part II

The following sentence is Victor Piñeiro's combined sentence from *Time Villains*.

> She's in third grade, and her life goal is to become the president's bodyguard, a professional vigilante, or warrior empress of the world. I think she'll probably end up doing all three.

Reflective Questions on Meaning and Effect

- Why do you think Victor combined the sentences in this way?

- Is there another combination that would be effective?

- Why do you think your combination was different from or the same as the author's?

- If your combination was different from Piñeiro's, which do you prefer, and why?

> We study authors' choices, not because they're the only answer, but because they are an option. Writers need options.

6.14 Printable

Invitation to Combine: Part I

We continue to focus our revision work with *Time Villains* describing a scene where protagonist Javi Santiago finds his sister Brady ready to help him send the famous pirate Blackbeard back to his own time.

Read each of these sentences below. Refer to the **Reviser's DRAFTboard**.

Combine these five sentences into one:

____

I opened the bedroom door.

Brady stood there.

She was in full camo gear.

She had shoe polish spread all over her face.

She carried a camo backpack.

____

6.14 Printable

Invitation to Combine: Part I

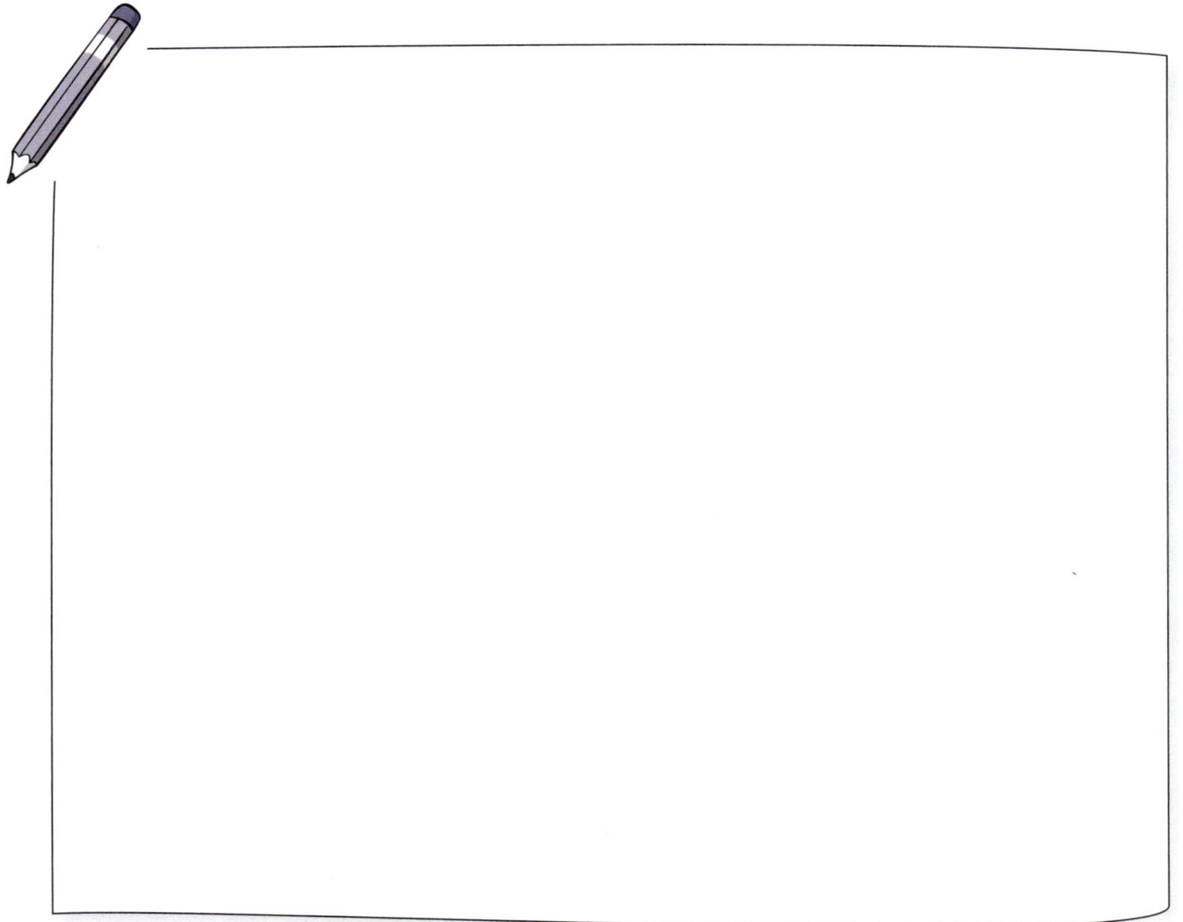

- When you finish, read your new sentence aloud to your group to see if the revised combination works.

- Compare your version with other groups or pairs in your class.

- Compare and contrast your version with the author's original text.

6.14

Invitation to Combine: Part II

Original Text from *Time Villains*

The sentence below shows Victor Piñeiro's combined sentence in *Time Villains*:

When I opened the bedroom door, Brady stood there in full camo gear with shoe polish spread all over her face, carrying a camo backpack.

Reflective Questions on Meaning and Effect

- Why do you think the author combined the sentences in this way?

- Is there another combination that would be effective?

- Why do you think your combination was different from or the same as the author's?

- If your combination was different from the author's, which do you prefer, and why?

> We study authors' choices, not because they're the only answer, but because they are an option. Writers need options.

6.15 Don't Get Stranded in Revision

Lesson Overview

Revision goal connected to standards:

Develop and strengthen writing by combining ideas to avoid redundancy, add clarity, and improve fluency.

Model Text

They Lost Their Heads! What Happened to Washington's Teeth, Einstein's Brain, and Other Famous Body Parts
 – Written by Carlyn Beccia

Teacher Considerations

They Lost Their Heads! What Happened to Washington's Teeth, Einstein's Brain, and Other Famous Body Parts by Carlyn Beccia is another engaging and thought-provoking nonfiction text that students usually gravitate toward if it's on our bookshelf. We chose sentences from this book to highlight interesting facts about how hair used to be viewed like an autograph or selfie.

Most likely, you've introduced your sixth graders to AAAWWUBBIS, the mnemonic that helps students remember subordinating conjunctions often used to compose a complex sentence. The most important thing here is for students to consider which connectors would work best to combine the ideas. We recommend using the opener-sentence pattern visual to help students form complex sentences. Check out the *Patterns of Power* lesson suggestions if you feel your students would benefit from specific work with complex sentence creation beforehand.

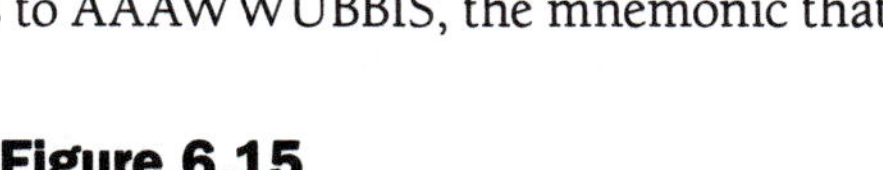

Figure 6.15
Sentence patterns: complex opener & semicolons.

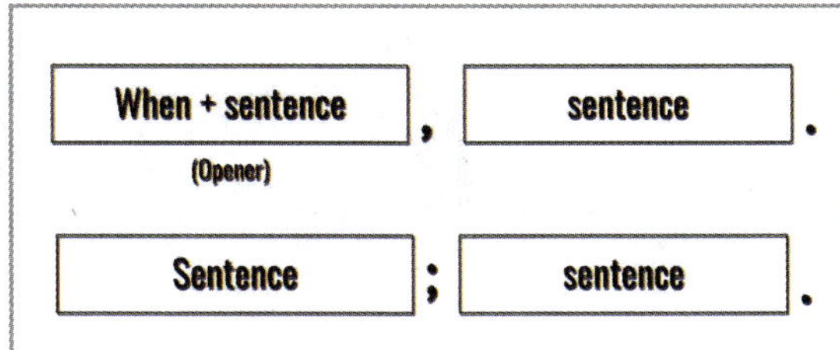

Patterns of Power **(6–8), Lesson 6.1** assists students in creating complex sentences using *when* to begin the opener (dependent clause) and how students can punctuate this type of sentence.

Patterns of Power **(6–8), Lesson 10.4 or 10.5** elevates the purpose and craft of semicolons. Both lessons include a semicolon in the author's original version.

Setting the Context

In the book *They Lost Their Heads!* by Carlyn Beccia, the author shares with readers how hair was viewed in history. You might start by telling students: "Can you believe there was a point in time where people preferred a lock of a famous person's hair to getting an autograph or taking a selfie with them? Let's check out this short text that highlights the content of this section of the book."

Hair can be used by scientists today to learn a lot about a person's health and overall well-being. But there was a time when people collected hair of friends, loved ones, and even famous people as a way to remember them. Because people collected and held onto strands of hair from famous historical figures, scientists today learned a lot about the health conditions of famous historical figures like Ludwig von Beethoven, Edgar Allan Poe, Charles Darwin, and Elvis from studying their hair.

Students may benefit from brief background building of the famous historical figures in the read aloud, although knowing these historical figures is not necessary for their success in revising the following sentences.

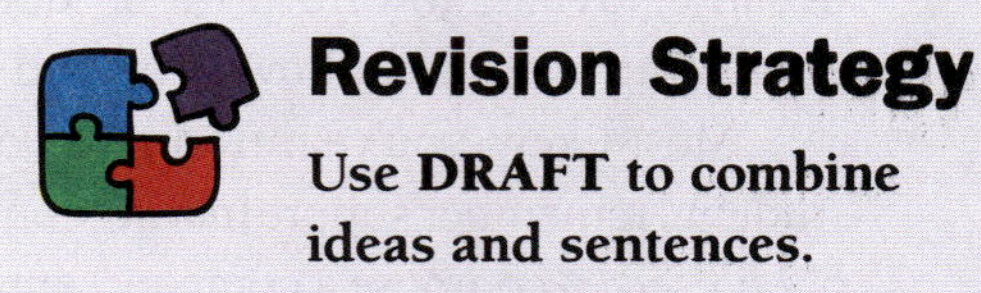

Revision Strategy

Use **DRAFT** to combine ideas and sentences.

Modeling

Use the **Reviser's DRAFTboard** along with printable, **6.15 Modeled Sentence Combo: Part I**, to explore the four sentences that need to be combined. "There are four sentences here that give us a brief history lesson about how hair was viewed in history. Let's see if we can use **DRAFT** to help us combine these four sentences into one. First, let's read aloud the sentences."

Modeling *(continued)*

Someone famous came to town.

They came to town two hundred years ago.

No one asked for their autograph.

They asked to take a snip of hair.

"Let's start by looking for anything repeated in each of the sentences. I notice the pronoun *they* is repeated in sentences two and four, and it's close to the pronoun *their* in sentence three. I also notice the words *came to town* show up in sentences one and two. Do we need all of these repeated words? Is there a way we can keep the same or similar ideas without repeating this so much?" Try out options yourself, writing those options where students can see your ideas. If students have gotten the hang of this process already, elicit their feedback about possible choices to delete one or more instances of the repeated pronoun or combine the two sentences that have the words *came to town* repeated.

"Next, let's take a look at how the sentences flow in order. Are there any parts that can be **Rearranged** to fit more effectively in a different part of the sentence?" Try rearranging the order of any of the sentences, placing them ahead or behind their current order. Elicit feedback from students about what choice(s) they would make.

Rearranging should lead to the need for **Adding a Connector** to show the relationship between the sentences. "Now I'm looking at two sentences and wondering how I might add a word or punctuation to show how they're connected." Refer students to **The Connectors chart** (page 90) to check out possible connection points, deciding on one or more to use. **Talk** through the possible choices and what they could sound like if added.

Once the class feels like they have an effective combination, reveal the author's original sentence to compare and contrast their version with Carlyn Beccia's using **6.15 Modeled Sentence Combo: Part II** (page 189). Prompt thinking with the following reflective questions as necessary:

- Why do you think Carlyn combined the sentences in this way?
- Is there another combination that would be effective?
- Why do you think your combination was different from or the same as the author's?
- If your combination was different from Beccia's, which do you prefer, and why?

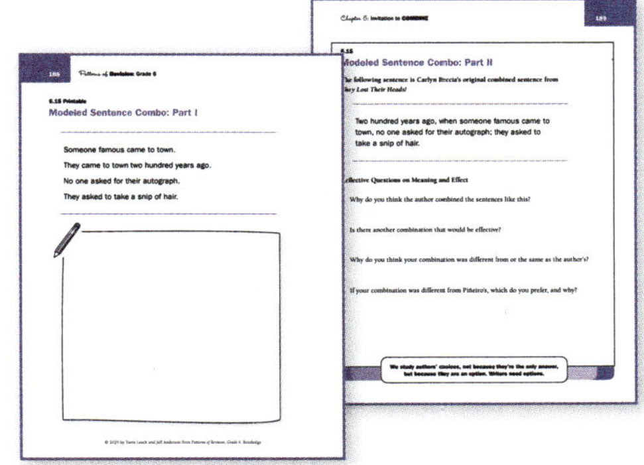

Collaborating Through Conversation

Distribute the printable, **6.15 Invitation to Combine: Part I** (page 190), to each student. Following the directions on the printable and using **DRAFT**, students collaborate through conversation with one or more classmates to combine the sentences. Have students decide on a workspace to combine sentences, whether it be on a copy of the printable, in their notebook, in a digital workspace, or somewhere else.

When ready, students compare their choices with other partnerships or groups. As with previous lessons, the conversation should be focused on effectiveness as opposed to getting the right answer. For comparative analysis, display **6.15 Invitation to Combine: Part II** on page 192 to share the author's original text. Use the reflective questions at the bottom to facilitate a conversation about meaning and effect.

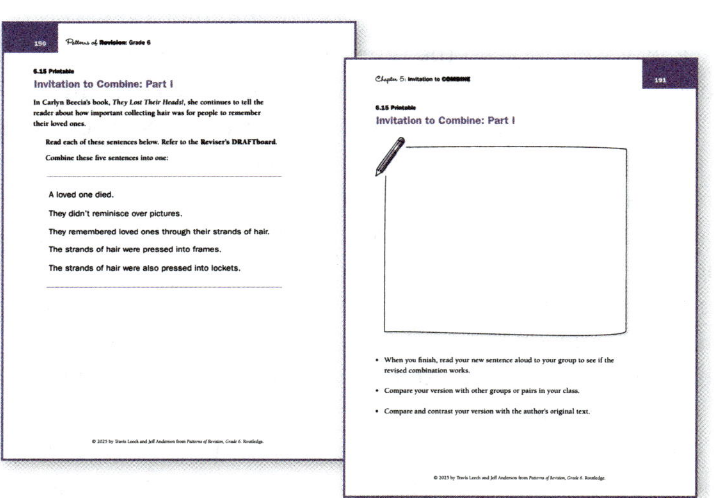

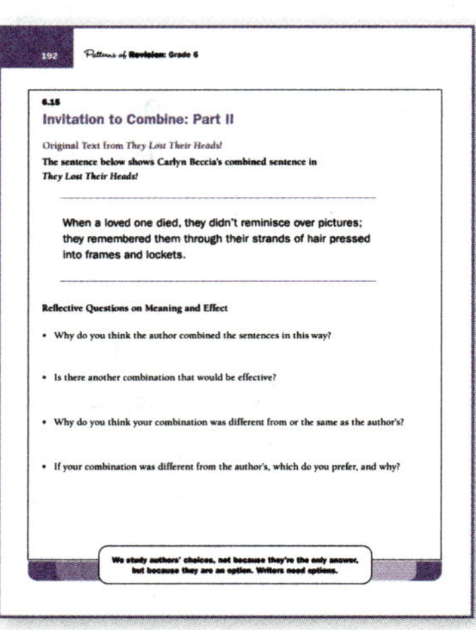

Quickwrite Opportunity (Optional)

1. Imagine you've just met a historical figure from the past. Write a letter to your best friend describing the encounter and how it has left you feeling inspired. (This prompt may require time for class brainstorming to generate a list of famous historical figures known by students.)
2. Write a short scene about an ordinary individual who unexpectedly becomes friends with a famous person. Explore some of the challenges and benefits of their friendship.

Applying Revision

To set students up for success, begin by modeling this revision process with your own writing. Display your writing for students to easily see, then begin talking through your process for finding a place to revise. When focusing on your writing, you may choose to connect your revision technique back to the work you did with either of the models in this lesson, such as adding a new or different connector word or punctuation to connect two ideas together. After revising, talk out the choices you made and explain why you think it creates more effective writing.

Students then return to their own writing to play with different revision options, using the **DRAFT** strategies and noticing the different effects. Invite them to choose one section or paragraph to focus on. One possible entry point for students could be connections between sentences, deciding on whether a different connector word or punctuation might be more effective.

Sharing Results

Invite one to three students to share their writing in front of the class. Give each of these students access to a way of easily displaying their writing for the rest of the class to see and prompt students to share their writing before and after they made the revisions. To extend student conversations, ask them to explain why they made each revision choice. If time allows, elicit positive feedback from classmates for each writer who shares.

6.15 Printable

Modeled Sentence Combo: Part I

Someone famous came to town.

They came to town two hundred years ago.

No one asked for their autograph.

They asked to take a snip of hair.

6.15

Modeled Sentence Combo: Part II

The following sentence is Carlyn Beccia's original combined sentence from
They Lost Their Heads!

Two hundred years ago, when someone famous came to town, no one asked for their autograph; they asked to take a snip of hair.

Reflective Questions on Meaning and Effect

- Why do you think the author combined the sentences like this?

- Is there another combination that would be effective?

- Why do you think your combination was different from or the same as the author's?

- If your combination was different from Piñeiro's, which do you prefer, and why?

We study authors' choices, not because they're the only answer, but because they are an option. Writers need options.

6.15 Printable

Invitation to Combine: Part I

In Carlyn Beecia's book, *They Lost Their Heads!*, she continues to tell the reader about how important collecting hair was for people to remember their loved ones.

Read each of these sentences below. Refer to the **Reviser's DRAFTboard**.

Combine these five sentences into one:

____

A loved one died.

They didn't reminisce over pictures.

They remembered loved ones through their strands of hair.

The strands of hair were pressed into frames.

The strands of hair were also pressed into lockets.

____

6.15 Printable

Invitation to Combine: Part I

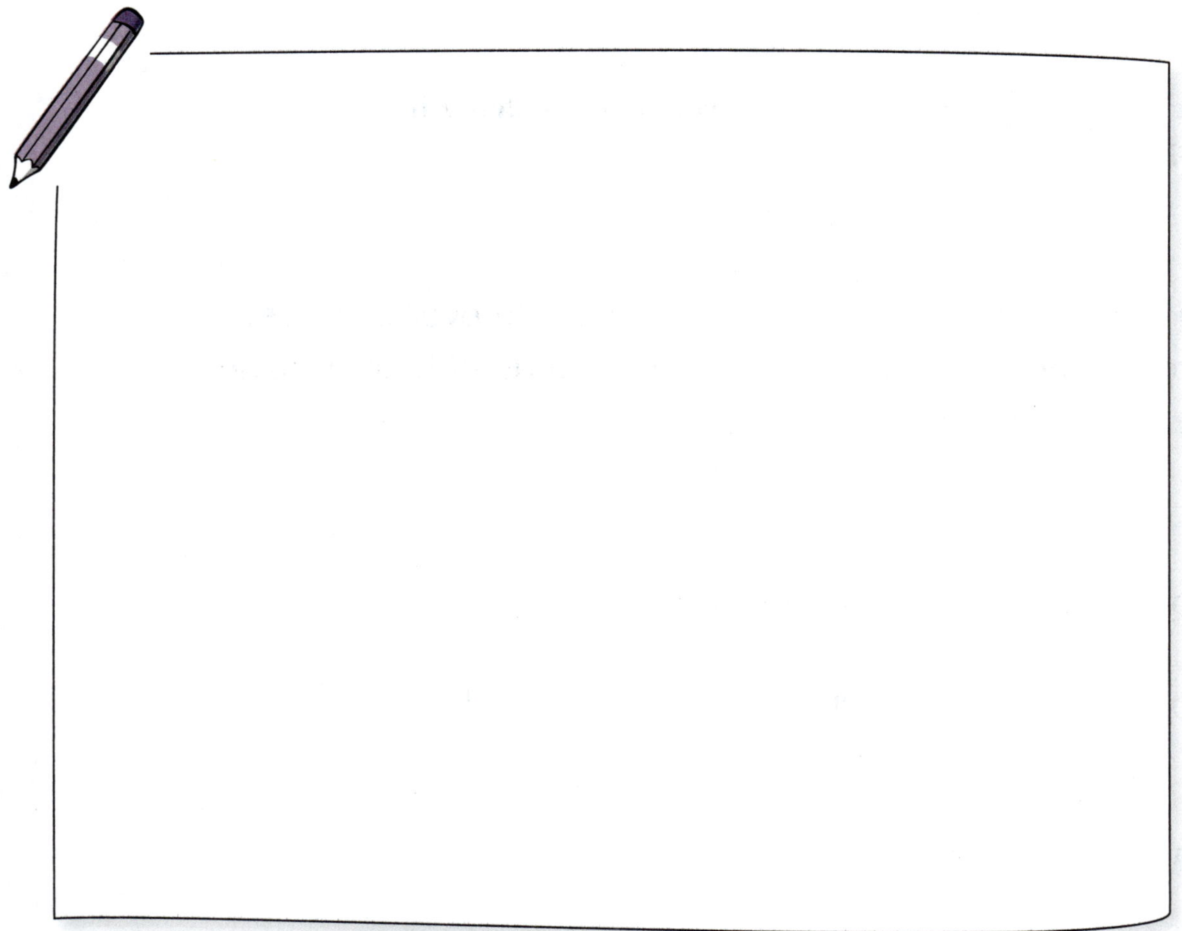

- When you finish, read your new sentence aloud to your group to see if the revised combination works.

- Compare your version with other groups or pairs in your class.

- Compare and contrast your version with the author's original text.

6.15

Invitation to Combine: Part II

Original Text from *They Lost Their Heads!*

The sentence below shows Carlyn Beccia's combined sentence in
They Lost Their Heads!

> When a loved one died, they didn't reminisce over pictures;
> they remembered them through their strands of hair pressed
> into frames and lockets.

Reflective Questions on Meaning and Effect

- Why do you think the author combined the sentences in this way?

- Is there another combination that would be effective?

- Why do you think your combination was different from or the same as the author's?

- If your combination was different from the author's, which do you prefer, and why?

We study authors' choices, not because they're the only answer,
but because they are an option. Writers need options.

6.16 **Adventures in Combining**

Lesson Overview

Revision goal connected to standards:

Develop and strengthen writing by combining ideas to avoid redundancy, add clarity, and improve fluency.

Model Text

Shipwreck at the Bottom of the World: The Extraordinary True Story of Shackleton and the Endurance
  – Written by Jennifer Armstrong

Teacher Considerations

With this lesson we are highlighting multiple aspects of **DRAFT** for students. As in previous lessons in this chapter, we've taken an original published text—this time from Jennifer Armstrong's *Shipwreck at the Bottom of the World*—and broken it up into multiple sentences so students can practice sentence combining strategies.

In the model lesson section, we focus on **Deleting** repeated material, **Adding Connectors** to combine sentences, as well as **Forming New Verbs** by changing a present tense verb into a participle. In the combining through collaboration section, students look at **Deleting**, and then **Rearranging** one of the ideas by moving it to the beginning of the first sentence.

Students should have some experience with semicolons if they've already experienced **Lesson 6.15: Don't Get Stranded in Revision**. If they haven't, and your students aren't familiar with the purpose and craft of a semicolon, you may consider introducing these through a mini lesson and posting an anchor chart beforehand to support their learning.

Both *Patterns of Power (6–8)*, **Lessons 10.4 or 10.5** include a semicolon in the model text and will give students a stronger understanding of the purpose and craft of semicolons.

Patterns of Power (6–8), **Lesson 7.5** will assist students in understanding how prepositional phrases ground the reader in time and space, strengthening the development of the setting.

Setting the Context

In *Shipwreck at the Bottom of the World*, Armstrong chronicles the true story of Ernest Shackleton's expedition to Antarctica on the Endurance and the ship's ultimate fate of getting stuck in ice and sinking to the ocean floor. To set a context for combining sentences in this lesson, read this chunk of text about the book.

Just imagine yourself in the most hostile place on earth. It's not the Sahara or the Gobi Desert. It's not the Arctic. The most hostile place on earth is the Antarctic, the location of the South Pole. North Pole, South Pole—what's the difference? The Arctic is mostly water—with ice on top, of course—and that ice is never more than a few feet thick. But under the South Pole lies a continent that supports glaciers up to two miles in depth.

Then, continue by reading the sentences below that highlight facts about the ice on the continent of Antarctica.

The ice never melts.	The ice clings to the bottom of the world.
The ice spawns winds.	The ice spawns storms.
The ice spawns weather.	The weather affects the whole planet.

Explain to students, "Here, we learn quite a few things about the ice in Antarctica from author Jennifer Armstrong. One thing writers can do when they revise is take short sentences or ideas with repetitive information and combine them into one."

Display the **Reviser's DRAFTboard chart**, showing the **DRAFT** mnemonic, or invite students to refer to it in their notebook if they have it.

"Writers, remember that we can use **DRAFT** to combine some sentences or ideas. We're going to try it out with some ideas from *Shipwreck at the Bottom of the World*."

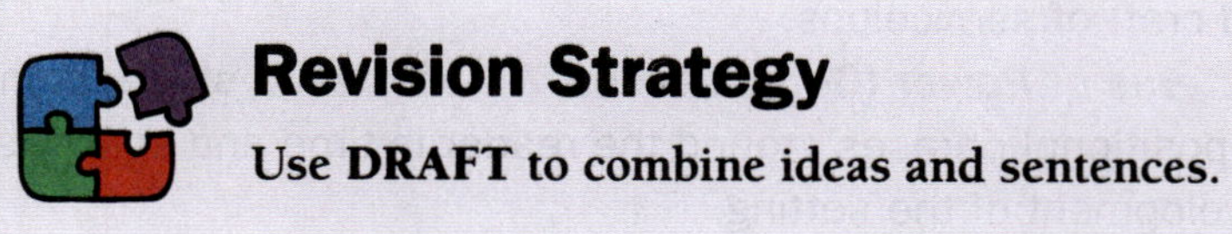

Revision Strategy
Use **DRAFT** to combine ideas and sentences.

Modeling

Use the **Reviser's DRAFTboard** along with printable, **6.16 Modeled Sentence Combo: Part I**, to explore the six sentences that need to be combined. "There are six sentences here about the ice on the continent of Antarctica. Let's see if we can use **DRAFT** to help us combine the sentences into one. Let's look again at the sentences we just read."

The ice never melts.

The ice spawns winds.

The ice spawns weather.

The ice clings to the bottom of the world.

The ice spawns storms.

The weather affects the whole planet.

"We are going to talk out ways we could combine these sentences, using any of the **DRAFT** strategies that help." Return to the **Reviser's DRAFTboard** and work through its mnemonic as you review how to use **DRAFT** as a guide to combine the sentences. "Let's start with **Deleting**. Do you see some words that are repeated? Talk it out with a neighbor. What else do you see that is repeated?" Model how to cross through repetitive words like "The ice" in sentences one through five and "spawns" in sentences three through five. "Now, let's think about how we might rearrange the words we have left. Do we need to **Add Connectors**? Remember that connectors are both words and punctuation marks. Let's talk this out." Your students may already have **The Connectors chart** glued into their notebooks, or you may have it hanging in your classroom. If not, the printable can be found on page 90.

Think aloud as you model rearranging and adding connectors. Write out some of the possibilities for students to see. After each one, read it aloud and orally share your thinking process as you continue to play some more. Perhaps you might say, "Okay, this one makes sense, but I wonder if I could rearrange some more or use a different connector to make it even more effective. Let me try . . ."

Here are a few possibilities to try and discuss:

The ice never melts, so it clings to the bottom of the world.

The ice never melts; instead it clings to the bottom of the world.

The ice never melts; it clings to the bottom of the world.

The Connectors

Prepositions
What do they do? They show time and place as well as introduce examples, contrasts, or comparisons.

Function	Example
Time	at, in, on
Extended Time	by, during, for, from, since, to, until, with(in)
Direction	in, into, on, onto, to, toward
Location	above, across, against, ahead of, along, among, around, at, behind, below, beneath, beside, between, by, from, in, inside, near, of, off, on, out, over, through, toward, under, within
Introduce Examples and Comparisons or Contrasts	as, despite, except, for, like, of, per, than, with, without

Subordinating Conjunctions (AAAWWUBBIS)
Although
As
After
While
When
Until
Because
Before
If
Since
What do they do? They show relationships, sometimes making one idea more or less important.

Function	Example
Time	after, before, during, since, until, when, whenever, while
Cause-Effect	as, because, since, so
Opposition	although, even though, though, whatever, while
Condition	as long as, if, in order to, unless, until, whatever

Relative Pronouns
What do they do? Introduce and link additional information to the noun before it.

Function	Example
Link **ideas and things** to more detail	that, what, which
Link **people** to more detail	who, whoever, whom, whose

Coordinating Conjunctions (FANBOYS)
For
And
Nor
But
Or
Yet
So
What do they do? They make connections that are equal to each other. They join sentences (thereby making compound sentences), and they can show a relationship between a pair or a list.

Connector Punctuation
What do they do? They combine, introduce, and enclose information.

Combines	Introduces	Encloses	Function	Example
Comma ,		Comma ,	Combine	and
Dash —	Dash —	Dash —	Opposition	but, nor, yet
Semicolon ;	Colon :	Parentheses ( )	Cause-Effect	for, so
		Quotation Marks " "	Choice	or

Modeling *(continued)*

"Okay, let's read this aloud. Does it make sense? Let's continue with **DRAFT** to see what else we could do with this combination." Then, refer back to the **Reviser's DRAFTboard**. "We've deleted, added, and rearranged. Let's think more about the verbs." Highlight or circle the verbs: *melts, clings, spawns, affects*. "Take a look at our **Form New Verbs chart**. I'm noticing my verbs are in the present tense. When I look at my **Form New Verbs chart**, one thing I could do is change a verb to an infinitive by adding *to* in front of it. Hmmm. Maybe I can change spawns to *to spawn*. Let's try it.

The ice never melts; it clings to the bottom of the world to spawn winds, storms, and weather . . .

Well, that is definitely one option. Look at the examples on the chart. Talk it out with a partner." After a brief turn and talk, model how to change the verb from *to spawn* to *spawning*. Then, think aloud as you compose a new sentence:

The ice never melts; it clings to the bottom of the world, spawning winds, storms, and weather . . .

"Writers, you may remember from our work with **Forming Verbs** that this is how you could change the verb by adding –ing at the end. Which one of these combinations seems most effective to you? Talk it out."

Once the class feels like they have an effective combination, reveal the author's original sentence. Invite students to compare and contrast their version with Jennifer Armstrong's using **6.16 Modeled Sentence Combo: Part II** on page 200, prompting things along with the following reflective questions as necessary.

- Why do you think Jennifer combined the sentences in this way?
- Is there another combination that would be effective?
- Why do you think your combination was different from or the same as the author's?
- If your combination was different from Armstrong's, which do you prefer, and why?

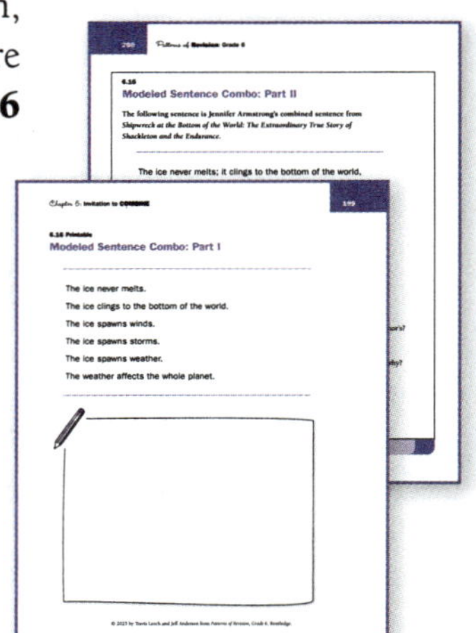

Collaborating Through Conversation

Distribute the printable, **6.16 Invitation to Combine: Part I** (page 201), to the class. Create groups for students to collaborate to combine these sentences. Facilitate a first read of the directions and invite students to record their possibilities on the lines provided on the printable. They may need reminders to access any of the charts either hanging in your classroom or glued into their notebooks that would help them make choices.

As you move around the room to support groups, be mindful of a few possible entry points for combinations you might share with groups to nudge their work forward, such as looking for repeated information within the sentences.

After groups have combined the sentences, display **6.16 Invitation to Combine: Part II** on page 203 to share the author's original text. Use the reflective questions at the bottom to facilitate a conversation about meaning and effect.

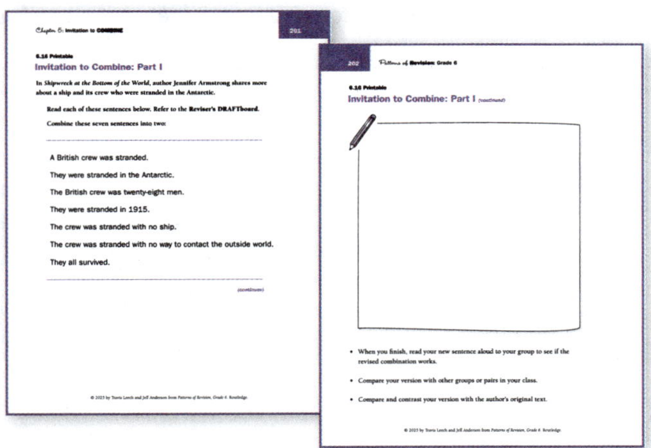

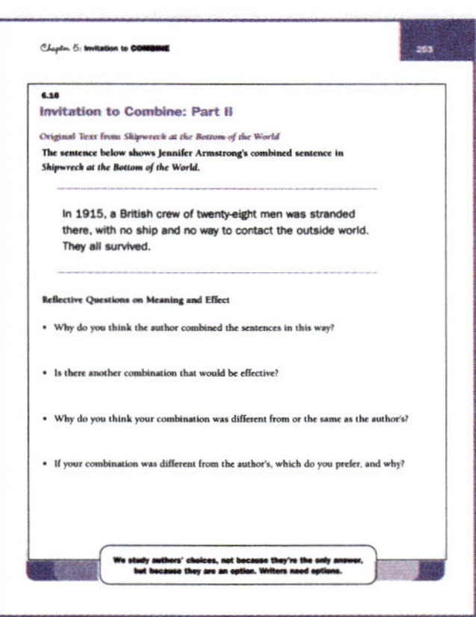

Quickwrite Opportunity (Optional)

1. Before embarking on an expedition, explorers must plan carefully and pack essential items. Describe five critical things you would take with you on a daring adventure to Antarctica or another extreme environment.

2. Creativity is the key to survival in the unknown. Invent a unique tool or gadget that could help explorers on their journey through frozen landscapes. Describe its features and how it would aid in their adventure.

Applying Revision

Students return to their own writing to play with different sentence combos, using the **DRAFT** strategies and noticing the different effects. Invite them to choose one section or paragraph to revise. You may want to focus students on looking at connections from one sentence to another as an opportunity to reconnect sentences with a semicolon to show a closer relationship. Giving them opportunities to play with the possibilities is the goal, showing students that they have options.

Tip

Not all revisions make writing better. Some won't work. We just need to flex our revision muscles. That's an important discovery for students to make about revision.

Sharing Results

To celebrate the revision your writers did in this lesson, consider taking them on an adventure to another teacher's classroom to share their revisions with someone new. Partnered with students there, they explain the revisions they made to their writing and explain why they made that choice, and their new partner shares how that helps them as a reader. You may then decide to hang these revised pieces in the hallway, showcasing student revision work.

6.16 Printable

Modeled Sentence Combo: Part I

The ice never melts.

The ice clings to the bottom of the world.

The ice spawns winds.

The ice spawns storms.

The ice spawns weather.

The weather affects the whole planet.

6.16

Modeled Sentence Combo: Part II

The following sentence is Jennifer Armstrong's combined sentence from
*Shipwreck at the Bottom of the World: The Extraordinary True Story of
Shackleton and the Endurance.*

The ice never melts; it clings to the bottom of the world,
spawning winds, storms, and weather that affects the
whole planet.

Reflective Questions on Meaning and Effect

- Why do you think the author combined the sentences in this way?

- Is there another combination that would be effective?

- Why do you think your combination was different from or the same as the author's?

- If your combination was different from the author's, which do you prefer, and why?

> We study authors' choices, not because they're the only answer,
> but because they are an option. Writers need options.

6.16 Printable

Invitation to Combine: Part I

In *Shipwreck at the Bottom of the World*, author Jennifer Armstrong shares more about a ship and its crew who were stranded in the Antarctic.

Read each of these sentences below. Refer to the **Reviser's DRAFTboard**.

Combine these seven sentences into two:

A British crew was stranded.

They were stranded in the Antarctic.

The British crew was twenty-eight men.

They were stranded in 1915.

The crew was stranded with no ship.

The crew was stranded with no way to contact the outside world.

They all survived.

(continues)

6.16 Printable

Invitation to Combine: Part I *(continued)*

- When you finish, read your new sentence aloud to your group to see if the revised combination works.

- Compare your version with other groups or pairs in your class.

- Compare and contrast your version with the author's original text.

6.16

Invitation to Combine: Part II

Original Text from *Shipwreck at the Bottom of the World*

The sentence below shows Jennifer Armstrong's combined sentence in *Shipwreck at the Bottom of the World*.

In 1915, a British crew of twenty-eight men was stranded there, with no ship and no way to contact the outside world. They all survived.

Reflective Questions on Meaning and Effect

- Why do you think the author combined the sentences in this way?

- Is there another combination that would be effective?

- Why do you think your combination was different from or the same as the author's?

- If your combination was different from the author's, which do you prefer, and why?

We study authors' choices, not because they're the only answer, but because they are an option. Writers need options.

6.17 Combining Is No Secret: Use DRAFT!

Revision goal connected to standards:

Develop and strengthen writing by combining ideas to avoid redundancy, add clarity, and improve fluency.

Model Text

Code Breaker, Spy Hunter: How Elizebeth Friedman Changed the Course of Two World Wars
- Written by Laurie Wallmark
- Illustrated by Brooke Smart

Teacher Considerations

In this lesson, students will revise by adding extra information about a character between either commas or dashes. We refer to this as adding an *interrupter* within a sentence, which adds nonessential but often important information to the sentence. We chose the biography of Elizebeth Friedman, *Code Breaker, Spy Hunter: How Elizebeth Friedman Changed the Course of Two World Wars*, written by Laurie Wallmark, as our text for this lesson. We love that this book highlights an important historical figure in the STEM field, and Wallmark is adept at crafting details about Elizebeth Friedman.

Patterns of Power (6–8), Lessons 7.2 and 7.3 both highlight how writers add extra information within a sentence using commas to *interrupt* the sentence.

Patterns of Power Lesson (6–8), Lesson 10.6 shows students how to use dashes to add extra information within a sentence.

Setting the Context

Elizebeth Friedman was an American code breaker who helped the U.S. outsmart the Nazis in World War II and take down criminals with her code breaking skills. To set a context, read aloud the excerpt of *Code Breaker, Spy Hunter: How Elizebeth Friedman Changed the Course of Two World Wars* by Laurie Wallmark.

As a child, Elizebeth loved to read, especially poetry. One of her favorite poets was William Shakespeare. His poetry showed structure and patterns, just like she would later look for in coded messages.

Revision Strategy

Use **DRAFT** to combine ideas and sentences.

Modeling

Use the printable **6.17 Modeled Sentence Combo: Part I** on page 209 to explore the four sentences that you'll combine into one. "There are four sentences here. Let's play with revision and see if we can make these four sentences into one. First let's read aloud the sentences."

Elizebeth Smith Friedman agreed to work with the FBI.

She agreed to work with them on a top-secret project.

She was a cryptanalyst.

She had a stellar reputation as a cryptanalyst.

"Let's spend some time talking out ways we could combine these sentences, remembering that we can use any of the **DRAFT** strategies that help reduce the sentences to one." Model how to combine the sentences, saying things like, "I see a word I haven't seen before in the last two sentences: *cryptanalyst*. I can guess that based on our read-aloud it might have something to

Modeling *(continued)*

do with codes and might be a job. Is there a way we can combine the last two sentences into one? Talk it out with a neighbor. What else do you see is repeated? How could you rearrange the words and add connectors?" Providing a list of connector words will help students to talk through this combination. (See **The Connectors** printable on page 90.) Allow students time to continue combining, or if they are unsure of how to move forward continue modeling the revision process.

Once the class feels like they have an effective combination, reveal the author's original sentence. Students compare and contrast their version or the class version with Laurie Wallmark's using **6.17 Modeled Sentence Combo: Part II** on page 210. Use the following reflective questions as necessary:

- Why do you think Laurie combined the sentences like this?
- Is there another combination that would be effective?
- Why do you think your combination was different from or the same as the author's?
- If your combination was different from Wallmark's, which do you prefer, and why?

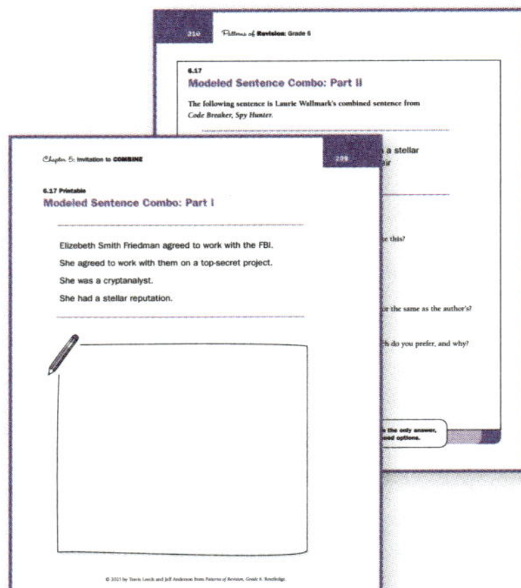

As students complete a comparative analysis of their combination with the author's original, highlight how the author uses an appositive phrase bracketed within the sentence to rename Elizebeth and give the reader more information about her. Highlight how the author adds extra information through renaming Elizebeth as *a cryptanalyst with a stellar reputation* to help the reader better understand why the FBI would want to work with her on a top-secret project.

Figure 6.17
Sentence with interrupter patterns.

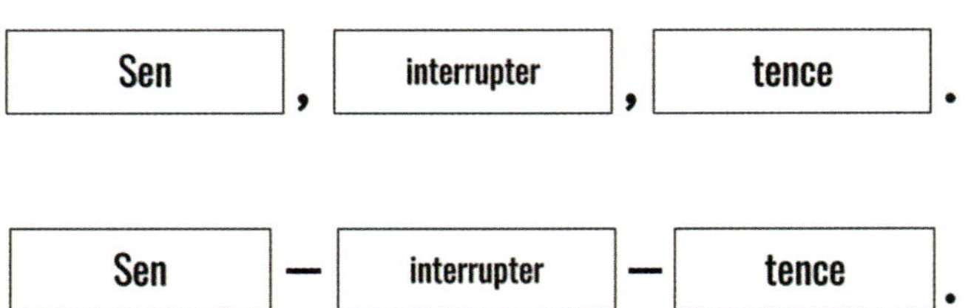

Collaborating Through Conversation

Distribute the printable, **6.17 Invitation to Combine: Part I** on page 211, to each student. Using **DRAFT** and the directions on the printable, students collaborate with one or more classmates to combine the sentences. Ensure writers have decided on where to record their possibilities, whether on the printable, in their notebooks, or in a shared digital space.

As soon as students are ready, they compare their choices with those of others. For comparative analysis, display **6.17 Invitation to Combine: Part II** on page 213 to share the author's original text. Use the reflective questions at the bottom to facilitate a conversation about meaning and effect.

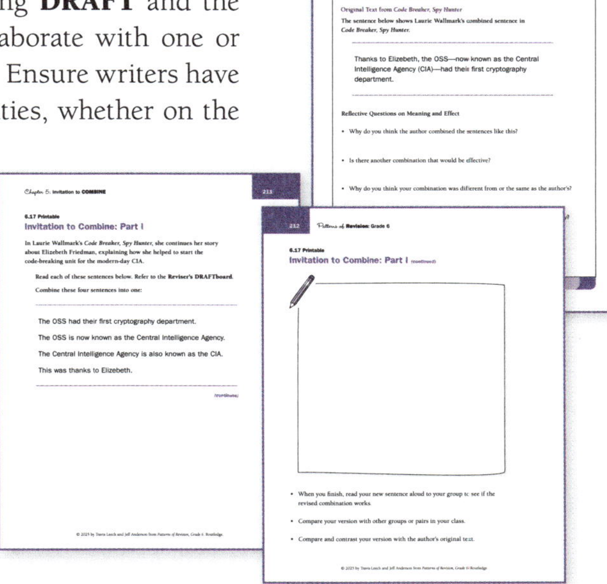

Quickwrite Opportunity (Optional)

1. Explain the importance of science or mathematics in everyday life and for any future careers that interest you. Discuss how science or math skills are crucial for problem-solving and decision-making in your daily life or as you imagine yourself in a career that interests you.
2. Author Laurie Wallmark has researched and written about other famous women in the STEM field. Choose one of the following famous women in STEM, spend some time researching them, and write out your findings:
   - **Ada Byron Lovelace:** a 19th-century mathematician and writer who is considered the world's first computer programmer.
   - **Grace Hopper:** a computer scientist and naval officer who played a significant role in the development of computer programming languages.
   - **Hedy Lamarr:** an actress and inventor who co-developed a frequency-hopping system that laid the groundwork for modern wireless communication technologies.
   - **Maria Mitchell:** the first female professional astronomer and astronomy professor.

Applying Revision

Students return to the writing they just generated or a piece they've already created in their writer's notebook to play with different sentence combinations, using any of the **DRAFT** strategies. If they have a hard time finding sentences in their own writing to combine, invite them to think about additional things they want to say about a character, a setting, or another noun that is the focus of their writing. Then writers use a sticky note or space in their writer's notebook to try different ways to enclose extra information about one or more nouns using this lessons models to guide their thinking.

Sharing Results

Students share their results with partners. Celebrate the revision writers did today either directly in their writing, in their practice boxes, or in another format. Share the revision strategy used by one or two students with the class, prompting students to name how the writer combined sentences using **DRAFT**.

6.17 Printable

Modeled Sentence Combo: Part I

Elizebeth Smith Friedman agreed to work with the FBI.

She agreed to work with them on a top-secret project.

She was a cryptanalyst.

She had a stellar reputation.

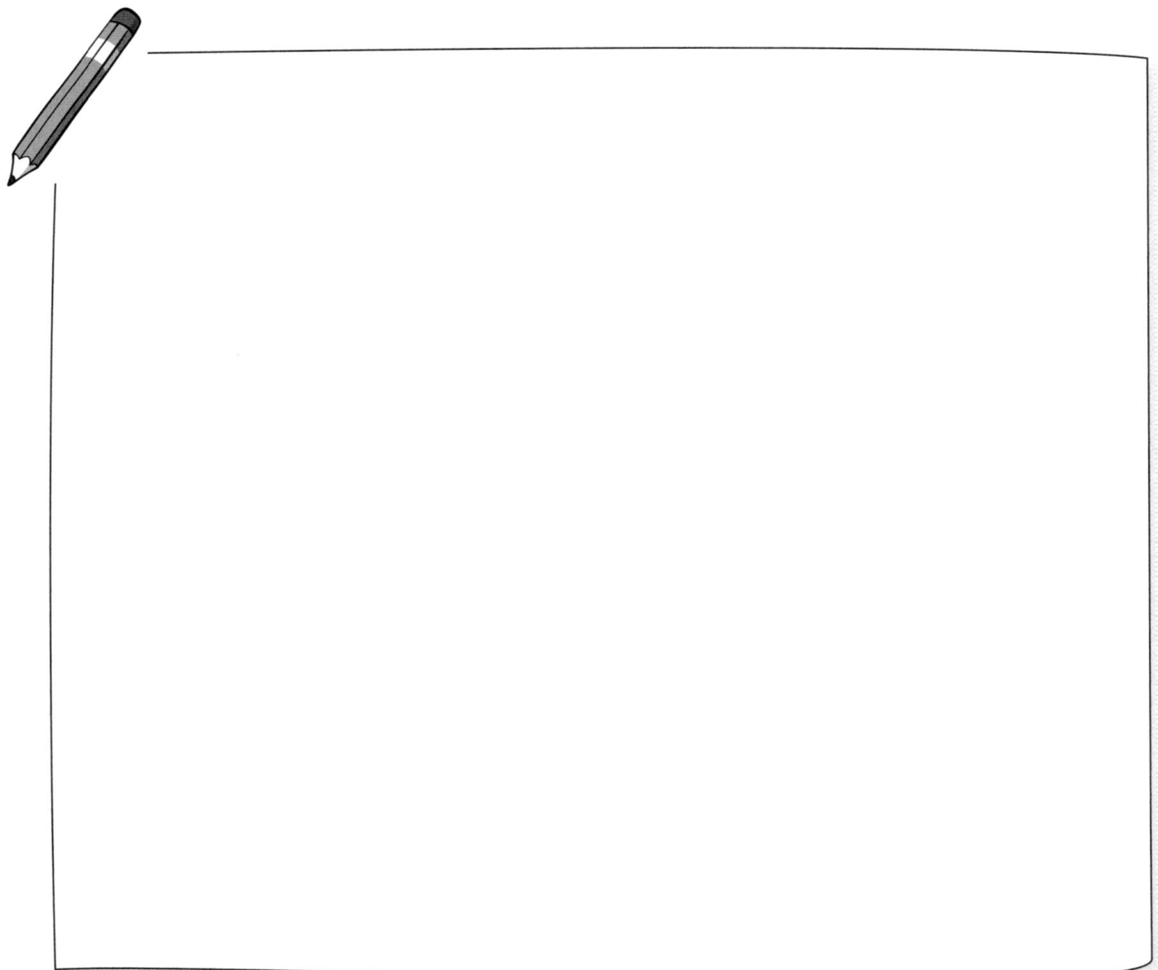

6.17

Modeled Sentence Combo: Part II

The following sentence is Laurie Wallmark's combined sentence from *Code Breaker, Spy Hunter.*

Elizebeth Smith Friedman, a cryptanalyst with a stellar reputation, agreed to work with the FBI on their top-secret project.

Reflective Questions on Meaning and Effect

- Why do you think the author combined the sentences like this?

- Is there another combination that would be effective?

- Why do you think your combination was different from or the same as the author's?

- If your combination was different from the author's, which do you prefer, and why?

> **We study authors' choices, not because they're the only answer, but because they are an option. Writers need options.**

6.17 Printable

Invitation to Combine: Part I

In Laurie Wallmark's *Code Breaker, Spy Hunter*, she continues her story about Elizebeth Friedman, explaining how she helped to start the code-breaking unit for the modern-day CIA.

Read each of these sentences below. Refer to the **Reviser's DRAFTboard**.

Combine these four sentences into one:

____

The OSS had their first cryptography department.

The OSS is now known as the Central Intelligence Agency.

The Central Intelligence Agency is also known as the CIA.

This was thanks to Elizebeth.

____

(continues)

6.17 Printable

Invitation to Combine: Part I (continued)

- When you finish, read your new sentence aloud to your group to see if the revised combination works.

- Compare your version with other groups or pairs in your class.

- Compare and contrast your version with the author's original text.

6.17

Invitation to Combine: Part II

Original Text from *Code Breaker, Spy Hunter*

**The sentence below shows Laurie Wallmark's combined sentence in
Code Breaker, Spy Hunter.**

Thanks to Elizebeth, the OSS—now known as the Central Intelligence Agency (CIA)—had their first cryptography department.

Reflective Questions on Meaning and Effect

- Why do you think the author combined the sentences like this?

- Is there another combination that would be effective?

- Why do you think your combination was different from or the same as the author's?

- If your combination was different from the author's, which do you prefer, and why?

We study authors' choices, not because they're the only answer,
but because they are an option. Writers need options.

6.18 Don't Let Sentence Combining Plague You

Lesson Overview

Revision goal connected to standards:

Develop and strengthen writing by combining ideas to avoid redundancy, add clarity, and improve fluency.

Model Text

Legend
 – Written by Marie Lu

Teacher Considerations

We continue combination revision work, using Marie Lu's book, *Legend*. We chose this book not only for its action-packed story line, but also for its descriptive world building. Marie Lu's writing offers numerous options for studying more complex sentence structures with students, including a compound-complex sentence that we'll work with in the Modeling part of the lesson. In the Collaborating Through Conversation section, students will add extra information within a sentence in a variety of ways, possibly using commas as connectors both to interrupt a sentence with extra information and to set up information that acts as a closer to the sentence.

***Patterns of Power* (6–8), Lesson 13.1:** this lesson highlights one possibility for creating compound-complex sentences. Studying this sentence structure with students will give them shared language for discussion as well as options for adding connector words and punctuation.

In both models presented in ***Patterns of Power* (6–8), Lesson 4.5,** the author's original text contains two verbs within the closer; students studying that lesson before experiencing the one presented here will have an eye for effective ways to connect two verbs together.

Setting the Context

In *Legend*, author Marie Lu imagines a not-too-distant future where a plague has affected our world and The Republic has taken control of the U.S. The story begins with the reader experiencing a plague-ridden California through the eyes of main character, Day, and his partner, Tess. Day and Tess watch over their old neighborhood while Republic soldiers inspect houses for signs of people carrying the plague. You may need to explain this to students before reading the excerpt aloud to them.

The plague has hit the Lake sector hard. In the glow of the Jumbotrons, Tess and I can see the soldiers at the end of the street as they inspect each home, their black capes shiny and worn loose in the heat. Each of them wears a gas mask. Sometimes when they emerge, they mark a house by painting a big red X on the front door. No one enters or leaves the home after that—at least, not when anyone's looking.

A shriek echoes from the other end of the street. My eyes dart toward the sound and my hand whips to the knife sheathed at my belt. Tess sucks in her breath.

After finishing the read aloud, explain to students they'll be reading on to see who or what made that shriek from the other end of the street.

Revision Strategy

Use **DRAFT** to combine ideas and sentences.

Modeling

Use the **Reviser's DRAFTboard** on page 162 along with printable, **6.18 Modeled Sentence Combo: Part I** on page 220, to explore the sentences that need to be combined. "Let's see who or what made that shriek from the read aloud. We're going to read six sentences and see if we can use **DRAFT** to help us combine them down to two. First, let's read aloud the sentences."

Modeling *(continued)*

It's a plague victim.   She must've been deteriorating for months.

Her skin is cracked.   Her skin is bleeding everywhere.

I find myself wondering.

I wonder how the soldiers could have missed this one during previous inspections.

"The first thing I notice when reading these sentences is that we have a few different pronouns: It, she, her, and I. In this part of the story, the character Day is the narrator, so that is probably who *I* is referring to. Who are the pronouns *she* and *her* referring to?" Give students a moment to discuss and connect back to the *plague victim* from sentence one. "Okay, now that we have those pronouns settled, let's think about our revision options from **DRAFT**. What do you see that is repeated? Can we already start deleting any information and combining ideas?"

Students may suggest combining sentences two and three to read something like this:

Her skin is cracked and bleeding everywhere.

"How about the last two sentences? I notice *I* and *wonder/wondering* are repeated. What options do we have for combining these two sentences together? One option could be to keep the start of the fifth sentence and then add the content of the sixth. It might look like this:

I find myself wondering how the soldiers could have missed this one during previous inspections.

Another option could be completely deleting the fifth sentence and just using sentence six.

I wonder how the soldiers could have missed this one during previous inspections.

Now, let's look at how we might **Add Connectors** to combine some of these sentences. When I look at sentence two, I notice it sounds like the reason why the plague victim's skin could be cracked and bleeding everywhere. Let's try some connectors that might highlight this relationship." Model trying out one or more of the following connected sentences.

Modeling *(continued)*

She must've been deteriorating for months, so her skin is cracked and bleeding everywhere.

She must've been deteriorating for months, because her skin is cracked and bleeding everywhere.

She must've been deteriorating for months; her skin is cracked and bleeding everywhere.

Students discuss which option they think is most effective and why. Then, offer options for how they might connect the last sentence together with this chunk of text. Model trying out one or more of these options, or create your own option for connection:

She must've been deteriorating for months, so her skin is cracked and bleeding everywhere, and I find myself wondering how the soldiers could have missed this one during previous inspections.

She must've been deteriorating for months, because her skin is cracked and bleeding everywhere, so I find myself wondering how the soldiers could have missed this one during previous inspections.

She must've been deteriorating for months, because her skin is cracked and bleeding everywhere; therefore I find myself wondering how the soldiers could have missed this one during previous inspections.

Have students discuss the connections between the sentences and their effectiveness as they read the combinations aloud or to themselves.

Once the class feels like they have an effective combination, reveal the author's original sentence. Students compare and contrast their version with Marie Lu's using **6.18 Modeled Sentence Combo: Part II** on page 221, prompting things along with the following reflective questions as necessary.

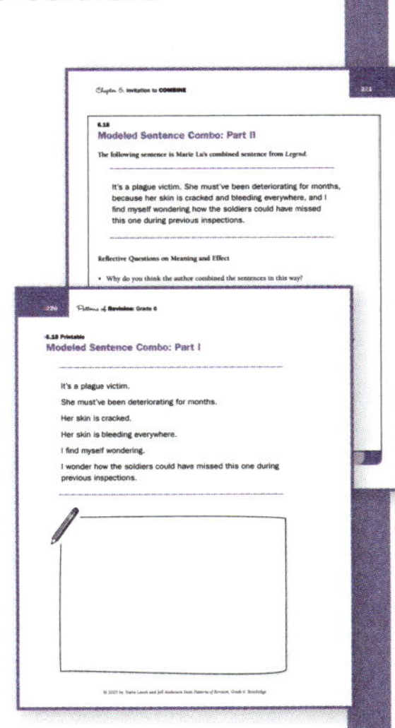

- Why do you think Marie combined the sentences in this way?
- Is there another combination that would be effective?
- Why do you think your combination was different from or the same as the author's?
- If your combination was different from Lu's, which do you prefer, and why?

Collaborating Through Conversation

Distribute the printable, **6.18 Invitation to Combine: Part I** on page 222, to the class. Following the directions on the printable and using **DRAFT**, students collaborate through conversation with one or more classmates to combine the sentences into one. Keep in mind that writers will most likely discover many different ways to combine the sentences provided.

When students are ready, display **6.18 Invitation to Combine: Part II** on page 224 to share the author's original text. Reflective questions at the bottom can help facilitate a discussion about meaning and effect.

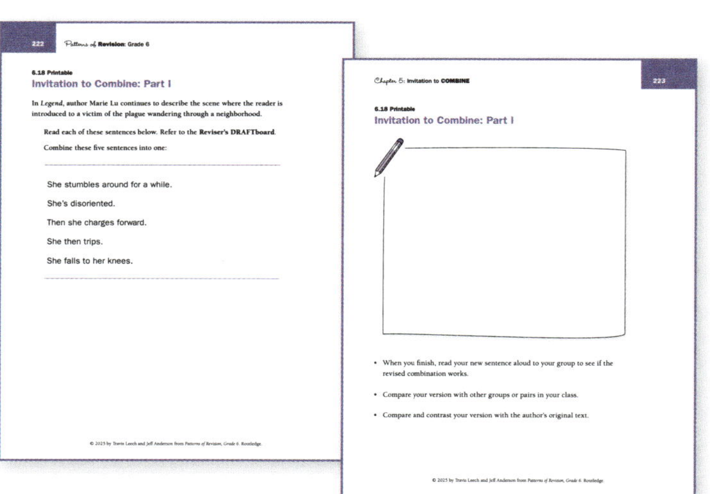

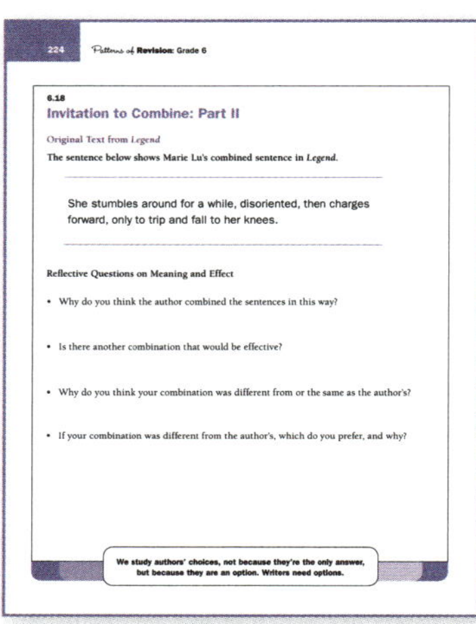

Quickwrite Opportunity (Optional)

1. Write about a time you were sick, describing either how you felt while you were sick or describing one scene of your time being sick.
2. Imagine you were observing a place that is important to you. Describe that place with as much detail as you can and create a scene of what could be happening at that place.

Applying Revision

Students return to their own writing or their writer's notebook to play with different sentence combinations, using the **DRAFT** strategies. Students notice the different effects. If students need support with finding a part of their writing to revise, invite them to think about two or three additional things they want their reader to know and combine those thoughts into one sentence. Remind students to use **The Connectors** printable (page 90) to help them connect their ideas. Then, they may choose which new combinations they will add to their piece.

Sharing Results

Each student highlights one thing from their writing they want to share with their new partner: a golden line.

- Students pair up.
- While one partner shares, the other partner listens.
- The partner who listens then shares one effective thing they noticed and/or one thing they want to know more about the writing they heard.
- Then partners switch and repeat the process.
- If time allows, students return to their writing and add more information to answer and develop the one thing their partner wanted to know more about.

6.18 Printable

Modeled Sentence Combo: Part I

It's a plague victim.

She must've been deteriorating for months.

Her skin is cracked.

Her skin is bleeding everywhere.

I find myself wondering.

I wonder how the soldiers could have missed this one during previous inspections.

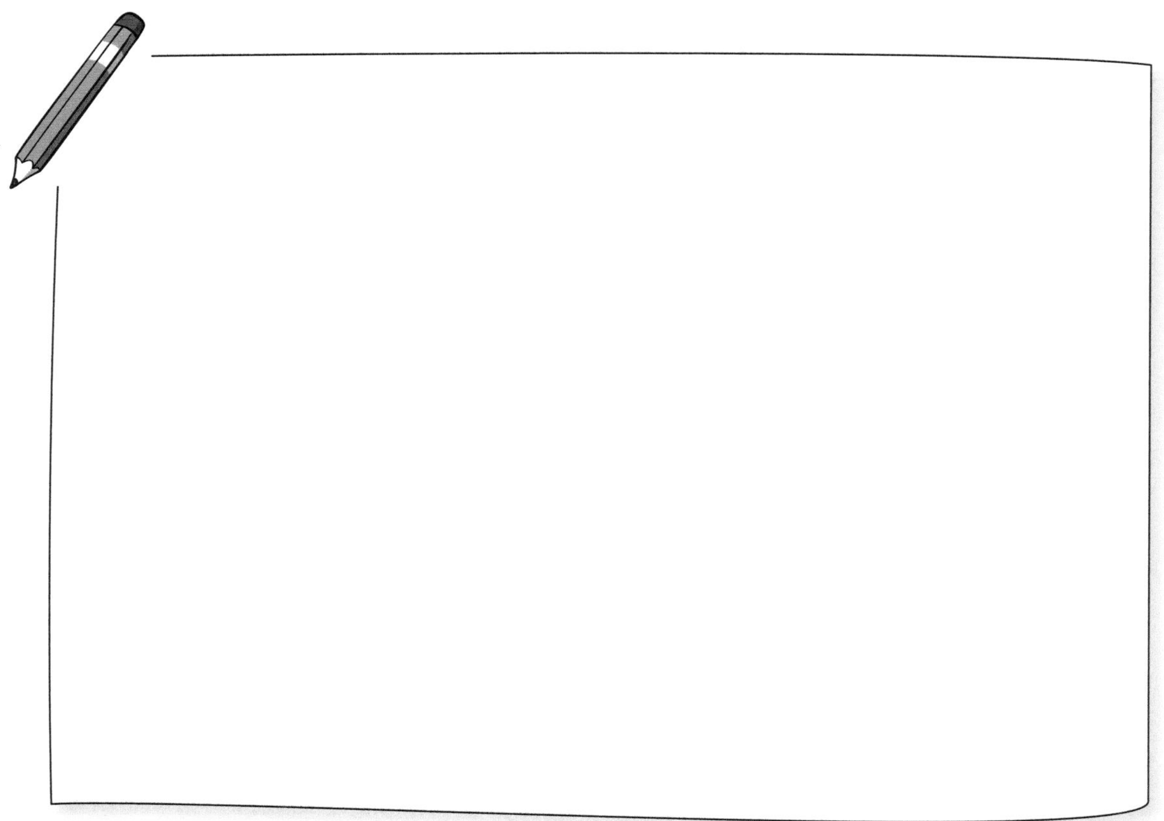

6.18

Modeled Sentence Combo: Part II

The following sentence is Marie Lu's combined sentence from *Legend*.

It's a plague victim. She must've been deteriorating for months, because her skin is cracked and bleeding everywhere, and I find myself wondering how the soldiers could have missed this one during previous inspections.

Reflective Questions on Meaning and Effect

- Why do you think the author combined the sentences in this way?

- Is there another combination that would be effective?

- Why do you think your combination was different from or the same as the author's?

- If your combination was different from the author's, which do you prefer, and why?

> **We study authors' choices, not because they're the only answer, but because they are an option. Writers need options.**

6.18 Printable

Invitation to Combine: Part I

In *Legend*, author Marie Lu continues to describe the scene where the reader is introduced to a victim of the plague wandering through a neighborhood.

Read each of these sentences below. Refer to the **Reviser's DRAFTboard**.

Combine these five sentences into one:

____

She stumbles around for a while.

She's disoriented.

Then she charges forward.

She then trips.

She falls to her knees.

____

6.18 Printable

Invitation to Combine: Part I

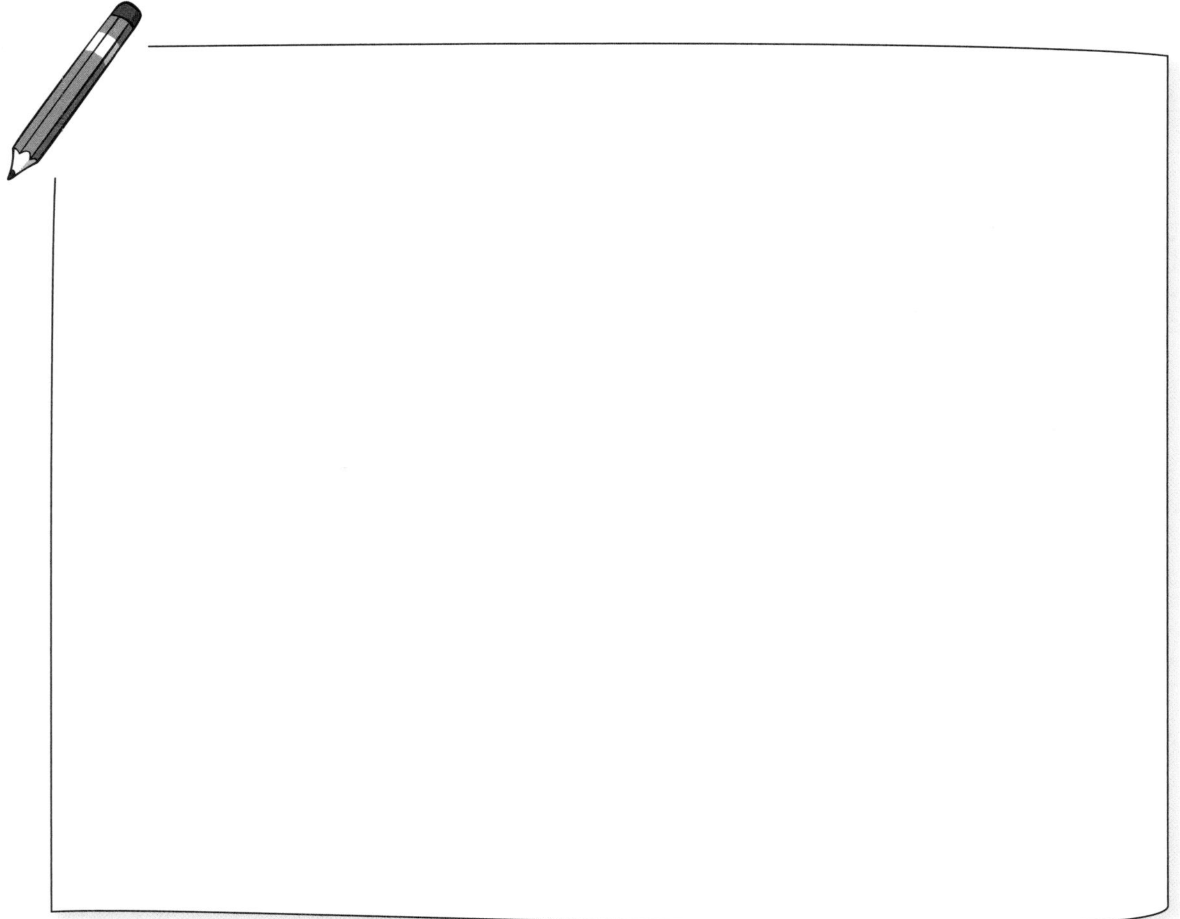

- When you finish, read your new sentence aloud to your group to see if the revised combination works.

- Compare your version with other groups or pairs in your class.

- Compare and contrast your version with the author's original text.

6.18

Invitation to Combine: Part II

Original Text from *Legend*

The sentence below shows Marie Lu's combined sentence in *Legend*.

She stumbles around for a while, disoriented, then charges forward, only to trip and fall to her knees.

Reflective Questions on Meaning and Effect

- Why do you think the author combined the sentences in this way?

- Is there another combination that would be effective?

- Why do you think your combination was different from or the same as the author's?

- If your combination was different from the author's, which do you prefer, and why?

We study authors' choices, not because they're the only answer, but because they are an option. Writers need options.

6.19 Getting a Complex Understanding of Revision

Lesson Overview

Revision goal connected to standards:

Develop and strengthen writing by combining ideas to avoid redundancy, add clarity, and improve fluency.

Model Text

Thirst
 – Written by Varsha Bajaj

Teacher Considerations

In this lesson, we take some time for a lighter review of combination revision work, using Varsha Bajaj's book *Thirst*. We chose this book because Bajaj creates characters relatable to middle schoolers while highlighting the real issues of people accessing clean water—an issue many students might not be familiar with.

Both examples you'll be working with highlight the use of complex sentences, as students play with **Adding Connectors** to combine sentences, exploring ways complex sentences can be structured differently within the author's original excerpts.

Patterns of Power **(6–8), Lessons 6.1 and 6.2:** these lessons highlight the structure of and help elevate conversations around complex sentences, showing both the dependent clause as an *opener* (6.1) and as a *closer* (6.2).

Setting the Context

In *Thirst*, author Varsha Bajaj tells the story of a teen girl who lives in a family struggling to get by in Mumbai, India. People who live in her neighborhood have difficulty accessing many of the basics they need to survive. The main character, Minni, shares some of the struggles her family faces with accessing clean water. Explain this to students, then read-aloud this section of the text.

Sanjay and I sit on the top of the hill and stare out at the huge, never-ending Arabian Sea. The salty breeze brings a little relief from the heat.

"It feels like the world is made of water from up here," I say. "That there's enough of it for everyone."

But I know there isn't.

Figure 6.19 Sentence patterns: complex opener & closer.

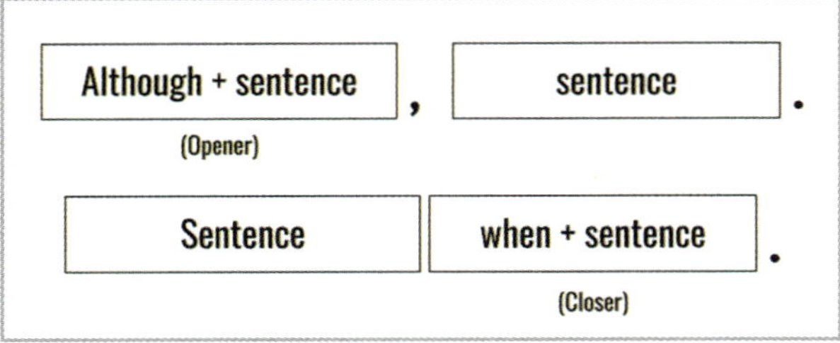

Use **DRAFT** to combine ideas and sentences.

Modeling

Use the **Reviser's DRAFTboard** on page 162 along with printable, **6.19 Modeled Sentence Combo: Part I** on page 231, to explore the sentences that need to be combined. "Let's continue reading about the narrator's life in her neighborhood in Mumbai. We're going to read four sentences and see if we can use **DRAFT** to help us combine them down to one. First, let's read aloud the sentences."

Water surrounds my city.   Most of the people I know are always struggling.

My city is an island.   They struggle to get enough.

Modeling *(continued)*

"The first thing I notice when reading these sentences are some repeated words in the first two sentences, as well as in the last two sentences. Let's mark where we see repetition.

Water surrounds my city.

My city is an island.

Most of the people I know are always struggling.

The people I know struggle to get enough.

"Can we start deleting any information and combining ideas?"
Students may suggest combining sentences one and two to read something like this:

Water surrounds my island city.

My city is an island that is surrounded by water.

"How about the last two sentences? What options do we have for combining them? Prompt students for options to combine these sentences or begin crafting options for students to see, talking through the reasoning behind your combining choices. Some options may look like this:

Most of the people I know are always struggling to get enough.

The people I know are always struggling to get enough.

"Now, let's look at how we might **Add Connectors** to combine some of these sentences. When I look at these sentences, I notice that there is a relationship here between the amount of water that is around the city and the struggle for people in the city to access it. Let's think about how we can show that relationship effectively by adding a connector." This is a great opportunity to visit the **Add Connectors chart** (page 90) and discuss the effectiveness of specific connector words that could be used to combine these two sentences. Try some options for students, including these possibilities:

Modeling *(continued)*

*Water surrounds my island city, **but** most of the people I know are always struggling to get enough.*

***While** water surrounds my island city, most of the people I know are always struggling to get enough.*

***Although** my island city is surrounded by water, the people I know are always struggling to get enough.*

Students discuss which option they think is most effective and why. Once they have decided on an effective combination, reveal the author's original sentence. Students compare and contrast their version with Varsha Bajaj's using **6.19 Modeled Sentence Combo: Part II** on page 232, prompting things along with the following reflective questions as necessary.

- Why do you think Varsha combined the sentences in this way?
- Is there another combination that would be effective?
- Why do you think your combination was different from or the same as the author's?
- If your combination was different from Bajaj's, which do you prefer, and why?

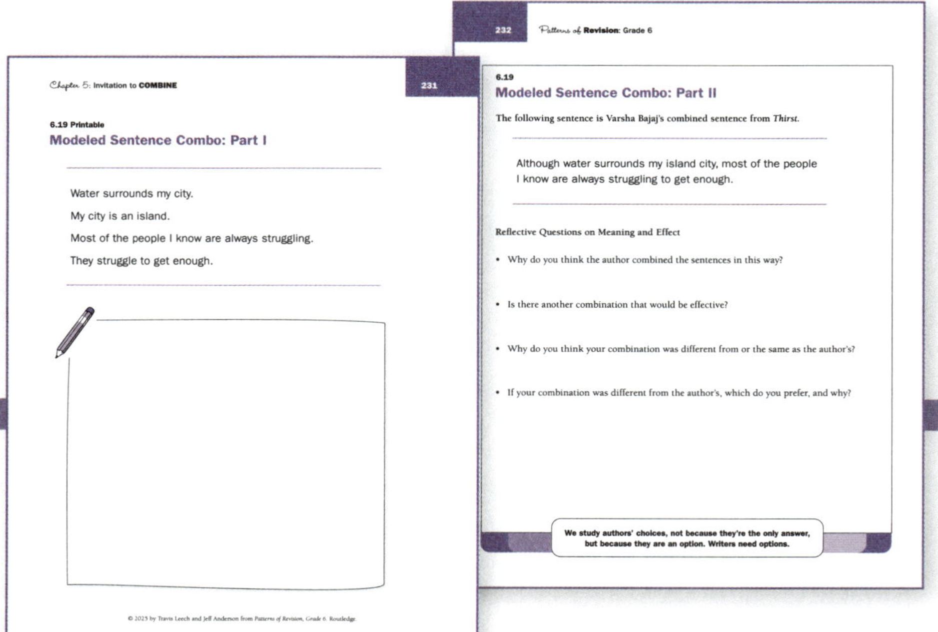

Collaborating Through Conversation

Distribute the printable, **6.19 Invitation to Combine: Part I** on page 233, to the class. Following the directions on the printable and using **DRAFT**, students collaborate through conversation with one or more classmates to combine the five sentences into one. Then move around the room to check in with and support learners as they combine sentences. Struggling groups may benefit from discussions around adding specific connector words to show relationships between the sentences in this section. This is another effective place to call back to the **Add Connectors chart** (page 90) to aid in discussing options with groups who need a nudge in the right direction.

When students are ready, display **6.19 Invitation to Combine: Part II** on page 235 to share the author's original text. Reflective questions at the bottom can help facilitate a discussion about meaning and effect.

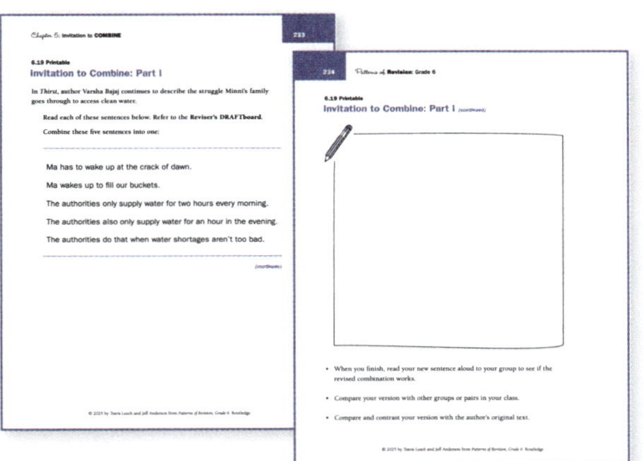

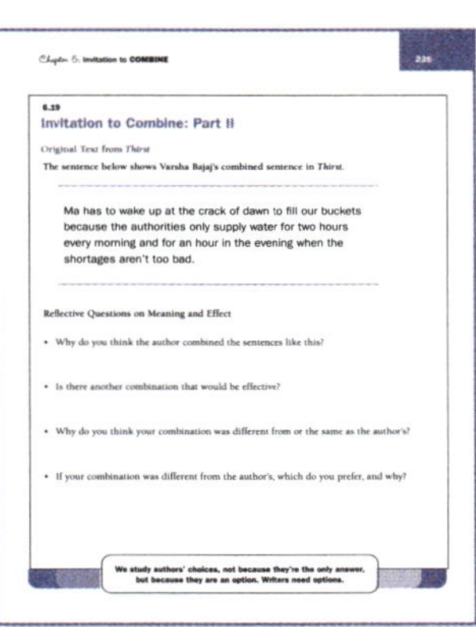

Quickwrite Opportunity (Optional)

1. Make a list of all of the times during a typical day that you use water. Then, write about what you might do if you could only use clean water for one or two things on that list. How might that make your day look different?
2. In this story, the main character, Minni, reflects on her daily life by journaling, often by writing in poetry. Write a brief journal entry that reflects on your feelings about a recent day in your life. If you're up for the challenge, write your entry as a poem.

Applying Revision

Each student selects a piece of writing to revisit. This can be writing from a previous class or writing generated during class in response to a prompt. Start by modeling this process with your own writing to support student clarity. Show the class your writing, then explain any sections you might like to revise. When focusing on your writing, you may choose to connect your revision technique back to the work you did with either of the models in this lesson, such as **Adding** a new or different connector word to connect two ideas together. Since the class has now had some experience with sentence combining, this would be a great opportunity to ask them to collaborate with you and offer one or more revision choices.

Students then return to their own writing to play with different revision options, using the **DRAFT** strategies and noticing the different effects. Invite them to choose one section or paragraph to focus on. One possible entry point to prompt students toward is to find a spot where adding more dialogue would add detail or clarity to the piece, being mindful of applying their learning about dialogue tags and using a colon to introduce new dialogue.

Sharing Results

Water Fountain Conversations: Take students out in the hallway with their revision work in hand.

- Line up students in a novel way (like by height or age).
- Group students into pairs, facing each other.
- Students share their revisions with each other.
- One line of students then shifts one student to the left or right, with the student who no longer has a partner rotating all the way to the other side of the line.
- Students share one more time with a new partner. Repeat this sharing process as many more times as it makes sense to do.
- If time allows, gather students back into a group and ask for volunteers to share their revisions.

6.19 Printable

Modeled Sentence Combo: Part I

Water surrounds my city.

My city is an island.

Most of the people I know are always struggling.

They struggle to get enough.

6.19

Modeled Sentence Combo: Part II

The following sentence is Varsha Bajaj's combined sentence from *Thirst*.

Although water surrounds my island city, most of the people
I know are always struggling to get enough.

Reflective Questions on Meaning and Effect

- Why do you think the author combined the sentences in this way?

- Is there another combination that would be effective?

- Why do you think your combination was different from or the same as the author's?

- If your combination was different from the author's, which do you prefer, and why?

> **We study authors' choices, not because they're the only answer, but because they are an option. Writers need options.**

6.19 Printable

Invitation to Combine: Part I

In *Thirst*, author Varsha Bajaj continues to describe the struggle Minni's family goes through to access clean water.

Read each of these sentences below. Refer to the **Reviser's DRAFTboard**.

Combine these five sentences into one:

____

Ma has to wake up at the crack of dawn.

Ma wakes up to fill our buckets.

The authorities only supply water for two hours every morning.

The authorities also only supply water for an hour in the evening.

The authorities do that when water shortages aren't too bad.

____

(continues)

6.19 Printable

Invitation to Combine: Part I *(continued)*

- When you finish, read your new sentence aloud to your group to see if the revised combination works.

- Compare your version with other groups or pairs in your class.

- Compare and contrast your version with the author's original text.

6.19

Invitation to Combine: Part II

Original Text from *Thirst*

The sentence below shows Varsha Bajaj's combined sentence in *Thirst*.

Ma has to wake up at the crack of dawn to fill our buckets because the authorities only supply water for two hours every morning and for an hour in the evening when the shortages aren't too bad.

Reflective Questions on Meaning and Effect

- Why do you think the author combined the sentences like this?

- Is there another combination that would be effective?

- Why do you think your combination was different from or the same as the author's?

- If your combination was different from the author's, which do you prefer, and why?

We study authors' choices, not because they're the only answer, but because they are an option. Writers need options.

6.20 Zooming in on Revision

Lesson Overview

Revision goal connected to standards:

Develop and strengthen writing by combining ideas to avoid redundancy, add clarity, and improve fluency.

Model Text

New from Here
— Written by Kelly Yang

Teacher Considerations

In this final combination lesson, sixth graders will get a good test of their revision skills. These sentences are going to ask students to apply all of their understanding of the **DRAFT** strategies: **Deleting**, **Rearranging**, **Adding Connectors**, and **Forming New Verbs** while **Talking It Out**. We suggest completing the other lessons in this chapter before this one, so students feel comfortable and confident with the combination work required here.

Setting the Context

In *New from Here* by Kelly Yang, Knox Wei-Evans and his family are living in Hong Kong just as the coronavirus pandemic is beginning. Instead of Knox and his family celebrating Chinese New Year, they're cooped up in the house learning more about the coronavirus pandemic from the news. One of the new changes during the start of the pandemic is that Knox's father begins working from home, meeting with his coworkers on Zoom. Read the following excerpt to students.

The next day, I wake up to Dad's voice on a conference call. I forget for a second that he's working from home. When the virus news erupted, his office, like many offices in Hong Kong, had to close—I guess that's one good thing about the virus! I scramble out of bed in my pj's, excited to photobomb Dad's Zoom.

Do you think Knox will go through with photobombing his dad's Zoom? Let's continue reading to find out.

Revision Strategy

Use **DRAFT** to combine ideas and sentences.

Modeling

Use the **Reviser's DRAFTboard** along with printable, **6.20 Modeled Sentence Combo: Part I** (page 241), to explore the sentences that need to be combined. "There are seven sentences here that tell what Knox does next. Let's see if we can use **DRAFT** to help us combine them into two. First let's read aloud the sentences."

I scramble out of bed.

I'm in my pj's.

I'm excited to photobomb Dad's Zoom.

The bedroom of my parents is where I crawl into.

Modeling *(continued)*

My parent's bedroom is where Dad has set up his temporary office.

I try hard not to giggle.

I burst onto Dad's screen!

Talk students through each of the parts of **DRAFT**, prompting them to share their thinking connected to any of the revision strategies they could choose to use: **Deleting**, **Rearranging**, **Adding Connectors**, **Forming New Verbs**, while **Talking It Out** with a partner or with the whole class.

Once the class feels like they have an effective combination, reveal the author's original sentence, using **6.20 Modeled Sentence Combo: Part II**, on page 242, to set up a conversation that compares and contrasts the choices of the class with Kelly Yang's original. Use the following reflective questions as necessary:

- Why do you think Kelly combined the sentences like this?
- Is there another combination that would be effective?
- Why do you think your combination was different from or the same as the author's?
- If your combination was different from Yang's, which do you prefer, and why?

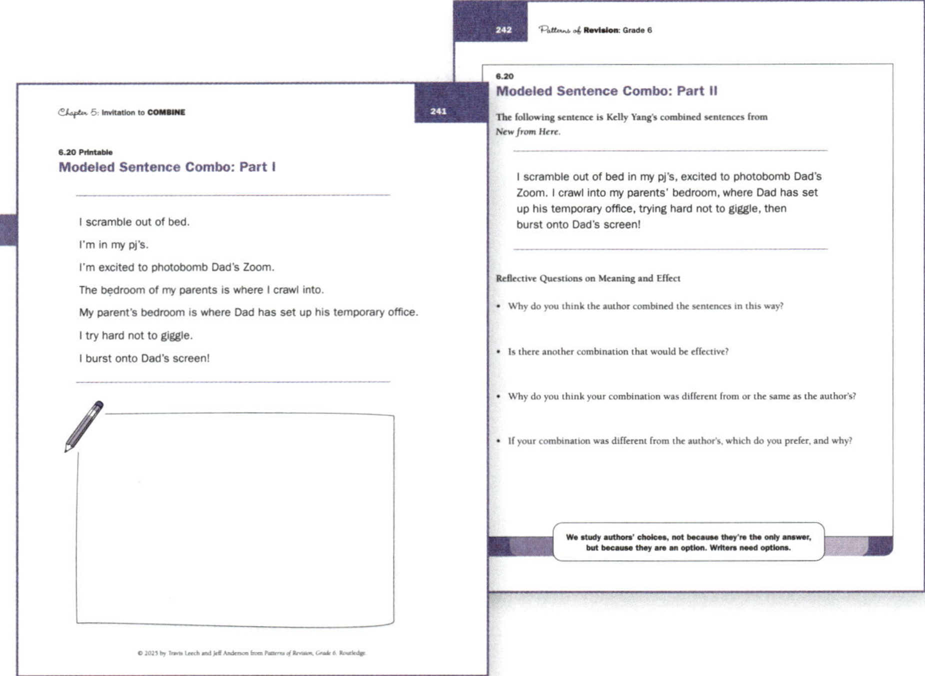

Collaborating Through Conversation

Distribute the printable, **6.20 Invitation to Combine: Part I** (page 243), to each student. Following the directions on the printable and using **DRAFT**, students collaborate through conversation with one or more classmates to combine the sentences into one. It is likely that your students will discover a few ways to combine the provided sentences. They can record their possibilities on the printable, in their notebooks, or in a digital space you have created for them.

Learners compare their choices to those of other partnerships or groups when they are ready. Discussions should be focused on effectiveness instead of getting the right answer, as in previous lessons. Share the author's original text in **6.20 Invitation to Combine: Part II** (page 245) for comparative analysis. Facilitate a discussion about meaning and effect by using the reflective questions at the bottom.

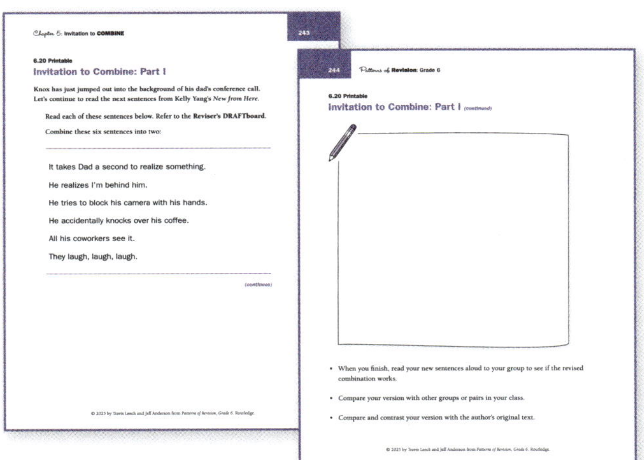

Quickwrite Opportunity (Optional)

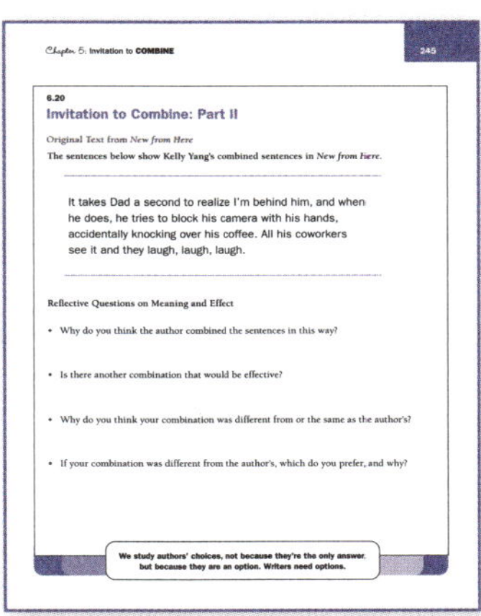

1. Reflect on a memorable bonding experience you had with family or friends indoors. How did you spend quality time together, and what made that moment so special?
2. Write about your favorite cozy or comforting spot. What makes it special, and how does it bring a sense of peace and relaxation?

Applying Revision

Everyone revisits a piece of writing: either one written in a previous class period or one that was inspired by one of the lesson's writing prompts. Begin by modeling the process with your own writing to support student clarity. Display your writing for students to see, then explain how you find a place to revise. When focusing on an aspect of your writing, you may choose to connect your revision technique back to the work you did with either of the models in this lesson. After revising, talk out the choice you made and explain why you think it creates more effective writing.

Students then return to their own writing to play with different revision options, using the **DRAFT** strategies and noticing the different effects. Invite them to choose one section or paragraph to focus on.

Sharing Results

Moving and Grooving to the Sound of Revision: Students write one of their revisions on a notecard and stand up by their desk or chair. Let them know they'll be moving around the room and sharing with other classmates.

- Start music and have students move around the class as the music plays.
- When the music stops, students group up into duos or trios and share the revision they wrote on their notecard.
- Repeat the process of students moving around the room to the music and stopping to share when the music stops as often as time allows.

Figure 6.20

Students meet up in a trio to talk about their revisions.

6.20 Printable
Modeled Sentence Combo: Part I

I scramble out of bed.

I'm in my pj's.

I'm excited to photobomb Dad's Zoom.

The bedroom of my parents is where I crawl into.

My parent's bedroom is where Dad has set up his temporary office.

I try hard not to giggle.

I burst onto Dad's screen!

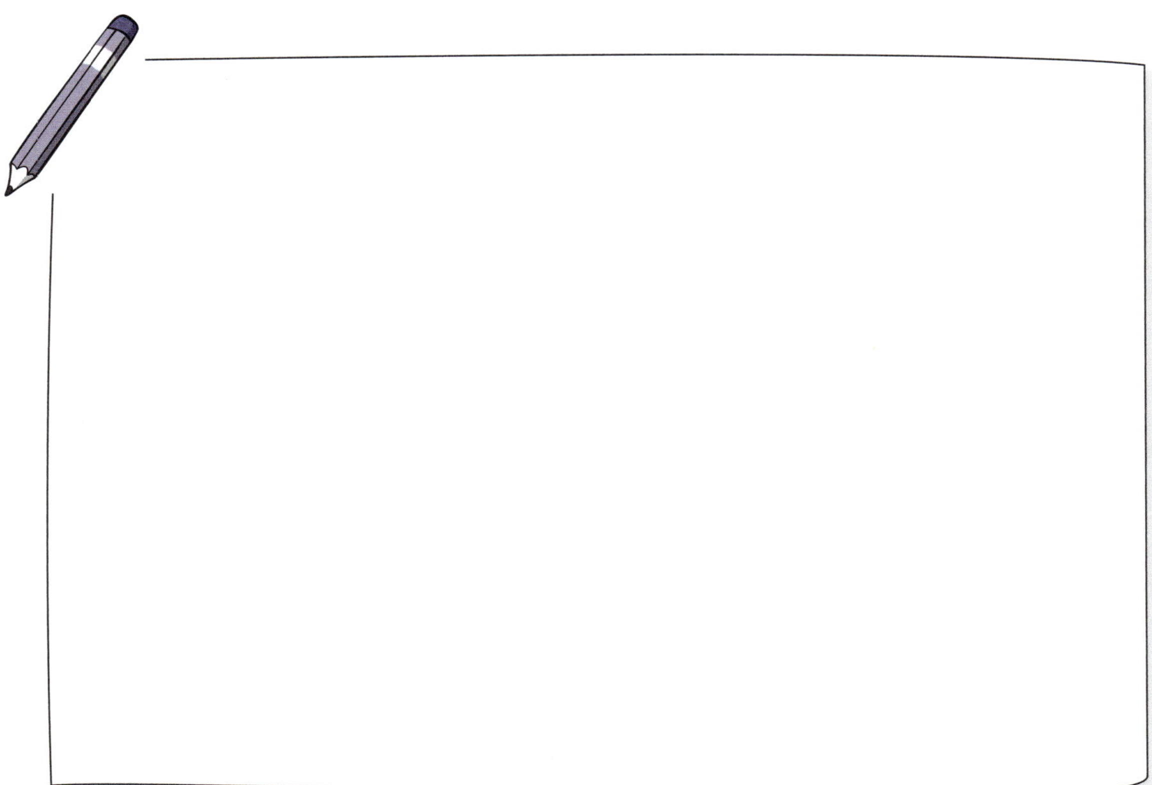

6.20
Modeled Sentence Combo: Part II

The following sentence is Kelly Yang's combined sentences from
New from Here.

I scramble out of bed in my pj's, excited to photobomb Dad's
Zoom. I crawl into my parents' bedroom, where Dad has set
up his temporary office, trying hard not to giggle, then
burst onto Dad's screen!

Reflective Questions on Meaning and Effect

- Why do you think the author combined the sentences in this way?

- Is there another combination that would be effective?

- Why do you think your combination was different from or the same as the author's?

- If your combination was different from the author's, which do you prefer, and why?

> **We study authors' choices, not because they're the only answer,
> but because they are an option. Writers need options.**

6.20 Printable

Invitation to Combine: Part I

Knox has just jumped out into the background of his dad's conference call. Let's continue to read the next sentences from Kelly Yang's *New from Here*.

Read each of these sentences below. Refer to the **Reviser's DRAFTboard**.

Combine these six sentences into two:

It takes Dad a second to realize something.

He realizes I'm behind him.

He tries to block his camera with his hands.

He accidentally knocks over his coffee.

All his coworkers see it.

They laugh, laugh, laugh.

(continues)

6.20 Printable

Invitation to Combine: Part I *(continued)*

- When you finish, read your new sentences aloud to your group to see if the revised combination works.

- Compare your version with other groups or pairs in your class.

- Compare and contrast your version with the author's original text.

6.20

Invitation to Combine: Part II

Original Text from *New from Here*

The sentences below show Kelly Yang's combined sentences in *New from Here*.

It takes Dad a second to realize I'm behind him, and when he does, he tries to block his camera with his hands, accidentally knocking over his coffee. All his coworkers see it and they laugh, laugh, laugh.

Reflective Questions on Meaning and Effect

- Why do you think the author combined the sentences in this way?

- Is there another combination that would be effective?

- Why do you think your combination was different from or the same as the author's?

- If your combination was different from the author's, which do you prefer, and why?

We study authors' choices, not because they're the only answer, but because they are an option. Writers need options.

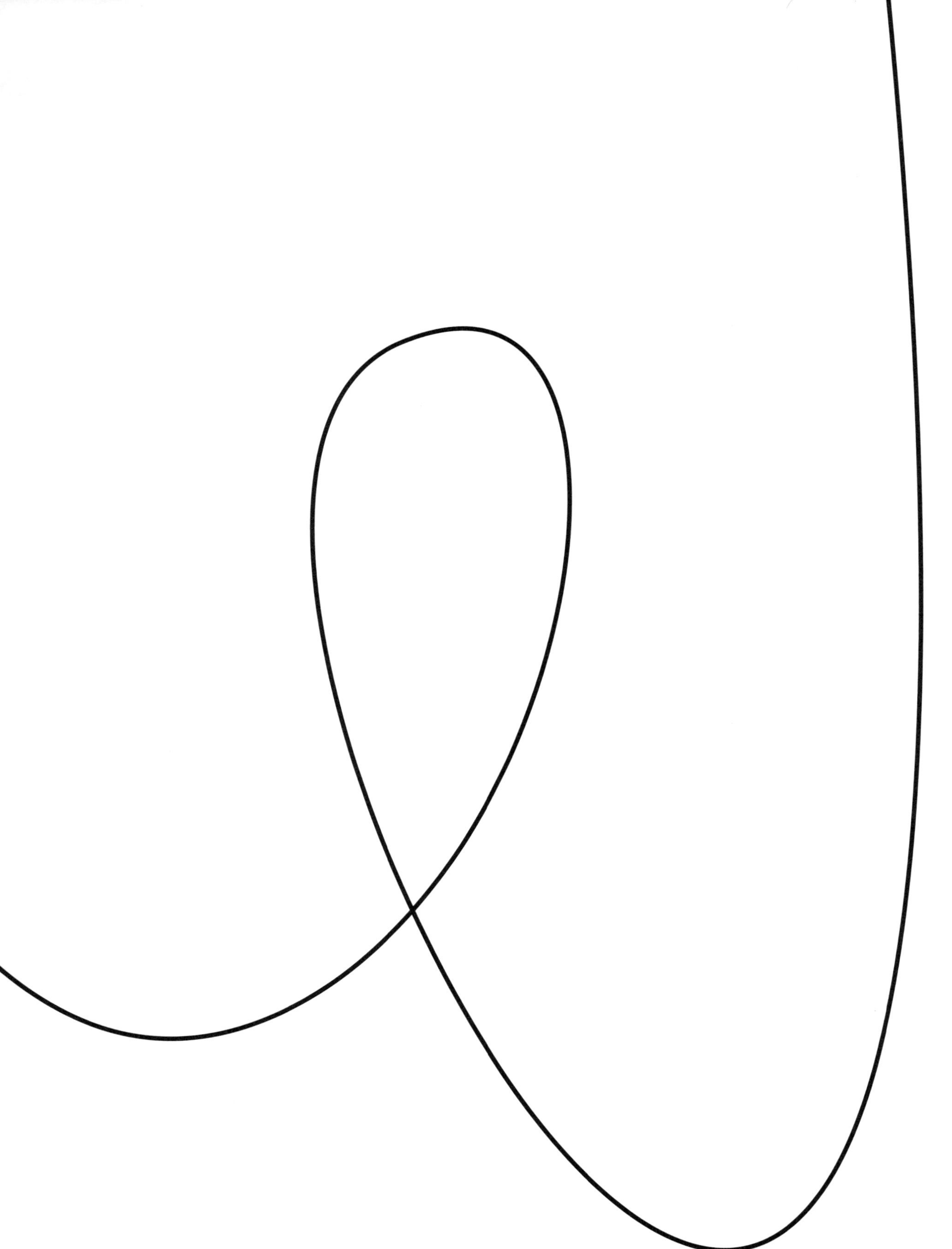

Conclusion

Living in a **REVISION** Mindset

Life is a balance between holding on and letting go.

— Rumi

Revision means change. Life is change and evolution. And if we're honest, we don't all love change—at first—and neither do middle graders. Change is new. Change can be difficult. Change takes time. Middle-grade writers would much prefer to write a draft and be done with it—no revision, no editing. But keep in mind and help students come to know: everything doesn't need to change all at once. Start in small chunks, and your students will be able to handle larger and larger chunks overtime.

Making the best changes in our writing includes making thoughtful decisions about what we'll keep and what we'll need to let go of. We know from professional writers that we learn the most about writing through revision. Like writing, we get better at revision by doing it. In *Patterns of Revision*, we designed the lessons to make the work of revision intriguing enough to be engaging, but also simple enough for middle graders to succeed at and use. As you navigate through the lessons included here, you'll begin to see that a limited set of options within the **DRAFT** mnemonic gives adolescent writers a bite-sized way into revision. One action at a time.

Patterns of Revision offers a structure with healthy doses of conversation and open-endedness, which provides the engagement that comes with choice, while keeping things simple enough that students don't become overwhelmed. Challenged, not frozen. Playful, not avoidant. Exploring, not ignoring. Over the span of the lessons, middle grade writers are intrigued enough that a few moves can make great improvement.

Revision is change.

Be open to change.

Listen.

Allow space.

Try not to resist the changes that come your way. Instead let life live through you. And do not worry your life is turning upside down. How do you know that the side you are used to is better than the one to come?"

— Rumi

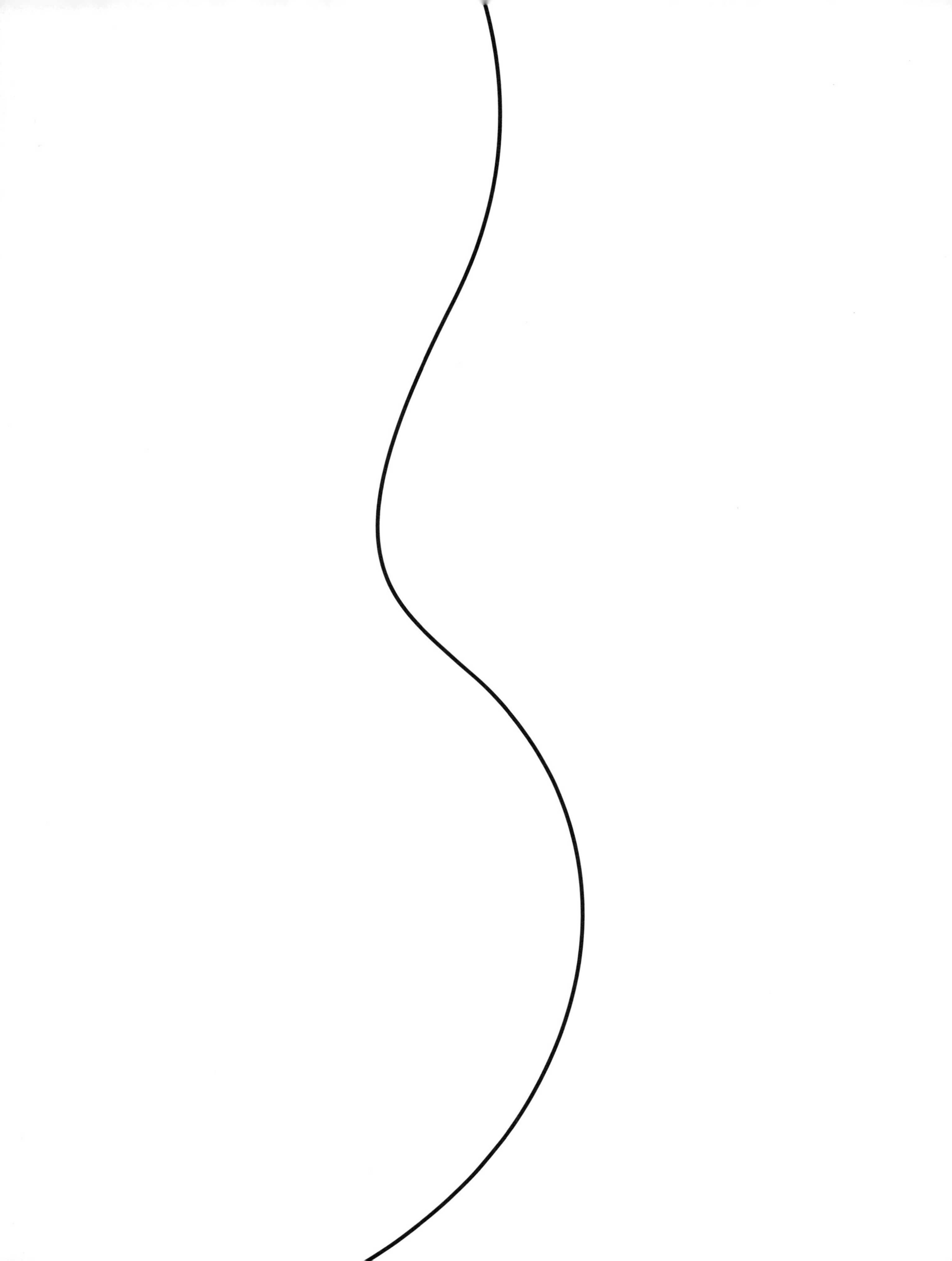

Young Adult Literature Bibliography

Albee, Sarah. 2010. *Poop Happened! A History of the World from the Bottom Up.* New York: Bloomsbury USA.

America's Test Kitchen Kids. 2018. *The Complete Cookbook for Young Chefs.* Naperville: Sourcebooks.

Armstrong, Jennifer. 2000. *Shipwreck at the Bottom of the World: The Extraordinary True Story of Shackleton and the Endurance.* New York: Random House.

Bajaj, Varsha. 2022. *Thirst.* New York: Penguin Young Readers Group.

Beccia, Carlyn. 2018. *They Lost Their Heads! What Happened to Washington's Teeth, Einstein's Brain, and Other Famous Body Parts.* New York: Bloomsbury USA.

Bruchec, Joseph. 2021. "The Save." In *The Hero Next Door: A We Need Diverse Books Anthology,* edited by Olugbemisola Rhuday-Perkovich. New York: Random House.

Gemeinhart, Dan. 2019. *The Remarkable Journey of Coyote Sunrise.* New York: Henry Holt and Company.

Gibbs, Stuart. 2014. *Space Case.* New York: Simon & Schuster for Young Readers.

Johnson, Varian. 2021. "The Definition of Cool." In *Black Boy Joy*, edited by Kwame Mbalia. New York: Random House Children's Books.

Kamkwamba, William and Bryan Mealer. 2015. *The Boy Who Harnessed the Wind: Young Reader's Edition.* New York: Penguin Young Readers Group.

Keller, Tae. 2020. *When You Trap a Tiger.* New York: Random House Children's Books.

Kelly, Erin Entrada. 2017. *Hello Universe.* New York: Hapercollins.

Lu, Marie. 2013. *Legend.* New York: Penguin Young Readers Group.

Magoon, Kekla. 2018. *The Season of Styx Malone.* New York: Random House Children's Books.

McAnulty, Stacy. 2019. *The Miscalculations of Lightning Girl.* New York: Random House Children's Books.

Mundial. 2020. *The Big Book of Soccer.* London: Wide Eyed Editions.

Piñeiro, Victor. 2021. *Time Villains.* Naperville: Sourcebooks.

Sanchez, Anita. 2018. *Itch! Everything You Didn't Want to Know About What Makes You Scratch.* New York: HaperCollins.

Thimmesh, Catherine. 2018. *Girls Think of Everything: Stories of Ingenious Inventions by Women.* Boston: Houghton Mifflin.

Wallmark, Laurie. 2021. *Code Breaker, Spy Hunter.* New York: Abrams.

Yang, Kelly. 2022. *New From Here.* New York: Simon & Schuster for Young Readers.

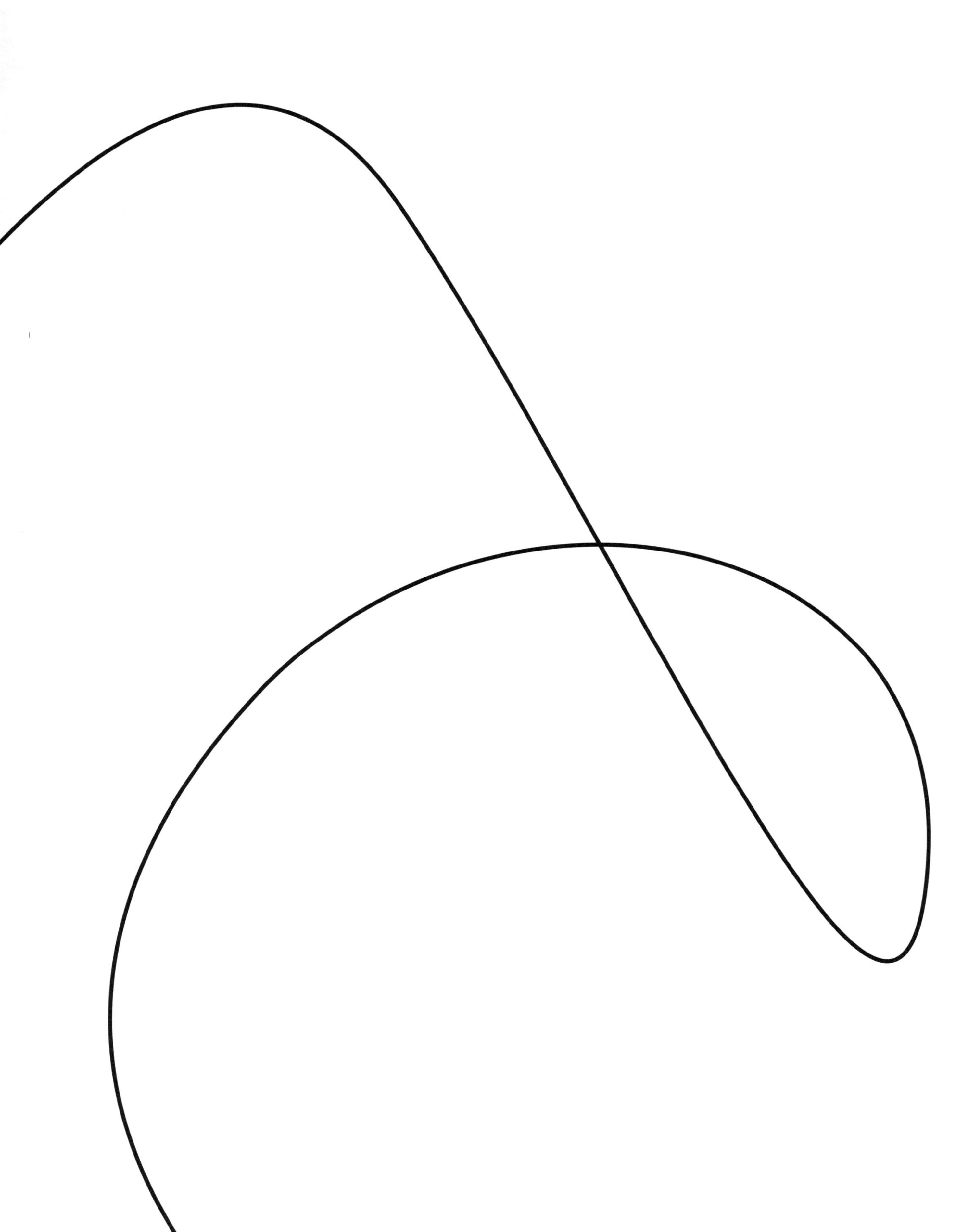

Professional Bibliography

Anderson, Jeff. 2011. *10 Things Every Writer Needs to Know*. Portland, ME: Stenhouse.

Anderson, Jeff, and Deborah Dean. 2015. *Revision Decisions: Talking Through Sentences and Beyond.* Portland, ME: Stenhouse.

Anderson, Jeff, with Travis Leech and Melinda Clark. 2017. *Patterns of Power: Inviting Adolescent Writers into the Conventions of Language, Grades 6-8*. Portland, ME: Stenhouse.

Christensen, Francis. 2007. *Notes Toward a New Rhetoric*. United States: Booklocker.com.

Graham, Steve, and Delores Perin. 2007. *Writing Next: Effective Strategies to Improve Writing of Adolescents in Middle and High School*—A Report to Carnegie Corporation of New York. Washington, DC: Alliance for Education.

Qarooni, Nawal. 2023. *Nourishing Caregiver Collaborations*. NY: Stenhouse.

Rief, Linda. 2018. The *Quickwrite Handbook*. Portsmouth, NH: Heinemann.

University of Chicago Press. 2017. *The Chicago Manual of Style*. 17th ed. Chicago, IL: University of Chicago Press.

Vygotsky, Lev S. 1978. *Mind in Society: The Development of Higher Psychological Process*. Ed. and trans. Michael Cole, Vera John-Steiner, Sylvia Scribner, and Ellen Souberman. Cambridge, MA: Harvard University Press.